formation address:

SAGE Publications, Inc.
2455 Teller Road
Newbury Park, California 91320

SAGE Publications Ltd.
6 Bonhill Street
London EC2A 4PU
United Kingdom

SAGE Publications India Pvt. Ltd.
M-32 Market
Greater Kailash I
New Delhi 110 048 India

d in the United States of America

ry of Congress Cataloging-in-Publication Data

an Keung.
ority children and adolescents in therapy / Man Keung Ho.
        p.   cm.
udes bibliographical references and indexes.
N 0-8039-3912-4 (cl.)   —ISBN 0-8039-3913-2 (pb)
Children of minorities—Mental health— United States. 2. Child
otherapy—Social Aspects—United States. 3. Adolescent
otherapy—Social Aspects—United States.   I. Title.
NLM: 1. Ethnic Groups—psychology. 2. Mental Disorders—in
cence.   3. Mental Disorders—in infancy & childhood.
ority Groups—psychology. 5. Psychotherapy—in adolescence.
chotherapy—in infancy & childhood. WS 350.2   H678m]
M54H6   1992
2'8914'08693—dc20   91-41972

03 94 95 96   10 9 8 7 6 5 4 3 2 1

Production Editor: Diane S. Foster

Minority C
and Adole
in Therapy

Man Keung

Pr

Li

H

p
P

a

SAGE PUBLICAT
The International Profess
Newbury Park   London

57

Contents

Preface

The non-Whites in the United States have increased dramatically over the last 3 decades. Demographics indicate that non-White youth—Blacks, Hispanics, American Indians, and Asian Americans—who are under the age of 18 will constitute 30% of the nation's youth population in the year 2000 and 38% by 2020 (U.S. Bureau of the Census, 1987a). This changing demographic tapestry promises not only the richness and vitality that diversity brings but also many difficult challenges.

Historically, ethnic minorities have often found themselves at the bottom of the economic, social, and political order. They are disproportionately represented among the poor, the uneducated, the unemployed, the sick, and the homeless. Many are totally unprepared for equal participation in American society. Minority children and youth especially need help to realize their potential.

In 1978, the U.S. President's Commission on Mental Health noted that low-income minority children and adolescents were particularly at risk for psychological disorders and behavioral problems because of their low socioeconomic status, their often stressful environments, and their lack of access to mental health services. This situation has not improved, and ethnic minority children are still greatly disadvantaged by their ethnicity, their poverty, and their social isolation (Children's Defense Fund, 1987). The latest health statistics indicate that infant mortality in some ethnic minority communities, especially the Black community, is double that in the White community;

1

half of all Black children and one third of all Hispanic children live in poverty (U.S. Bureau of the Census, 1987a). School dropout rates for minority youth in some urban areas exceed 60% (Reed, 1988). Ethnic minority youth also show three times the rate for White youth in psychiatric hospitalizations (Milazzo-Sayre, Olmeda, Benson, Rosenstein, & Manderscheid, 1986) and teenage pregnancies (Children's Defense Fund, 1986), and twice the rate for White youth in suicides (U.S. Department of Health and Human Services, 1986) and in substance abuse (Dembo, 1988).

As the population of minority youth continues to mount, it has become increasingly clear that most of the human services and mental health professionals who serve them lack up-to-date information, ethnic-specific and applicable training, and insufficient resources to respond to the minorities' pressing problems and needs. Ozawa (1986) labels the population trends a "demographic imperative" and challenges social institutions that serve minority youth to modify their White middle-class orientation. Agencies must modify traditional programs and services in order to serve these minority youth more effectively. Hodgkinson (1990) also observes that the need and motive for working with minority youth should not be political liberalism or obligation but enlightened self-interest.

Although minority youth are the most rapidly growing segment of the youth population in America, only very limited literature exists to inform practitioners, educators, and health professionals about their problems and needs (Gibbs, Huang, and Associates, 1989; Phinney & Rotherman, 1987; Powell, Yamamoto, Romero, & Morales, 1983). What little literature is available pertaining to working with minority youth is often written in a fragmented, eclectic, unsystematic fashion. My experience in the last 25 years as a practitioner, educator, supervisor, and consultant in transcultural therapy has helped me to recognize the need for a theory-based comprehensive book on the sociopsychological assessment and treatment of minority children.

Purpose and Organization of This Book

The primary purpose of *Minority Children in Therapy* is to provide theory specification, integration, and systematization for clinical assessment and treatment of minority children and adolescents from four major minority groups: (a) Asian and Pacific Americans, (b) American Indians and Alaskan natives, (c) Hispanic Americans, and (d) Black Americans.

Five important features frame the organization of this book. First, it introduces a culturally relevant theoretical framework from which appropriate assessment and therapeutic guidelines for work with minority children and adolescents are derived (Chapter 1). Second, it provides practitioners and students with an up-to-date resource for understanding and clinically assessing minority children who are experiencing political, social, educational, and/or economic problems. Using the ecological perspective as an organizing framework, materials relevant to each minority group are organized and presented according to a standard outline (Chapters 2, 3, 4, and 5). This outline includes (a) historical background; (b) mental health problems and issues; and (c) individual, family, school, and societal systems and issues. Adherence to a single outline facilitates organization, comparison, and integration of common core knowledge and inter- and intragroup differences in assessing minority children. Third, with an ecological perspective providing a common thread linking different minority groups, the book's organization facilitates the integration of the conventional with the more culturally specific methods, techniques, and skills of treatment with minority children (Chapter 5, 6, 7, and 8). Fourth, it provides a theory-based "how to"—that is, specific guidelines and suggestions on culturally relevant, theoretically and empirically based ego-psychodynamic theory with individual therapy; systems-oriented therapy with the family; and group-dynamic, process, and theory-based therapy with the group. Fifth, because this is a practice-oriented book, it will be infused with case vignettes to illustrate the role of sociocultural and psychological factors in the assessment of problems and for the development of alternative cultural-specific intervention strategies.

It is hoped that the organization of this book will provide students and practitioners with a comprehensive, up-to-date examination of therapy with minority children. It also will provide an analytical and functional format that lends itself to the scientific ordering of clinically and empirically based information and a promising challenge of quality for practice theory with minority children. Specification of therapy knowledge should facilitate the learning process of both undergraduate and graduate students. Practicing therapists will find that the book presents theory-based practical information that they can readily use in their work with minority children.

It is generally recognized that not only is there considerable inter-ethnic group diversity among the minorities, but there is also marked and significant intraethnic minority group heterogeneity. In an attempt to delineate and systematize practice knowledge with minority children, the possibility of stereotyping, obviously, is great. Aware of this danger, I tried to avoid it and consulted a panel of nationally distinguished ethnic minority practitioners and educators. However, undoubtedly I have not been totally successful. If I have presented incorrect or stereotypical information, I apologize and invite reader's corrections. The lack of satisfactory gender-neutral pronouns in the English language has prompted me to use "he" or "she" throughout the book without any idea which has been favored. The case examples come mostly from my own practice. The few that do not are "gifts" from colleagues, trainees, or students at the Norman Transcultural Family Institute. All of the identifying information has been changed or omitted to protect client confidentiality.

Finally, I wish to thank the individuals who have helped me with this book. I owe particular thanks to Paul Keys (Hunter College), Rosa Jimenez-Vazquez (Virginia Commonwealth University), Edith Freeman (Kansas University), Daniel Lee (Loyola University), Ronald Lewis (Arizona State University), Derald Sue (University of California at Hayward), Toni Dobrec (Three Feathers Association), Janet Weber (Adam Elementary School), Muriel Yu (University of Texas at Arlington), and Deborah Golub (Smith College), who read and critiqued parts of the manuscript pertaining to each ethnic minority group. I want to express my appreciation to Leona Huffaker for editing an early draft of the manuscript and to the secretarial staff of the Information Processing Center of the University of Oklahoma, who typed the manuscript. Finally, I want to thank my wife, Jeannie, for her understanding, patience, and support, and my sons, Christopher Yan-Tak and Steve Yan-Mong, who taught me what it is like to be today's teenagers.

—MAN KEUNG HO

PART I

Conceptual Framework

1

A Transcultural Framework for Assessment and Therapy with Ethnic Minority Children and Youth

Mental health and health professionals and practitioners who work with other minority children and youth require a comprehensive body of knowledge. It must be organized and integrated in both theoretical and practice terms and applicable both in a clinical or a prevention setting. Ideally, this knowledge should include a full awareness of human development and behavior, including sociocultural factors (ethnics, racial and cultural background, social role, familial forces); biological factors (anatomical and physiological underpinnings, organicity); and psychological factors (personality, individual psychodynamics, family and group psychodynamics).

The following three major content areas provide an optimal basis for the organization and integration of theoretical concepts, empirical data, and technical application in work with ethnic minority children: (a) an ethnicity and cross-cultural mental health perspective, (b) a psychosocial developmental perspective, and (c) an ecological perspective.

Ethnicity and Cross-Cultural Mental Health

Ethnicity refers to membership in a group of people "who share a unique social and cultural heritage that is passed on from generation to generation" (Mindel, Habenstein, & Wright, 1988, p. 5). It refers to one's sense of belonging to a group and the part of one's thinking, perceptions, feelings, and behavior that is due to ethnic group membership. *Ethnic identity* is conceptually and functionally separate from one's personal identity as an individual. Moreover, ethnic identity is distinguished from ethnicity in that the latter refers to group patterns and the former refers to the individual's acquisition of group patterns.

Ethnicity and ethnic identity have enormous implications in the assessment and treatment of minority youth and children. In addition to shaping the child's belief system about what constitutes mental health and mental illness, ethnicity influences the child's manifestation of symptoms, defensive styles, coping mechanisms, conceptualization of a mental health problem, and responses to "proper" treatment. Finally, ethnicity also determines the types of help-seeking patterns that parents employ to seek relief for adolescents and children.

Ethnic identity, when combined with membership in a minority race, presents a dual struggle as well as challenge to a child or adolescent. Minority refers to a group of political and economic individuals who are relatively powerless, receive unequal treatment, and regard themselves as objects of discrimination (Ho, 1987; Omi & Winant, 1986). Not only are children growing up in minority families exposed to different family structures and dynamics, school and neighborhood experiences, and community responses than children from mainstream Anglo families, but they also must cope with socioeconomic realities and barriers that profoundly limit their opportunities and negatively affect their normal development and mental health. The following discussions attempt to identity factors that minority group children uniquely encounter and that in turn affect their mental health. These factors include minority reality, impact of the external system on their cultures, biculturalism, language differences, social-class differences, color differences, belief systems, and help-seeking behavior.

Ethnic Minority Reality

Racism and discrimination profoundly affect the lives of many ethnic minorities. They affect a minority person from birth until death and affect every aspect of family life, from child-rearing practices and self-esteem to cultural and racial identification. They also influence the way in which a minority child relates to others and to the outside world.

Discrimination against minorities pervades all levels of society from theories about genetic inferiority (Jensen, 1969) and cultural pathology (Moynihan, 1965) to the segregation that existed blatantly in the South until the Civil Rights era in the 1960s. As a result of perpetuatory racism and discrimination, the socioeconomic status of ethnic minorities degenerates. When children are both poor and members of ethnic minorities, the negative and long-term impact of poverty increases significantly (Committee for Economic Development, 1987). Continued inequities in the United States are manifested today by the disproportionate numbers of minority people who are poor, homeless, living in substandard housing, in prisons, unemployed, and/or school dropouts. This process of discrimination is evident regardless of economic status, social-class levels, and job level. The processes of racism and discrimination also affect the minorities' help-seeking behaviors and contribute to the underutilization of helping professionals, who generally are monolinguistic, middle class, and ethnocentric in problem diagnosis and treatment (Acosta, Yamamoto, & Evans, 1982).

Impact of External System on Minority Cultures

Cultural differences in values, attitudes, the self, and activities and behaviors lead ethnic minority groups, especially children, to believe that their value system is inferior to that of White Americans. In contrast with middle-class White American cultural values, which emphasize human control of nature and the environment, most ethnic minority groups emphasize human harmony with the environment. Minority children are brought up with an emphasis on the being-in-becoming mode of activity and harmony. This behavior is often misconstrued as unmotivated or lazy by teachers who are middle-class White Americans with a strong "doing orientation" (Bellah et al., 1985).

In addition, the sociological structure of mainstream society addresses itself basically to the nuclear family, which also conflicts with
the extended family common to minority groups. In attempting to
reconcile the impact of their external systems, many minority group
members find themselves personally rejected by society. At the same
time, they may be getting inadequate support within their own
group. The negative impact that the external system has on the minority culture tends to alienate the minority individual. It may cause
conflict within the family and at the same time leave the minority
child without an adequate model to emulate.

Biculturalism

A member of an ethnic minority is inevitably part of two cultures.
Children raised in America to some degree may be *bicultural* or even
multicultural—that is, they may acquire the norms, attitudes, and behavior patterns of their own and one or more other ethnic groups.
Bicultural competence is the ability to understand and step in and out
of two cultural environments, adjusting one's behavior to the norms
of each culture in order to attain one's objectives (de Anda, 1984). For
example, a Hispanic student may behave according to hierarchical
vertical structure at home with his family and friends. At the same
time, he can behave competitively at public school, as the White
American culture requires.

A minority child can develop bicultural competence, but he or she
cannot have a bicultural self-identification. Children cannot label
themselves as belonging simultaneously to two different groups, except perhaps for children of intermarriage. Minority children have
no choice but to develop and differentiate between a personal identity and an ethnic or racial identity in order to form a cohesive sense
of self. When a minority child is forced to make a choice between his
or her own culture and the dominant culture, conflict is inevitable
(Stonequist, 1964).

However, current theories emphasize the advantages of socialization in more than one cultural group (Ho, 1984; Ramirez & Castanada,
1974). Children experiencing two cultures are seen as demonstrating
greater role flexibility and creativity. Children who possess bicultural competence can be expected to have higher self-esteem, greater
understanding, and higher achievement levels than others (Ramirez,
1983). Unfortunately, the stress of straddling two disparate cultures

may be overwhelming to some minority children (Welsh, 1988), especially in view of the disparaging messages received from mainstream society (Gibbs, 1987).

Ethnicity and Language

Ethnicity is experienced and persists through language. A native language provides a psychic bond or uniqueness that signifies membership in a particular ethnic group. Many minority children's school problems and family conflicts are related to language problems (Ogbu, 1985). Language facility and preference are important indicators of the level of one's acculturation. The various language preferences within a family may reflect significant family dynamics and points of acculturation and intergenerational conflicts or harmony.

Although many minority children are bilingual—and that bilingualism is a strong indicator of biculturalism—problems of miscommunication may still occur. Many minority children do not have parallel vocabularies or may not know various meanings of words. Whether the minority child or family speaks English or the native language, linguistic style tends to vary between public and private situations (Falicov, 1982; Ho, 1990a). In public, it may contain allusions, indirect statements, and guardedness, whereas in private, conversations—reserved only for intimate relationships—may be bolder and more straightforward.

Minority youth often use language as a means of artistic expression: for example, "rapping" and "playing the dozens" (Mancini, 1980). One way for therapists to communicate with ethnic clients is to respect nonstandard English used by the youth, plead ignorance to expressions they do not know, and encourage the youth to teach the therapist the language.

Ethnicity and Social Class

Although it has been well documented that social class and socioeconomic issues play an important role in the treatment of children (Cohen & Pearl, 1964), the impact of ethnicity differences on the therapeutic process cannot be overlooked. *Social class* refers to "differences in wealth, income, occupation, status, community power, group identification, level of consumption, and family background" (Duberman, 1975, p. 34). Social class is another dimension that

describes and defines the child's world by ascribing a particular position and value to his or her family's socioeconomic status. Thus
membership in a social class provides boundaries within which the
growing child and adolescent will experience a restricted range of
opportunities, choices, and challenges in particular social contexts.

However useful the definition of social class may be for categoriz-
ing children for some purposes, by itself it may not be adequate for a
full appreciation of ethnic differences as they relate to assessment
and treatment. Children and other family members may act in accordance with their perceived class interest in some situations and in
accordance with their cultural performances or minority identity
in others. Even when they are economically and materially successful, some ethnic minority members still experience difficulty
in being accepted by the White middle-class society. At the same
time, they may feel alienated from their own ethnic group (Combs,
1978). Moreover, the influence exerted by value patterns that were
acquired throughout childhood is often considerable even among
those whose behavior is highly westernized (Mass, 1978). Rather
than a "declining significance of race," as erroneously indicated by
Wilson (1987), a therapist working with minority children should not
lose sight of the "continuing significance of race and ethnicity" in
determining the psychological well-being of minority children (M.
Thomas & Hughes, 1986).

Ethnicity and Skin Color

For children, any deviation from the norm may garner undesired
attention. Conformity in appearance and skin color is highly valued.
For the minority child who differs in physical appearance and skin
color, this may be a very sensitive point. Even within minority
groups some family members may identify with the dominant culture and incorporate the prejudicial belief that "White is beautiful;
White is right."

Skin color has many different levels of symbolism for minority
Americans. It affects a child's thoughts, attitudes, and perceptions
about beauty, intelligence, worth, and self-esteem (Walker, 1982).
Many minority children view their color proudly, as a badge of pride
and honor; others are negative or at best ambivalent and view their
color as a "mark of oppression." In some Black families dark-skinned
members are preferred, and light skin color is seen as a constant

reminder of the abuse of Black women by White men. For many light-skinned minority children, the dilemma of not being identified as an in-group member can cause pain, discomfort, and personality disturbance.

Ethnicity, Belief Systems, and Mental Health Symptoms

The child's belief system about what constitutes mental health and mental illness is heavily shaped by ethnicity, which in turn influences the child's manifestation of symptoms, defensive styles, and patterns of coping with anxiety, depression, fear, guilt, and anger. The influence of ethnicity in symptomatic behavior was well illustrated by studies (Mostwin, 1976; Opler, 1967) showing that different ethnic patients manifested different symptoms, even though they suffered from the same disorder. Enright and Jaeckle (1963) reported for a study of paranoid schizophrenic patients that the Japanese American group expressed more depression, withdrawal, disturbance in thinking, and inhibition, whereas the Filipino American group exhibited greater delusions of persecution and overt signs of disturbed behavior. Most ethnic minority groups have negative attitudes toward mental illness. This attitude affects individual clients and the extended family as a whole during the therapy process.

Ethnicity and Help-Seeking Behavior

Ethnicity generally dictates the help-seeking behavior that minority group parents employ to find relief for children or adolescents with dysfunctional behaviors or symptoms. Studies indicate that ethnic minority parents do not consider mental health services a solution to their children's emotional and mental problems (Casas & Keefe, 1978; Kleinman & Lin, 1981; McAdoo, 1977). All ethnic minorities consider the family and extended family their primary source of support. Reliance on natural support systems produces fewer feelings of defeat, humiliation to self and to the family, and powerlessness.

There are eight major reasons for the underutilization of health and mental services. These are (a) distrust of therapists, especially White therapists; (b) cultural and social-class differences between therapists and clients; (c) an insufficient number of mental health facilities and professionals who are bicultural; (d) overuse or misuse of a physician for psychological problems; (e) language barriers; (f) reluctance to recognize the urgency for help; (g) lack of awareness of the existence of mental health clinics; and (h) confusion about the relationship between mental health clinics and other agencies such as welfare, courts, or schools.

As we have seen, ethnic minority children encounter many social factors that affect their mental health. Next let us direct our attention to the psychosocial and developmental perspective of ethnic minority children.

Psychosocial Development

To fully comprehend and appreciate the maturational and developmental processes of an ethnic minority child, three separate but related theoretical perspectives are considered. These are (a) Erikson's stage-related theory, (b) Norton's dual-cultural perspective, and (c) the ethnic socialization process.

Erikson's Stage-Related Theory

Erikson's theory focusing on the psychosocial tasks of growing up in American society offers the following four major advantages to the therapist to help understand and assess minority children and youth.

1. Erikson (1959) proposes that human psychological development continues throughout the life cycle. Ascertaining and understanding the phase-specific normative developmental issues, conflicts, and anxieties is a key element in assisting or advancing the development of a child in a given age period.

2. Erikson's longitudinal emphasis on continuity includes both the child and the adult as participants in the same continuous process of development; thus the status of each can be assessed in identical terms—the degree of attainment of age-appropriate individuation and the extent of freedom from development-arresting forces in the individual and in the environment. Environmental influences contribute to an individual's problem formations and remain important in the present as an ongoing factor in adaptation. Hence, assessment of a child's relationships with significant others is vitally important in the prevention, rehabilitation, and treatment of the child's problem.

3. In keeping with its emphasis on the continuity of development throughout the life cycle, the developmental view also stresses the recapitulation of earlier developmental issues—however well resolved or unresolved—in later developmental phases. This concept is particularly well illustrated by the separation-individuation theory (Bowby, 1958; Mahler, 1972), which focuses on the development of the capacity for human relationship and for adaptation, as these arise from progressive ego development and self-object differentiation.

4. The developmental orientation views mental problems not in the medical model of disease, but in the model of functional disturbances that impair current functioning and also impede further development in one or more of its lines or aspects. The aim of treatment is to enhance and facilitate those developmental processes that have been arrested.

Erikson's emphasis on environment as an important ingredient for the child's development may lead one to assume that the self-concept of minority children is negatively affected by the stigma of membership in a devalued ethnic group. However, recent studies (Powell, 1985; Taylor, 1976) indicate that this is not the case. The dual-cultural perspective explains the differences and, therefore, is essential in the assessment of the psychosocial development of a minority child or youth.

Norton's Dual-Cultural Perspective

The dual-cultural perspective (Norton, 1983) of the minority child's environment is a concept that can be defined as a conscious and systematic process of simultaneously perceiving, understanding, and comparing the values, attitudes, and behaviors of the larger societal system with those of the child's immediate family and community system. According to Norton (1983), every minority child is embedded simultaneously in at least two systems: that of his immediate social and physical (nurturing) environment and that of the larger major society (sustaining environment). Although the sustaining system houses the instrumental needs of a person (goods, services, economic sources, etc.), the nurturing system can be compared to Erikson's "significant others," those closest and most important in the determination of a child's sense of identity.

The dual perspective is vitally significant to the assessment of ethnic minority children and youth, because the degree of difference between the systems may be very diverse, thus causing value and behavioral conflict between the systems. By employing the dual-perspective framework, a therapist can evaluate the psychosocial development of a minority child by looking at the complexities from two different perspectives and from within the subsystems of each of the two major systems involved.

Ethnic Socialization Process

Closely related to the dual-cultural perspective, assessment of the psychosocial development of ethnic minority children and youth will be incomplete if the ethnic socialization process is not considered. *Ethnic socialization* refers to the developmental processes by which children acquire the values, perceptions, attitudes, and behaviors of a particular ethnic group and come to see themselves and others as members of such groups (Rotherman & Phinney, 1987).

When children are at the early-elementary age, ethnicity affects them primarily through the immediate environment of family, peers, and school. The development of ethnic identity can be based on objective criteria, such as learning about the ethnicity of their parents. As these children reach middle childhood and their understanding of the world increases, they learn about discrimination, political power, and the economic resources of their ethnic group. As they approach and enter adolescence, young people develop their personal identity. They begin to deal more consciously with ethnicity and at the same time are increasingly influenced by the wider mainstream culture. Their ethnic identity includes both the objective criteria of ethnicity and the subjective criteria reflecting the individual's choice of reference group.

As youth become more aware of their own ethnicity, their ethnicity also is more evident to other children. They are more often faced with a conflict between the values of their own group and those of the majority culture. Rather than the degree of acculturation, the lack of bicultural involvement and flexibility appears to be a particular source of personal and family stress for minority children (Szapocznik & Kurtines, 1980b).

Ecological Perspective

Although many theories of therapy with children are conceived as being directed at the process of conflict, anxiety, and defense systems within the individual, the ecological perspective as proposed by Bronfenbrenner (1979) maintains that unbalance and conflict may arise from any focus in the interlocking transactional systems, ranging from the microsystems of the individual, family, and the school to the macrosystem of governmental social and economic policies. The level of emphasis upon each of these systems, in turn, depends on the specific nature of the child's problem. At the individual level, the focus is on the biopsychological endowment each child possesses, including physical appearance, personality strengths, level of psychosocial development, cognition, perception, problem-solving skills, emotional temperament, level of acculturation, habit formation, and interpersonal competence and language skills.

The family-level focus is on family-life style, immigration history, culture, family organization, gender-role structure, division of labor, affective styles, tradition, rituals, and management of internal or external stress. At the cultural level, the focus should be on understanding the value systems, belief systems, and societal norms of the host-culture, as well as those of the original or native culture. At the environmental level, the focus should be on understanding the economic, social, and political structures of American society that discriminate and oppress individuals in minority groups.

There are five psychotherapeutic principles that are particularly relevant to therapy that uses the ecological perspective with minority children and youth.

First, a child's problems are seldom conceived as an illness. Problems or difficulties are understood as a lack or deficit in the environment (as in the case of newly immigrated children), as dysfunctional transactions between systems (social service organizations and mental health care delivery systems), or as adaptive strategies (culture shock and conflict). A therapist can focus on the interface between or among systems or subsystems.

Second, the principle of *equifinality* allows and encourages the therapist to apply a number of different interventions that produce similar effects or outcomes. Such flexibility and creativity in seeking alternative routes to change provide the therapist the option to relate

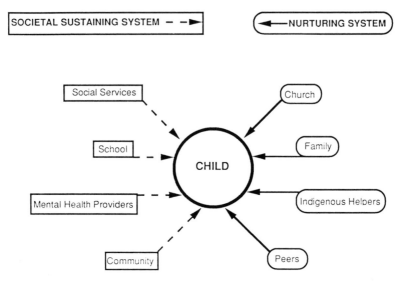

Figure 1.1. An Ecological Framework For Assessment

interventive strategies to existing child therapy theories or to apply innovative strategies of change based on the child's unique cultural background and life space.

Third, therapeutic strategies make use of the life experiences and natural systems of the child. Emphasis on the child's life space and family as a natural helping system places the therapist in a role as cultural broker instead of intruder or manipulator.

Fourth, the ecological principle that a change in one part of the system affects all other parts of the system allows the therapist the flexibility to intervene in a child's problem without gaining access to the family or other parts in the subsystem in the change process.

Finally, the ecological model mandates an interdisciplinary perspective and employs multitheoretical orientations and modalities to involve indigenous helpers in treatment.

Implications and Guidelines for Assessment

By employing the ethnicity, psychosocial, and ecological perspectives, a therapist can acquire a comprehensive framework in the understanding and assessment of a minority child or youth. Figure 1.1 provides a guideline in which a minority child's level of development and functioning can be assessed (Gibbs et al., 1989; Powell et al., 1983; Looney & Lewis, 1983). This assessment guideline includes a minority child's or youth's (a) individual level of psychosocial adjustment, (b) relationships with family, (c) school adjustment and achievement, (d) relationships with peers, and (e) adaptation to the community.

Individual Psychosocial Adjustment

Questions to be addressed in the assessment of variations in the individual child's psychosocial adjustment include the following: To what extent is the child's problem a function of his or her

physical appearance, which can be affected by malnutrition, improper diet, height, weight, skin color, and hair texture and unfavorably compared with preferred Anglo norms?

affect expression, which may be culturally appropriate but may be in direct conflict with the mainstream norm? Does it emphasize directness and overt assertiveness?

self-concept and self-esteem, which is germane to the child's native culture and is appropriate criteria for self-evaluation but is in conflict with the mainstream criteria for self-concept and self-esteem?

interpersonal competence, which differs according to different sociocultural milieu?

definition of and attitudes toward autonomy, which may be in serious conflict with the norms of the child's school or community milieu or is adaptive within the child's overall life situation?

attitudes toward achievement, which are culturally appropriate but are in conflict with the traditional channels of educational achievement enforced by the public school system?

management of aggression and impulse control, which can enhance or impede his or her school performance and interpersonal competence?

coping and defense mechanisms that may be dysfunctional in certain sociocultural contexts and environments?

Relationships with Family

Questions to be addressed in the child's relationships with his or her family include the following: To what extent is the child's problem a function of his or her

family structure, which is in transition because of immigration, acculturation, or life-cycle processes?

roles within the family, which are in conflict with the traditional structure
favoring older-age and male-gender hierarchies?

family communication conflict from hierarchical to egalitarian caused by
acculturation and family life processes?

parental use of discipline, which may enhance or impede the child's performance at school or at home?

culturally defined dominant dyad, which is in conflict with the Anglo-
American nuclear family ideals that define father-mother as the
dominant dyad?

culturally defined autonomy, which is in conflict with the Anglo-American
nuclear family ideals that define autonomy as physical departure
from family of origin and financial independence?

School Adjustment and Achievement

The importance of school as an institution to the socialization of
latency-aged children and adolescents is second after family. School
is also an arena where minority children first experience cultural conflict and behavioral adjustment problems. Questions to be addressed in
the evaluation of a child's school adjustment and achievement include
the following: To what extent is the child's school adjustment problem a function of his or her

psychological adjustment, which may be attributed to parental lack of education, parental negative attitudes toward the school, the child's
unfamiliarity with the norms and expectations of the classroom
and school environment, social-class differences, and/or language difficulties?

social adjustment, which may require moving away from a familiar
neighborhood school to a larger school where there are greater
cultural, racial, and economic differences?

behavioral adjustment, which may be related to an unstable home situation, poor nutrition, poor physical health, or the inability to handle overwhelming anxiety and stress?

academic achievement, as measured by culturally biased achievement
tests and/or verbal skills, motivation for learning, attitude toward a particular class or toward the school in general, study habits, and family support?

Relationships with Peers

A minority child's relationships with peers reflects his or her psychosocial adjustment and may influence academic achievement at school. Questions to be addressed in the evaluation of a minority child's relationships with peers include the following: To what extent are the child's relationships with peers a function of his or her

> *ability* to display empathy, to form friendships, to engage in cooperative and competitive activities, and to manage aggressive and sexual impulses?
>
> *social skills* to form peer relationships at school and within his or her own community and the effects of these peer relationships on overall psychosocial functioning?

Adaptation to the Community

Evaluation of a minority child's adaptation to the community should be age related. Three specific questions should be addressed in the evaluation of the child's adaptation to the community: To what extent is the child's adaptation to the community a function of his or her age-related

> *quality activities and participation* in church, youth groups, and language- and ethnic-related classes?
>
> *quality participation* in organized sports, arts activities, volunteer activities, and/or part-time jobs?
>
> *inappropriate or excessive activities* that create family conflicts or dysfunctional behavior, such as delinquency, drug abuse, or poor academic behavior?

A summary of the assessment guidelines for the development and functioning of an ethnic minority child or youth is presented in Table 1.1.

Implications and Guidelines for Treatment

The transcultural framework for therapy with ethnic minority children and youth requires that the therapist pay close attention to three major variables: (a) client or child variables; (b) therapist variables; and

Table 1.1 Ecological and Psychosocial Assessment Guidelines for Ethnic
Minority Children and Youth

To what extent is the individual child's adjustment a function of the following?

INDIVIDUAL LEVEL OF PSYCHOSOCIAL ADJUSTMENT

1. Physical appearance, which can be affected by malnutrition, improper diet, height, weight, skin color, and hair texture and unfavorably compared with preferred Anglo norms

2. Affect expression, which may be culturally appropriate but may be in direct conflict with the mainstream norm. Does it emphasize directness and overt assertiveness

3. Self-concept and self-esteem, which are germane to the child's native culture and are appropriate criteria for self-evaluation but are in conflict with the mainstream criteria for self-concept and self-esteem

4. Interpersonal competence, which differs according to different sociocultural milieu

5. Definition of and attitudes toward autonomy, which may be in serious conflict with the norms of the child's school or community milieu or is adaptive within the child's overall life situation

6. Attitudes toward achievement, which are culturally appropriate but are in conflict with the traditional channels of educational achievement enforced by the public school system

7. Management of aggression and impulse control, which can enhance or impede his or her school performance and interpersonal competence

8. Coping and defense mechanisms that may be dysfunctional in certain sociocultural contexts and environments

RELATIONSHIPS WITH FAMILY

9. Family structure that is in transition because of immigration, acculturation, or life-cycle processes

10. Roles within the family, which are in conflict with the traditional structure favoring older-age and male-gender hierarchies

11. Family communication conflict from hierarchical to egalitarian caused by acculturation and family life processes

12. Parental use of discipline, which may enhance or impede the child's performance at school or at home

13. Culturally defined dominant dyad, which is in conflict with the Anglo-American nuclear family ideals that define father-mother as the dominant dyad

14. Culturally defined automony, which is in conflict with the Anglo-American nuclear family ideals that define autonomy as physical departure from family of origin and financial independence

SCHOOL ADJUSTMENT AND ACHIEVEMENT

15. Psychological adjustment, which may be attributed to parental lack of education, parental negative attitudes toward the school, the child's unfamiliarity with the norms and expectations of the classroom and school environment, social-class differences, and/or language difficulties

Table 1.1 Continued

---

16. Social adjustment, which may require moving away from a familiar neighborhood school to a larger school where there are greater cultural, racial, and economic differences
17. Behavioral adjustment, which may be related to an unstable home situation, poor nutrition, poor physical health, or the inability to handle overwhelming anxiety and stress
18. Academic achievement as measured by culturally biased achievement tests and/or verbal skills, motivation for learning, attitudes toward a particular class or toward the school in general, study habits, and family support

RELATIONSHIPS WITH PEERS

19. Ability to display empathy, to form friendships, to engage in cooperative and competitive activities, and to manage aggressive and sexual impulses
20. Social skills to form peer relationships at school and within the child's own community and the effects of these peer relationships on overall psychosocial functioning

ADAPTATION TO THE COMMUNITY

21. Quality participation in church activities, youth groups, and language- and ethnic-related classes
22. Quality participation in organized sports, arts activities, volunteer activities, or part-time jobs?
23. Inappropriate or excessive activities that create family conflicts or dysfunctional behavior, such as delinquency, drug abuse, or poor academic behavior

---

(c) client-therapist therapeutic process variables, including the agency setting. Table 1.2 presents this transcultural therapeutic framework.

Two important child-related variables are personal experiences and life experiences. The child's or youth's personal sociocultural variables include biological and psychological predisposition (gender, race, sexual preference); culture (world views and adaptive behaviors); cognitive styles (information processing, biased thinking, and stereotyping); self-perception (self-esteem, ethnic identity, acculturation level); aptitudes; abilities; interests; hopes; expectations; and behaviors. The child's life-experience variables include place of birth, nationality, immigration status, physical appearance, socioeconomic status, family characteristics, living environment (segregated/integrated, available support systems), educational history, and health status.

Two important therapist variables include personal sociocultural factors and professional factors. The personal sociocultural charac-

Table 1.2 A Transcultural Framework for Therapy with Ethnic Minority Children and Youth

THERAPIST

Personal
Biological/psychological predisposition
Gender
Race
Age
Sexual preference
Life experiences
Culture
World views
Beliefs
Values
Attitudes
Congitive styles
Information processing
Biased thinking
Sterotyping
Self-Perception
Ethnic idenity
Acculturation level

Racial sensitivity

Behaviors

Professional
Culture
Assumptions
Beliefs
Values
Attitudes
Training
Philosophy
Theories
Techniques
Skills

Behaviors

THERAPIST/CHILD

Child
Expectations met
Expectations of therapist's personal and professional attributes
Credibility
Problem solving process
Problem-solving techniques and skills

Follow through

Termination

Therapist
Providing cultural revelant settng
Professional and objective use of self
Ability to establish "cultural relationships"
Ability to specify real problem

Formulation cultural-relevant goals
Applying cultural-sensitive techniques and skills in problem solving

Ablity to follow through

Termination

CHILD

Personal
Biological/psychological predispostion
Gender
Race
Age
Sexual preference
Culture
World views
Beliefs
Values
Attitudes

Cognitive styles
Information processing
Biased thinking
Stereotyping

Self-perception
Self-esteem
Ethnic identity
Acculturation level
Aptitude , abilities
Motivation, expectations
Behaviors

Life Experiences
Place of Birth
Nationality
Immigration status
Health status
Physical apperance
Family characteristics
Level of acculturation
Singe/two-parent home
Child-rearing practices
Living enviroment

School adjustment

Relationship with peers

Adaptation to the community

teristics of the therapist are the same as those of the client (child), with one exception being the level of the therapist's racial consciousness and sensitivity. The professional factors influence how the therapist views the child's culture. Therapists should be reminded that the professional training many receive in mental health, medicine, and education has not gone beyond the Eurocentric and White-American middle-class orientation. Such a monocultural narrow focus has impeded cross-cultural therapeutic processes (Mizo & Delaney, 1981). The therapist's personal variable of professional training in the philosophical assumptions of therapeutic theories, techniques, and skills also can enhance or impede the cross-cultural therapeutic process.

Client-therapist therapeutic process variables include the client's family and their conception of the child's problem and how familiar the family is with the therapy process (Casas & Keefe, 1978; Kleinman & Lin, 1981).

On the other hand, the therapist's sensitivity and culturally relevant skills and techniques and the agency's responsiveness to minorities are all important. Together they greatly influence the therapy process and its outcome.

To be culturally competent in therapy with a minority child, a therapist needs to master certain skills that correspond with six interactive phases in the therapeutic process. These phases are (a) precontact, (b) problem identification, (c) problem specification, (d) mutual goal formation, (e) problem solving, and (f) termination.

Unfamiliarity with therapy and bad experiences with the social welfare bureaucracy cause most minority children and their parents to have negative attitudes about the helping professions. The skills and sensitivity which the therapist exhibits at the precontact phase will determine whether the child will return for therapy. The therapist's understanding of the child's ethnic reality, race, language, social class, birth place, and acculturation level will help him or her to be culturally sensitive. Children will recognize and appreciate a therapist's sensitivity and acceptance of their ethnic differences. This will help the child trust the therapist and certainly will enhance the therapeutic process.

In view of the complexity of the minority child's problems, the presenting problem which brings the child to therapy may not be the exact or real problem. The therapist's skill is essential during the problem-identification phase, which incorporates the ecological perspective to "tune in" to the child's cultural dispositions, behaviors, and family structure. The therapist's ability to discuss openly racial and ethnic differences and issues and to adapt to the child's interactive style may free the child to disclose other matters that really concern him or her (Ho & McDowell, 1973). The therapist's ability to elicit and understand the child's conceptualization of the problem and previous attempts to solve the problem also will facilitate the interactive process of this phase.

Using cultural mapping as a means to ascertain the child's problem has been helpful (Pendagast & Sherman, 1977) in the problem-specification phase of therapy. The therapist's skill in identifying the ecosystem sources of a minority child's problems and in linking the ecosystem source to the individual child's concerns or problems is important at this phase of therapy. What the therapist suggests in problem specification should consider each child's cultural reality. For example, the closeness in the mother-child dyad should not be misconstrued as enmeshment among Hispanic American and Asian American families. Similarly, a minority adolescent's development of autonomy should not be determined solely by moving from home or the adolescent's ability to support himself or herself.

At the mutual-goal-formation phase, it is important that the therapist clearly delineate agency functions and respectfully inform the child of his or her professional expectations of the child. Therapeutic goals formulated should be consistent with the child's emphasis on collectivism and interdependence. It is essential that the therapist be able to differentiate and select from three categories of goals: situational stress (e.g., social isolation, poverty), cultural transition (e.g., conflictual family and school practices, intergenerational conflicts, acculturation conflicts), and transcultural dysfunctional patterns (e.g., developmental arrests or impasses, repetitive interactional behaviors). It is also important for goals to be growth focused, structured, realistic, concrete, practical, cultural specific, and readily achievable (Acosta et al., 1982; Edwards & Edwards, 1984).

Therapeutic skills required by the therapist in the problem-solving phase include the therapist's ability to reaffirm the child's life skills and coping strategies within a bicultural environment. The therapist's ability to "frame" the change within the traditional family and to use culturally acceptable language will reduce resistance. Similarly, the therapist's ability to suggest a change or new strategy as an expansion of the "old" cultural stress or problem-solving response will be welcomed by the child and will usually generate positive results.

Finally, the therapist's suggestions and applications of change strategies should be consistent with the child's developmental needs and problems, degree of acculturation, motivation for change, and comfort in responding to the therapist's directives.

Assessment of the accomplishment of therapeutic goals at the evaluation and termination phases should be conducted according to the child's collective culture. For example, the therapist's effort to help the child individuate should be evaluated according to how the child can best get along with others, including his or her family or extended families. Termination is in order when the child is reconnected to his or her larger world or environment and can incorporate the new changes independent of the therapist's interaction. Finally, effective termination also requires that the therapist consider the ethnic minority child's concept of time and space in a relationship during termination and makes sure the termination is natural and gradual.

A summary of guidelines for therapeutic intervention skills with ethnic minority children is presented in Table 1.3. The Ethnic-Competence-Skill Model in Psychological Interventions with Ethnic Minority Children and Youth is constructed based on these guidelines (see the Appendix). The primary purpose of this model is to assist therapists to assess and to build their therapeutic intervention skills with ethnic minority children and youth.

Table 1.3 Guidelines for Therapeutic Intervention Skills with Ethnic Minority Children

Intervention Phase	Intervention Skills
Precontact	Ability to realize the child's ethnic minority reality, including the effects of racism and poverty on the child
	Ability to understand the child's ethnicity, race, language, social class, and differences in minority status, such as refugees, immigrants, and native born
	Ability to objectify and make use of worker's own culture/ethnicity and professional culture (psychiatry, social work, psychology, etc.), which may be different from the child's culture and ethnicity
	Ability to be sensitive to the child's fear of racist or prejudiced orientations
Problem Identification	Ability to understand and "tune in" to the child's cultural dispositions, behaviors, and family structures that may include close extended-family ties
	Ability to discuss openly racial/ethnic differences and issues and respond to culturally based cues
	Ability to adapt to the child's interactive style and language, conveying to the child that the worker understands, values, and validates his or her life strategies
	Ability to understand the child's help-seeking behavior, which includes the child's conceptualization of the problem and the manner by which the problem can be solved
Problem Specification	Ability to use cultural mapping to ascertain the child's problem
	Ability to identify the ecosystematic sources (racism, poverty, prejudice) of a minority child's problems
	Ability to identify the links between ecosystematic problems and individual concerns or problems
	Ability to consider the implications of what is being suggested in relation to each child's cultural reality (unique dispositions, life strategies, and experiences)
Mutual Goal Formation	Ability to clearly delineate agency functions and respectfully inform the child of the worker's professional expectations of him or her
	Ability to formulate goals consistent with the child's emphasis on collectivism and interdependence
	Ability to differentiate and select from three categories of goals: situational stress (e.g., social isolation, poverty), cultural transition (e.g., conflictual family-school practice), and transcultural dysfunctional patterns (e.g., developmental impasses and repetitive interactional behaviors)

Table 1.3 Continued

	Ability to engage the child to formulate a goal that is problem or growth focused, structured, realistic, concrete, practical, and readily achievable
Problem Solving	Ability to reaffirm the child's life skills and coping strategies within a bicultural environment
	Ability to frame the change within the traditional, culturally acceptable language
	Ability to suggest a change or new strategy as an expansion of the "old" cultural stress or problem-solving response
	Ability to apply new strategies that are consistent with the child's needs and problem, degree of acculturation, motivation for change, and comfort in responding to the worker's directives
Termination	Ability to assess the accomplishment of therapeutic goals according to the child's collectivist culture
	Ability to reconnect and restore the child to his or her larger world or environment
	Ability to assist the child to incorporate the new changes in the child's original life strategy independent of the worker's interaction
	Ability to consider the child's concept of time and space in a relationship during termination and make sure the termination is natural and gradual

PART II

Understanding and Assessing the Mental Health Problems of Ethnic Minority Children and Adolescents

Part I of this book introduced the transcultural theoretical framework from which appropriate assessment and therapeutic guidelines in therapy with ethnic minority children and adolescents are derived. Part II provides an up-to-date resource for the understanding and clinical assessment of ethnic minority children and youth experiencing political, social, educational, or economic problems. Using the ecological perspective as an organizing framework, I have included materials relevant to the following ethnic minority groups: Asian American, American Indian, Black American, and Hispanic American. This section is organized according to (a) historical background; (b) mental health problems and issues; and (c) individual child, family, school, and societal systems and issues. Adherence to a single outline facilitates organization, comparison, and integration of common core knowledge and inter- and intraethnic group differences in the assessment of minority children and youth.

2

Asian American Children and Adolescents

Historical Background

Asian Americans are often perceived as sharing the same or similar characteristics, but they actually comprise many diverse groups: Chinese, Japanese, Korean, Filipinos, Samoans, Guamanians, Hawaiians, and other Pacific Islanders. Other groups include recent immigrants and refugees from Vietnam, Thailand, Cambodia, Laos, and Indonesia; persons from India, Pakistan, and Ceylon; and children of mixed ancestry with one Asian parent (Marishima, 1978). There are obvious language, historical, social, and economic differences. Generational status (new immigrants vs. third and fourth generation) among groups and individuals should not be overlooked. Before accurate assessment of Asian American children and adolescents can take place, current demographics, immigration data, native culture, and family tradition must be reviewed.

Demographic Data

The Asian American population has doubled since 1970, now comprising about 2% of the total U.S. population (3.5 million), and it

Table 2.1 Asian Americans in the United States, 1970 and 1980

Year	Chinese	Filipino	Japanese	Korean	Vietnamese	Samoan	Guamanian
1970	435,062	343,060	591,290	70,000[a]	N.A.[b]	N.A.	N.A.
1980	806,042	774,652	700,974	354,593	261,729	41,948	32,158

SOURCE: U.S. Bureau of the Census. (1983). *Characteristics of the Population: 1980* (Vol. 1, pp. 9-20). Washington, DC: Government Printing Office.
a. Estimated.
b. N.A. = not available.

continues to increase. The population distribution of Asian Americans in 1970 and 1980 is shown in Table 2.1.

In 1970 the most populous Asian American group was the Japanese (591,290), followed by the Chinese (435,062) and the Filipinos (343,060). In 1980, however, the Chinese were the most numerous (806,042), followed by the Filipinos (774,652) and the Japanese (700,974). The Koreans showed a fivefold increase from an estimated 70,000 in 1970 to 354,593 in 1980. Other Asian groups identified by the U.S. Census but not included in Table 2.1 are the Asian Indians (361,531) and the native Hawaiians (166,814). The Immigration Act of 1965 and the U.S. policy on refugees that resulted from the Vietnam War are primarily responsible for the rapid Asian American population increase in the United States. Most Asian Americans live in coastal urban areas and in Hawaii. Despite a concentrated effort by the U.S. government to scatter recent Southeast Asian immigrants throughout the country, the majority resettled in California (135,308), Texas (36,198), and Washington state (16,286).

Immigration Data

The Chinese were the first immigrants from Asia to arrive in the United States. Their immigration from China during the 1840s was encouraged by the social and economic unrest in China at that time and by overpopulation in certain provinces (De Vos & Abbott, 1966). During this period, there was a demand in the United States for Chinese to help build the transcontinental railroad. However, a diminishing labor market and fear of the "yellow peril" later made the Chinese hesitant to immigrate. Chinese men were robbed, beaten, and murdered, especially if they tried to compete with Whites in the mining districts of western states. Eventually anti-Chinese sentiment culminated in the passing of the Federal Chinese Exclusion Act of 1882, the first exclusion act against any ethnic group. This racist immigration law was repealed in 1943 as a gesture of friendship toward China, who was an ally of the United States during World War II. The Immigration Act of 1965 finally abolished national-origin quotas. "Oldtimer" Chinese immigrants were characterized by demographers as primarily uneducated peasants, unskilled laborers, and men. Post-1965 immigrants have been well-educated urban families (Lai, 1980).

Early Japanese immigrants came to the United States from 1890 to 1924, after the Chinese exclusion laws were passed. They left a rapidly industrializing country and often got jobs as contract laborers on plantations in Hawaii. During World War II, anti-Japanese prejudice in the United States culminated in the forced removal in 1942 of over 110,000 Japanese, 75% of whom were American citizens, to guarded relocation centers. Unlike the Chinese, Japanese immigrants were allowed to start families by employing the *picture bride* (bride selected by photograph) method of marriage. Consequently, the acculturation process of their American-born children occurred much earlier than for immigrant Chinese children. Hence, in general, the Japanese are more acculturated than the Chinese, even though many Chinese trace family arrival in this country back further.

The Filipino population in the United States grew most rapidly after the Immigration Act of 1965. As a result of the Spanish-American War and the Treaty of Paris (1899), the Philippines at one time were actually a possession of the United States. The Tydings-McDuffie Independence Act conferred commonwealth status on the Philippines, and Filipinos then became aliens for the purpose of U.S. immigration. The earliest Filipino immigrants were unskilled laborers or students who were encouraged by the U.S. colonial government to attend American colleges and universities (Melendy, 1980). Immigrants who came in the 1960s were mostly young professionals, both men and women. Many of them experienced difficulties in obtaining U.S. licenses to practice their professions. The majority of the surviving early Filipino immigrants are now retired, living in cheap one-room hotels and apartments. They experience health care problems, limited recreational opportunities, and physical and psychological isolation.

The number of Korean immigrants just prior to the Immigration Act of 1965 was slightly over 7,000 (H. Kim, 1980). A high proportion of them were Christian, because American missionaries in Korea played a major role in Korean immigration. Kim estimated that 90% of the Korean immigrants have been here less than 15 years because the Immigration Act of 1965 went into effect in 1968. The largest Korean community, with a population over 150,000, is in Los Angeles. Generally, post-1968 Korean immigrants have had to endure less hostility and structural discrimination than the early Chinese and Japanese immigrants.

The Pacific Islanders include groups such as Samoans, Tongans, Guamanians, and a small number from Tahiti and the Fuji Islands. Samoan immigration began to increase after 1951, when the U.S. Navy closed its island base. Guamanian immigration was facilitated by the 1950 Organic Act, which conferred U.S. citizenship on inhabitants of the territory of Guam. Because of their ties with the Church of Jesus Christ of Latter-Day Saints, many Tongans have settled near Salt Lake City, Utah. The Pacific Islanders as a group are relatively few in number and have no visibly strong ethnic community in the United States in the 1990s.

Southeast Asians from Cambodia, Laos, and Vietnam came to this country primarily as refugees. Statistics from 1980 indicate that 415,238 Indochinese were in the United States, of which 78% were from Vietnam, 16% from Cambodia, and 6% from Laos. The majority of them have settled in California, Texas, and Washington (Montero & Dieppa, 1982). Cambodia, Laos, and Vietnam were part of the old French colonial empire and were lumped together as French Indochina. Cambodian culture was influenced by India, whereas the people of Laos are mainly ethnic Thai. The Vietnamese culture was heavily influenced by China and France. The exodus of Vietnamese refugees began in 1975 with the fall of Saigon and U.S. withdrawal from the country. The first wave of refugees was mostly well-educated professionals. A second wave was admitted to the United States after 1975 and consisted of less-educated people. The latter have experienced more difficulty than the former in adjusting to the United States.

Native Culture

To assess an Asian American child's world view, a therapist should focus on understanding the cultural values, belief systems, and societal norms of American culture as well as Asian traditional culture. In an attempt to understand Asian American clients and to work effectively with this unique ethnic group, Ho (1976b) lists seven salient cultural values operating among Asian Americans.

Filial Piety. The respectful love of parent is the cornerstone of morality and is expressed in a variety of forms. *Oya-KoKo,* a Japanese's version of filial piety to parents, requires a child's sensitivity, obligation, and unquestionable loyalty to lineage and parents. An Asian child is expected to comply with familial and social authority even to the point of sacrificing his or her personal desires and ambitions.

Shame as a Behavioral Influence. Shame (*tiu lien* in Chinese) and shaming are used traditionally to help reinforce familial expectations and proper behavior within and outside the family. If an individual behaves improperly, he or she will "lose face" and also may cause the family, community, or society to withdraw confidence and support. In Asian societal structures, where interdependence is very important, the actual or threatened withdrawal of support may shake a person's basic trust and cause him or her considerable anxiety at the thought of facing life alone.

Self-Control. Self-discipline is another concept highly valued by Asian Americans. The value *enryo* requires a Japanese individual to maintain modesty in behavior, be humble in expectations, and show appropriate hesitation and unwillingness to intrude on another's time, energy, or resources. To *Yin-Nor* for a Chinese is to evince stoicism, patience, and an uncomplaining attitude in the face of adversity and to display tolerance for life's painful moments.

Middle-Position Virtue. In training children, Asian parents emphasize a social norm that cultivates the virtues of the middle position, in which an individual should feel neither haughty nor unworthy. Middle-position virtue is quite different from the perfectionism and individualism highly valued by the middle-class White American population. The Asian American emphasis on middle position brings an individual in step with others instead of ahead or behind others. Thus, it fosters the individual's sense of belonging and togetherness.

Awareness of Social Milieu. An Asian's concern for the welfare of the group also is related to his or her acute awareness of social milieu, characterized by social and economic limitations and immobility.

The individual is highly sensitive to the opinions of peers and allows the social nexus to define his or her thoughts, feelings, and actions. In the interest of social solidarity, one subordinates oneself to the group, suppressing and restraining any disruptive emotions and opinions. Despite an individual's wealth and social status, compliance with social norms, which provides social esteem and self-respect, is strictly observed.

Fatalism. Constantly buffeted by nature and by political upheaval over which they had little control, Asian Americans adopted a philosophical detachment. This resignation allowed people to accept their fate with equanimity. Other than trying to philosophize or ascertain underlying meaning in life events, Asians met life pragmatically. It is unfortunate that this pragmatic adaptability, the very factor that often contributed to their success in the United States, later became a serious handicap. Asian Americans' continuing silence sometimes cause them to fall further behind in an alien American culture that encourages, and indeed demands, aggressiveness and outspoken individualism. This fatalistic attitude of Asian Americans has partly contributed to their unwillingness to seek outside professional help. Unfortunately, this pragmatic adaptability is often misconstrued by some mental health and social services providers as resistance.

Inconspicuousness. Fear of attracting attention was particularly acute among the thousands of Asian immigrants who came to the United States illegally. Experiences with racist segments of American society further convinced Asian immigrants of the need for and value of silence and inconspicuousness. Fear and distrust still linger today among the descendants of early immigrants. It is understandable why Asians are extremely reluctant to turn to government agencies for aid, even in cases of dire need. Asian Americans' silence and inconspicuousness tend to make them verbally passive members in politics, group work, and community activities.

Family Tradition

The cohesive extended network of the traditional Asian American family is structured and prioritized, fed with male dominance, and with parental ties paramount. A male child has distinct obligations and duties to his parents that assume a higher value than obligations to his siblings, children, or wife. Sibling relationships are considered second in priority and are frequently acknowledged through cooperative adult activities. Concepts and teachings, such as working hard, responsibility, family obligations, and collaborations, pervade parent-child relationships. Members of the older generation are responsible for transmitting guidelines for socially acceptable behavior, educating younger people in how to deal with life events, and serving as a source of support in coping with life crises (Coelho & Stein, 1980). A traditional Asian American family becomes the primary caretaker of its members' physical, social, and emotional health.

Mental Health Issues and Problems

Epidemiological Data

There is very little literature dealing with the mental and psychological problems of Asian American children and youth. Asian American patients have been found to be similar to White patients in mental health diagnoses, except they are more likely to receive psychotic diagnoses (S. Sue, 1977). This difference may be explained by the fact that less severely disturbed Asian Americans avoid using mental health services.

Many investigators have suggested that Asian Americans as a group consume less alcohol and have fewer cases of alcoholism than Whites and other ethnic groups (Comberg, 1982). This is attributed to the genetic-racial differences in alcohol sensitivity and aversion and Asian American attitudes and values toward the use of alcohol. Some observers have predicted that alcoholism among Asian Americans may increase in the future in response to urbanization, cultural conflict, and changes in family structure.

At the First National Asian American Conference on Drug Abuse Prevention, participants generally felt that drug abuse is as prevalent in Asian American communities as in other communities (Multicultural Drug Abuse Prevention Center, 1976). These references are almost 15 years old. One would expect more drug abuse in 1990. Lyman (1977) believes organized drug dealings in San Francisco's Chinatown provided revenues for the *tongs* (Chinese associations) and gained a foothold.

Crime and juvenile delinquency are low in Asian American communities (Kitano, 1976). However, it is generally recognized that

criminal acts in urban Asian American communities are underre-
ported (Petersen, 1978). Youth gangs' violent activities have increased
recently in various Chinatowns throughout the country. Lyman (1977)
attributes the increased formation of gangs to (a) an increase in the
number of immigrant youths, (b) frustration over racism and powerlessness, (c) inability to succeed in school because of English-
language problems and cultural conflicts, and (d) the financial gains
obtained through gang activities (p. 136).

The relatively low statistical rates of psychological and behavioral
problems of Asian American children and youth in big school districts, such as those in Los Angeles county and Seattle, should not be
misconstrued—that these children do not suffer from psychological
difficulties. Instead, fewer documented cases actually may reflect a
tendency by Asian American parents to deny or minimize certain behavioral problems in their children (Sata, 1983).

Several studies have indicated that Asian Americans tend to express psychological strain through somatic complaints (Kleinman &
Sung, 1979; Rahe & Ja, 1978; S. Sue et al., 1976). S. Sue and Morishima
(1982) offered the following speculations. First, because the Asian
American culture emphasizes a holistic view of psychological and
physical health, both emotional and somatic problems are likely to be
generated by stressors. Second, physical complaints have less negative stigma than emotional complaints, which imply mental disturbance. Third, because self-disclosure or the expression of strong
affects is discouraged by Asian American culture, physical complaints may be used to allow expression of personal and interpersonal problems.

Diagnostic Categories

According to the Los Angeles County Department of Mental Health
(1986), a total of 115 Chinese American children under 18 were
treated during the fiscal year of 1986. Diagnostically, these children
ranged from adjustment disorders to psychotic disorders.

A total of 14 Asian American adolescents were seen for suicidal attempts from 1985 to 1988 at the Asian Bicultural Clinic of Governeur
Hospital in New York City (Ma, Ma, & Chen, 1988). These adolescents'
diagnoses ranged from affective disorder (7), schizoaffective disorder
(2), schizophrenic disorder (1), and atypical psychosis (1) to adjustment disorder (2) and life circumstance problem (1).

Out of approximately 3,500 Korean children enrolled during the 2-year school period in the greater Chicago area, 52 were referred for psychological evaluations (Koh & Koh, 1982). Among those, 34 were boys and 18 were girls (2 to 1 ratio) with a mean chronological age of 12.5 years. Reasons for referral were classified into learning problems (50%), educational guidance (17%), poor peer relationships (10%), and other problems including behavioral and emotional problems. Evaluators also concluded that compared to bilingual children from European countries, Asian children require a longer period of acculturation in terms of language and culture. It may take 2 to 3 years for Asian children to acculturate, compared to 6 months to a year for European immigrant children to reach the same degree of acculturation.

Hisama (1980) also indicated that children of Asian immigrant families tend to internalize their distress, thus manifesting more anxiety reactions, psychosomatic disorders, and school phobia. Chinese American youth constituted 5% of the 8,000 juvenile offenders in 1986 in San Francisco, where approximately 12% of the population is Chinese American (Millard, 1987).

Dubanoski and Snyder (1980) reported that although Japanese Americans accounted for about 27% of the population in Hawaii in 1976 and 1977, only 3.45% of abuse and 4.65% of neglect cases were attributed to them. According to the authors, neglect was more common than abuse, which may reflect the Japanese American family's emphasis on shame and ostracism as forms of punishment as opposed to direct confrontations involving physical violence.

Problems Associated with Relocation

Studies indicate that relocations can be very stressful for children (Garmezy & Rutter, 1983; Hisama, 1980). The specific experience and manner of coping are related to the developmental stage of the child. For the infant and toddler, the impact of relocation is more often experienced through the parents' adjustment or anxiety level. For the latency-age child or adolescent, relocations or migrations are experienced directly as significant loss and great uncertainty. The problems of self-concept, identity conflicts, and generational conflicts with parents are typical issues confronting adolescents. Relocation seems to exacerbate these normal development conflicts.

The adolescent's search for a new identity can be seen as a persistent attempt to define and redefine himself or herself. Adolescents in their native homelands have had few choices in moral values. Traditionally, Asian culture and society have reinforced the morality taught in the family. However, after relocating to the United States, Asian youth often find that their traditional family values are inconsistent with those of American society. The American ways of encouraging youth to be more expressive, autonomous, and self-determining have become attractive to Asian youth. Hence, they begin to refuse guidance from parents and enter into situations and liaisons without parental consent.

Traditional Asian culture emphasizes achieving one's identity and sense of worth through close relationships with adult family members and by being a member of an established lineage and extended family system. The process of relocation and immigration often disrupts and separates many Asian families, especially refugee families. Such discontinuity, coupled with rapid exposure and socialization in an age-segregated American society, enhances the importance and influence of a peer group. Asian adolescents' frequent rejections by American peer groups and conflict with their parents can be detrimental to their development. Studies of minority immigrants indicate self-depreciation and low self-worth among these adolescents (Nann, 1982; Osborne, 1971). Naditch and Morrissey (1976) speculate that minority immigrant youths' conflicts and role stresses may result in deviant behavior and, occasionally, serious psychopathology.

Two physiological systems, respiratory and digestive, have been found to be primary somatic targets for Asians experiencing immigrational stress (Holmes & Masuda, 1974, p. 175). Denial is the defense mechanism most frequently used by recent Vietnamese refugees. This denial defense is congruent with the Asian cultural values of self-sacrifice, submission for the common good, harmony, and consignment to fate. When the use of denial fails to protect a refugee from some of the harsh realities of immigration and when previous support systems are unavailable, psychosocial destruction such as psychosis may occur (Pfister-Ammeude, 1973). A national mental health needs assessment found some alarming facts concerning stress among Asian immigrants: (a) Mental health problems among Southeast Asian immigrants who arrived in 1975 only began to surface several years later; (b) depression was the most frequently reported problem; (c) anxiety, marital conflict, and intergenerational conflict were prevalent; and (d) the stress of the uprooting and cultural adjustment led to many emotional problems (Bureau of Research and Training, 1979).

Ecological Approach to Assessment

Therapy with ethnic minority children and youth should focus on the interaction between the child and the environment. The goal of the therapy is to enhance and restore the psychosocial functioning of the child or to change oppressive or destructive social conditions that negatively affect the mutually beneficial interaction between the child and the environment. In assessing an Asian American child's needs for services, the therapist should seek to understand the child's feelings and attitudes about oppressive experiences and destructive factors and their negative impacts.

The ecological approach is adopted for analysis of sociopolitical and psychological factors affecting the Asian American child. The ecological approach consists of four interconnected levels: personal, family, school, and societal. Analysis of each level as it affects the life, social condition, and performance of an Asian American child follows.

The Personal System

Level of Acculturation

To combat social isolation and to gain a feeling of belonging and acceptance, an Asian American child is forced to find reference groups in the United States. The child may identify entirely with traditional Asian culture, reject Asian culture as old fashioned and dysfunctional, or find an intermediate position (i.e., become bicultural). Unfortunately, regardless of what value system a child adopts, there are potential adjustment problems.

E. Lee (1982) has suggested four criteria to determine a child's degree of acculturation: (a) years in the United States—as a whole, the longer the child lives in the United States, the more he or she is acculturated; (b) age at time of immigration—an 8-year-old is more easily acculturated than an 18-year-old; (c) country of origin, political, economic, and educational background—a Chinese student from Hong Kong (a British Colony) is more easily acculturated than a young adult from mainland China; and (d) professional background of the parents—a child of an English-speaking medical doctor is more easily acculturated than a child whose parents work in a Chinese restaurant. The child's family immigrational history is important in the assessment of the child's acculturation level. If the child is born in this country and is, for example, a third-generation Japanese American (*Sensei*) who speaks fluent English, ethnicity and cultural issues may be less of an issue than for a child who has recently arrived in the United States.

Accurate assessment of a child's acculturational level not only assists the therapist in data collection, analysis, and interpretation, it also may determine if the child will return for future therapy sessions. Understanding the child's level of acculturation will enable the therapist to be sensitive and responsive in the engagement phase of the therapeutic process.

Physical Appearance

Most Asian American children, American or foreign born, eventually become conscious of their physical appearance (D. Lee, 1975). Some Asian American children view their Asian features negatively and even perceive their physical characteristics as ugly, inferior, or shameful. Their negative perception makes them susceptible to teasing by their peers. Some children overreact to being teased, whereas others may resent being Asian, thus affecting their personality development and healthy positive self-concept (B. Kim, 1977-1981).

Skin color is another stress affecting Asian children's perception of their physical appearance. Many Asian children and youth equate being light-complected with being beautiful or handsome and think that to be American is to be White. If Asian children feel inferior because of skin color, this affects their self-image and feelings of self-worth. Negative self-concepts based on skin color are further reinforced by the growing realization that other dark-complected ethnic minorities do not enjoy the same social and economic status as their White counterparts.

The generally smaller physique of Asian American children often causes them to be vulnerable to the "heightism" so prevalent in American society (Okie, 1988). Some children blame their parents for their "inferior" physical attributes and differences. Thus, it may exacerbate the already stressful adolescent-parent relationship.

Speech and Language

It is important to assess the degree of fluency in English and in the native Asian language, especially if this may be affecting competence in schoolwork or relationships with family and peers. Asian American children often experience special language problems. According to the U.S. Department of Health, Education, and Welfare (1974), about 70% of Asian children under the age of 14 years still speak their native language in their homes. The more recent needs assessment surveys (B. Kim, 1978; Wang & Louie, 1979) also reported that the lack of English proficiency seemed to exacerbate virtually every problem area of Asian Americans. It also limits the availability of problem-solving strategies.

Asian Americans' general lack of proficiency in the English language is further complicated by the Asian culture's de-emphasis of verbal skills in meaningful interpersonal exchange. Indeed, among the Japanese, there is a distrust of verbal skills as connoting glibness, possible dishonesty, or lack of trustworthiness (Lebra, 1976).

Depending on the acculturation level of Asian American children, most of them are bilingual. Their bilingualism can drastically reverse the hierarchical role of their parents, who may be monolingual or have a poor command of English. The children's rejection of their parents' culture also is manifested in their unwillingness to learn and speak their parents' native language. The language differential between children and their parents and grandparents may widen the generational and cultural rift within Asian American families, especially among those whose parents are immigrants and whose children are American born (Wake, 1983).

Affective Behavior

Studies have indicated that Asian American children and youth are more emotionally restrained and unexpressive than Caucasian American youth (Han, 1985; Jourard, 1971). However, their affective behavior may be culturally appropriate. Fenz and Arkoff (1962) reported that Asian American children learn self-control and detachment by modeling their parents' behavior. Problem behaviors are clearly spelled out; aggression, antisocial behavior, and disobedience bring shame to the entire family and are strictly discouraged. Emotional displays are discouraged in the home because of the formal relationship that exists between parents and children (Sung, 1971). In comparison to other ethnic groups, Asian American mothers are more likely than Black or Caucasian mothers to describe their children as shy, self-effacing, and overcontrolled (Tuddenham, Thomas, & Stuart, 1974).

The affective behavior of an Asian American youth also depends upon the acculturation level of the youth and his or her family. The more acculturated the youth is, the more expressive he or she will become. Although the youth's expressiveness may be highly rewarded in school, he or she may run into conflict within the youth's home environment, where emotional restraint and self-control are taught and reinforced.

Interpersonal Relations

For Anglo-American youth, independence is a virtue in itself. However, Asian American youth are taught at an earlier age that there is a pervasive awareness of mutual interdependence. The common forms of communication include those that reveal the awareness of the dependence of Asian American youth upon one another. Obviously, close family relationships should come first. These should be followed by close relationships within school groups, and then by occupation or company groups. Through life, an Asian American learns that one's sense of identity, belonging, and mutual interdependence are related to groups. As an Asian American child struggles to belong to groups at school, he or she can easily be influenced by American peers striving for independence. To be accepted by American peers at school may require the Asian child to detach himself somewhat from his family or origin. This can then cause the child to experience cultural and family conflict.

Attitude Toward Self

Research indicates Asian American children and youth display less sense of control over the environment than White children and adolescents (Coleman et al., 1972). Japanese American children aged 9 to 12 years have a less positive self-concept than their Caucasian American peers with respect to physical characteristics (Arkoff & Weaver, 1966). Chinese students were found to have suffered from more stress than White students, especially in feelings of isolation, loneliness, rejection, and anxiety.

Asian American children's and youths' attitude toward self is often negatively influenced by a society that only gives lip service to equality. These children are constantly bombarded by the mass media, which upholds Western values as superior. Additionally, Asian children may have experienced ethnicity-related insults, ranging from simple teasing at school to recurrent derogatory comments by other significant persons, including their teachers. Once the children internalize these negative experiences, they deny their own ethnicity, and this reduces their positive attitudes toward themselves.

Anxiety and Patterns of Defense

To express anxiety and emotional distress, Asian American students are more likely than Caucasian American students to exhibit somatic symptoms, such as headaches, weakness, pressures on the chest or head, insomnia, and tenseness (Kleinman & Lin, 1981; Marsella, Moore, & Guzman, 1973; Rahe & Ja, 1978). However, a therapist should not view the Asian child's physical complaints solely as a reflection of an underlying emotional problem. Successful treatment often requires intervention at the level of dysfunctioning, which includes the primary malfunctioning in biological and psychological processes as well as the secondary psychosocial and cultural responses to the dysfunctioning.

Three speculations help explain why Asian American children tend to express anxiety and distress by somatization. First, there is an interconnectiveness between the physical and psychological status (Wa, 1980). Second, expression of strong affects are prohibited, but physical complaints are acceptable (Kleinman & Lin, 1981). Third, physical disturbance is less stigmatized than mental disturbance (Murase, 1980) and, therefore, is more acceptable in Asian American culture.

Issues of Sexuality

Most Asian American children grow up with minimal direct sex education from parents and other elders. Much of what they know about sex is learned from their peers at school and the news media. Language differences between parent and child may cause a communications barrier in the discussion of sexuality within the family. However, recent data from Abramson and Imai-Marquez (1982) suggest that even parents who do not have a communication barrier with their children experience similar problems.

Ironically, among many traditional Asian groups, holding hands, hugging, and touching among those of the same sex and between children and the aged, regardless of sex, are viewed as normal. As the children grow older, the norms of the peer group and those of the

American society are the exact opposites of the norms they have been socialized in.

In regard to sexual behavior, many traditional Asian parents apply double standards to their children. A daughter is not afforded the same degree of freedom and liberty in dating as the son. According to traditional Asian standards, dating and all activities related to it should have one basic purpose: choosing a marriage partner. The socializing and entertainment aspects of dating are viewed as incidental, frivolous, and may render the young people, especially daughters, unfit for marriage.

If an Asian American child's general dissatisfaction with his or her physical characteristics endures into early adolescence, the onset of dating may present very stressful times. This is the time when the realities of their ethnicity may generate difficulties, especially with their date's parents if they have negative attitudes toward Asians.

Because of American media, Asian American girls may have been conditioned to expect the Asian boys they date to behave assertively and confidently in the traditional Western manner (Weiss, 1970). They often reject Asian American boys who do not fit this image. Many Asian American boys then find themselves heir to two different cultures but belonging to neither.

The Family System

Immigration History and Level of Acculturation

The traditional Asian American family structure provides stability, interpersonal intimacy, social support, and a relatively stress-free environment for its members (Hsu, 1972). However, the process of immigration and cultural transition exerts a severe blow to these families. Relatives and close friends often are no longer available to provide material and emotional support to needy members. The traditional hierarchical structure and rigidity of family roles often makes the expression and resolution of conflicts within the nuclear family very difficult. In turn, little or no interpersonal interaction outside the nuclear family forces greater demands and intense interaction *within* the nuclear family. This can leave members highly vulnerable and with many unresolved conflicts. Discrepancies in acculturation between husband and wife and between parents and children negatively affect the decision making and functioning of a family. An individual's acceptance of and compliance with Western values, such as individualism, independence, and assertiveness, especially in attitudes related to authority, sexuality, and freedom of choice, often make the hierarchical structure of a traditional Asian American family dysfunctional.

Although an Asian American family undergoes several stages in its attempt to help its members, different families may have different service needs and help-seeking patterns. Generally, social service workers see the following three types of Asian American families (Ho, 1987, p. 35).

Recently Arrived Immigrant Families. Initial requests for services by this type of family tend to be predominantly requests for information and referral, advocacy, and other concrete services such as English-language instruction, legal aid, and child care. Due to cultural differences, unfamiliarity with mental health resources, and language barriers, these families seldom seek personal or psychological help.

Immigrant-American Families. These families are characterized by foreign-born parents and American-born children and the great degree of cultural conflict between them. They usually require help in resolving generational conflicts, communication problems, role clarification, and renegotiation.

Immigrant-Descendant Families. These families usually consist of second- (Japanese *Nisei*) or third- (Japanese *Sansei*) generation American-born parents and their children. They speak English at home and are acculturated to Western values. They can seek help from mainstream human service agencies, mental health centers, and private practitioners with some degree of comfort.

Family Structure and Life Patterns

The cohesive extended network of the traditional Asian American family is structured and prioritized, fed with male dominance and strong parental ties. The roles and expectations of a parent-child subsystem within an Asian/Pacific American family are well-defined. The father is the head of the family. He makes the decisions, and his authority generally is unquestioned. In addition to being the breadwinner of the family, he is totally responsible for the welfare of the family as a whole. He makes and enforces the family roles and is the primary disciplinarian. Hence, the father is frequently perceived as somewhat stern, distant, and less approachable than the mother.

The mother, on the other hand, is recognized as a nurturer and caretaker of both her husband and children. Her energy and creativity are channeled primarily into taking care of her children. In addition to providing the children with physical care and emotional nurturance, the mother intercedes occasionally with the father on the children's behalf. She forms a strong emotional bond with her children, especially her firstborn son, who later is expected to provide economic and social security for her upon her husband's death. Due to the strong emotional attachment the oldest son feels toward his mother, the wishes of the mother are frequently respectfully attended to by this son.

Whereas the primary role of the father is to provide and enforce the rules, and the mother's role is to nurture and care for her children, the child's responsibility at home is to obey and to be deferential to his or her parents. The Asian/Pacific child is taught to behave in ways that will not bring shame to the family. The child is always reminded that the effect of his or her behavior on parents and clan must be the major consideration governing one's actions (Ritter, Smith, & Chan, 1965). Love and affection generally are not openly displayed in an Asian/Pacific family. When the child is an infant, both parents usually show no hesitancy in pampering the child publicly. After these early years, the child quickly becomes incorporated into his or her role in the family structure and learns to live by the more rigid guidelines and expectations of the family and the society. Generally, Asian/Pacific children grow up in the midst of adults, including their parents and their extended family. Children are seldom left at home with babysitters or other adults (Hsu, 1972). Having been exposed to the companionship of adults, an Asian/Pacific child also is taught strict control of aggression. Sollenberger (1962) found that 74% of Chinese parents demanded their children show no aggression under any circumstances.

Attitudes About Mental Health

To assist Asian Americans successfully, social workers need to understand their traditional cultural values toward dysfunctional behavior. The process of acculturation may have altered an individual's or a family's cultural values, but as Mass (1978) indicates, the influence exerted by the value patterns that were acquired throughout childhood is often considerable, even among those whose behavior is highly Westernized. Asian Americans feel stigma and shame in talking about their personal problems. The terms *Hajj* for the Japanese, *Hijj* for the Filipinos, *Tiu lien* for the Chinese, and *Chaemyoun* for the Koreans indicate the shame and loss of face these Asian groups feel when talking about personal issues (B. Kim, 1978).

Most Asian Americans do not seek psychiatric dynamics and psychological theories to account for behavioral difficulties (Lapuz, 1973). Instead, social, moral, and organic explanations are used. When an individual behaves dysfunctionally, he or she commonly attributes the cause to external events such as physical illness, the death of a loved one, or the loss of a job. The individual therefore is not to blame. Interpersonal duties and loyalties are held sacred by many Asian Americans. The dysfunction or suffering of an Asian American individual may be attributed to his or her violation of some duty, such as filial piety. Community elders or family members may be expected to exhort the individual to improve. In surveying a sample of Asian Americans in Los Angeles regarding their attitude toward seeking help for mental health problems, ministers, relatives, friends, and family doctors were mentioned as resources more frequently than professional workers (Okano, 1977). Over half the sample indicated that they would prefer to work out emotional problems on their own.

Help-Seeking Behavioral Patterns

Despite of their many mental health and social service needs, Asian Americans do not generally turn to these institutions and services for assistance. They are mostly referred by outside agencies, with less than 20% being self-referred or referred by families (Yamamoto & Yap, 1984). Literature on minority counseling and social service indicates that Western modes of service delivery have not been effective (Bromerly, 1987). Low utilization and early termination of services by Asian Americans support this premise (D. Sue, 1981). Miranda and Kitano (1976) have identified several barriers to Asian American clients' utilization of mental health and social services, including (a) fragmentation of services so that clients are referred from one worker to another, (b) discontinuity between the life of the professional and that of the client, (c) inaccessibility of services, and (d) the primary focus of the professional on being accountable to fellow professionals rather than to the ethnic community.

The School System

Racial/Ethnic Composition

The racial/ethnic composition of a school system can influence the educational achievement and behavioral adjustment of an Asian child or youth. The school system constitutes a child's reference group, which in turn influences how the child feels regarding specific values and preferences. An Asian American child in a predominantly White school will soon learn that many reference group values are in conflict with the cultural values being practiced at home. Such a conflict in values may hinder the child's development of self-identity and self-concept. An acculturated child or youth will be less influenced by the uneven racial/ethnic composition of the school system. Nevertheless, knowledge of the racial/ethnic composition of the school system can help the therapist assess the manner in which the child experiences peer relationships and internalizes the views of peers. The child's relationship with peers may in turn affect attitudes toward self, school performance, and family.

Attitudes of Teachers and Staff

In assessing the school performance of an Asian American child, the therapist should ascertain the attitudes of the teachers and staff toward Asian American students. Many teachers and staff are not knowledgeable about Asian culture and contributions made by Asians in the United States. Yee (1973) examined the content of 300 social studies textbooks for elementary and secondary schools and found that 75% of them made no mention of Asians at all. The others contained brief descriptions of Asian ghettos such as Chinatown, Chinese railroad workers, Japanese farm workers, laundry workers, and the culinary skills of Asians. Such an incomplete picture of Asians may directly or indirectly lower the self-esteem of Asian students, leaving them with little pride in their cultural identity.

Some teachers and staff have stereotyped impressions about Asians as a "model" minority group who excel in academic achievement. They are disappointed in Asian students who are unexpressive and passive in a learning environment that requires high verbal skills. These teachers and staff do not understand that competition in and of itself is not valued among Asians. Instead, the purpose of work and achievement is to enhance the status of the family (Hsu, 1971).

With the influx of Asian immigrants, so many students, especially those who reside outside major coastal cities, have limited English skills. Additionally, there are limited support services for these students. This situation is not only frustrating for school officials but also devastating to the students who are under extreme pressure by their parents to succeed (N. Young, 1972).

Societal Issues

Sociopolitical Climate

The designation of Asian Americans as a minority group that has experienced prejudice and discrimination is misunderstood by many who fail to assess accurately the status of Asian Americans and to conceptualize racial discrimination. Asian Americans have had a history of exploitation and racism in the United States (Lyman, 1977). Federal legislation has often restricted Asian immigration or, as in the case of the 1924 Immigration Act, prohibited their immigration entirely. Asian immigrants were placed in the category of "aliens ineligible for American citizenship." Anti-miscegenation laws, which prohibited interracial marriages, were passed. More than 110,000 Japanese Americans were relocated in detention camps during World War II.

Restrictions against Asian Americans covered many other areas of life as well. Employment and housing opportunities were limited, and the full use of public and private facilities was denied. Such sociopolitical and psychological constraints relegated Asian Americans to a second-class status.

Gains in civil rights and civil liberties occurred only after World War II, and more specifically in the 1960s. Today, Asian Americans are often considered "model" minorities, but many still face discrimination and prejudice (Asian American Advisory Council, 1973; B. Kim, 1978).

Prejudice and Discrimination

Asian Americans in the mid-1980s have increasingly been the targets of anti-Asian sentiment. Five Southeast Asian refugee elementary students were killed in the schoolyard of Cleveland Elementary School in Stockton, California, by a self-proclaimed anti-Asian Caucasian male (Wong, 1989). In 1982 a Chinese American draftsman and waiter was bludgeoned to death with a baseball bat by two White auto makers who, mistaking him for a Japanese, blamed him for the Detroit auto industry's problems. A 1986 U.S. Civil Rights Commission report concluded that anti-Asian violence was a national problem. According to a *Wall Street Journal* article ("Anti-Asian Sentiment," 1986), the U.S. Department of Justice indicated that anti-Asian incidents rose 62% in 1985.

The anti-Asian sentiment also spreads across the educational arena. Due to Asian American student's success in educational performance, many unofficial discriminatory quotas on admissions to colleges have been found (S. Sue, 1985; S. Sue & Zane, 1987) across American campuses.

Economic competition is also cited as a factor in the rise of anti-Asian sentiment. The economic success story from Japan and other Asian countries has spawned resentment in American communities that have lost jobs to the overseas competition. Prejudice, ignorance, and racism also account for why some Americans feel hostile toward Asian Americans.

Societal issues both directly and indirectly affect the performance and adjustment of Asian American children. Some of their problems may be directly related to institutional discriminatory practices by schools or other societal agencies. Other educational or behavioral problems encountered by Asian children may be caused by a child's low self-concept, fostered and reinforced by negative societal issues.

To serve Asian American children and adolescents is not always easy for mental health agencies and workers. Therapists are better equipped to deal with their Asian clients if they take the time to inquire about their historical background and look at unique mental health issues and problems of this minority group. Taking an ecological approach to the assessment, as discussed above, is also advised.

3

American Indian Children and Adolescents

Historical Background

Demographic Data

The American Indian population consists of Indians, Eskimos, and Aleuts. According to 1980 census figures, American Indians comprise 96% of the American Indian population, 3% are Eskimos and 1% are Aleut (U.S. Department of Commerce, 1983a, p. 14). American Indians include all tribes in the lower 48 states and the Athabascans of eastern Alaska. The Alaskan natives include the Athabascans, Eskimos, and Aleuts. The 1980 U.S. census indicated that the total population of American Indians and Alaskan Natives in the United States reached 1.8 million, an increase of 72% from the 1970 U.S. census. This large increase was the result of a higher birthrate, a lower infant mortality rate, and improved census reporting procedures (p. 2).

Alaskan natives constituted 16% of the population of Alaska and numbered 64,103 (U.S. Bureau of the Census, 1983a, p. 3). Of that number 21,869 were American Indians, 34,144 were Eskimos, and 8,090 were Aleuts. In the lower 48 states, one fourth of the American Indian population (339,836) lived on 278 federal and state reservations. Among the non-Indian residents on the reservations were non-Indian spouses, ranchers, farmers, merchants, health care professionals, and other government employees.

In the North American region, there were 13 distinct language groups, 130 major tribal groupings, and an undetermined number of subgroupings (Josephy, 1971). The Navajo Nation, which numbers about 150,000, was the largest tribe in the United States. However, most reservations had fewer than 1,000 American Indians.

Between the 1970 and 1980 census reporting periods, 54% of the American Indians became urban residents (U.S. Department of Commerce, 1984). Of the total American Indian population, 47% resided in four states as of 1980: 201,369 (approximately 15%) in California; 169,459 (about 13%) in Oklahoma; 152,745 (about 11%) in Arizona; and 107,481 (about 8%) in New Mexico. Nine states had American Indian populations of 30,000 to 99,000: Alaska, Washington, Montana, South Dakota, Minnesota, Wisconsin, Michigan, New York, and North Carolina. Eighty-one percent of California's Indian population resided in urban areas. Indians in Arizona and New Mexico and Eskimos and Aleuts in Alaska predominantly resided on reservations.

The median age of American Indians was 24.0 years. The median age of those in central cities and on farms was 24.8 years, and of the total rural population was 21.9 years. Of the 1,022,411 American Indians who were 16 years or older in 1980, 598,626 were in the labor force, with 507,614 employed and 76,865 unemployed. The median family income of American Indians was $13,678 (U.S. Congress, 1986), compared with $17,786 for Black families and $29,152 for White families (U.S. Bureau of the Census, 1986). The median income for families on reservations was only $9,942, and $9,320 for the 23% of Indian households headed by women.

Native Culture

It is difficult to describe general cultural traits of American Indians, because there are many diverse family practices that exist within and among tribes. However, the degree of diversity among the population is decreasing because of the extermination of many groups through the introduction of European pathogens. Within the last century, attempts to force acculturation to Anglo-European practices have also reduced the range and diversity of American Indian and cultural practices. Although no Indian tribes have identical cultural beliefs and practices, there are some unifying concepts that set them apart from the dominant society (Attneave, 1982; Lewis & Ho, 1976; Red Horse, 1988). Some of those indigenous cultural values are described below.

Sharing. The concept of sharing is deeply ingrained among American Indians, who hold it in greater esteem than the White American ethic of saving. Because one's worth is measured by one's willingness and ability to share, the accumulation of material goods for social status is alien to the American Indian. Sharing, therefore, is neither a superimposed nor an artificial value, but a genuine and routine way of life.

Concept of Time. In contrast to the general belief that they have no concept of time, American Indians are indeed time conscious. They deal, however, with natural phenomena—mornings, days, nights, months (in terms of moons), and years (in terms of seasons or winters). If an American Indian is on the way to a meeting or appointment and meets a friend, that conversation will naturally take precedence over being punctual for the appointment. In this culture, sharing is more important than punctuality.

Harmony with Nature. Nature is the American Indians' school, and they are taught to endure all natural happenings that they will encounter during life. They learn as well to be independent individuals who respect others. American Indians believe that to attain maturity—which is learning to live with life, its evil as well as its good—one must face genuine suffering. The resilience of the American Indian way of life is attested to by the fact that the culture has survived and continues to flourish despite the intense onslaught of the White man.

Fatalism and Humor. One of the strongest criticisms of American Indians has been that they are pessimistic; they are presented as downtrodden, low spirited, unhappy, and without hope for the future. However, as one looks deeper into their personality, another perspective is visible. In the midst of abject poverty comes "the courage to be"—to face life as it is while maintaining a tremendous sense of humor (Huffaker, 1967).

The Nature of Man. American Indians realize that the world is made up of both good and bad. There are always some people or things that are bad and deceitful. However, they believe that in the end good people will triumph just because they are good. This belief is seen repeatedly in American Indian folktales about Iktomi the spider. He is the tricky fellow who is out to fool, cheat, and take advantage of good people. But Iktomi usually loses in the end, reflecting the American Indian view that the good person succeeds while the bad person loses. Therefore, the pessimism of American Indians should instead be regarded as "optimistic toughness" (G. Bryde, 1971).

Being-in-Becoming. The White American culture has repeatedly demonstrated a value system that seeks to control, to be in charge, and that often destroys the balance of nature. This is done with the view that human beings are superior to all other forms of life and therefore have the right to manipulate nature and situations for their comfort, convenience, and economic gain. Contrarily, American Indians are taught to endure all natural and unnatural happenings that they encounter during their lives. They are alone, not only to others but also to themselves. They control their emotions, allowing no passionate outbursts over small matters. Their habitual mien is one of poise, self-containment, and aloofness, which may result from a fear and mistrust of non-Indians.

American Indian patience, however, can easily be mistaken for inactivity. Today, when young American Indians have to compete in a predominantly White school, this quality is often interpreted as laziness. The White man's world is a competitive, aggressive society that bypasses the patient man who stands back and lets the next person go first.

Individuality and Mutual Respect. American Indians believe that no matter where any individual stands, he or she is an integral part of the universe. Because every person is fulfilling a purpose, no one should have the power to impose values. For this reason, each person is to be respected and can expect the same respect and reverence from others. Hence, the security of this inner fulfillment provides them with an essential serenity that resists interference from outside.

Collateral Relationship with Others. Working together and getting along with each other are highly valued traits. American Indians believe the family and group should take precedence over the individual. This concept of collaterality reflects the integrated view of the universe where all people, animals, plants, and objects in nature have their place in creating a harmonious whole. American Indians' adherence to collaterality is sometime misconstrued by those who live within the dominant culture, which stresses individualism, high achievement and competition. Indian children in public schools are often mistakenly seen as "unmotivated," "lazy," or "unproductive."

Family Tradition

Because each American Indian tribe represents its own unique social system, it is difficult and at times inappropriate to discuss Indian family traditions in general terms. Nonetheless, American Indians traditionally maintain a relationship network that supports and nurtures strong bonds of mutual assistance and affection. American Indian family systems are extended networks, characteristically including several households. It is an active kinship system inclusive of parents, children, aunts, uncles, cousins, and grandparents. An unrelated individual can also become a family member by being a namesake for a child. This individual then assumes family obligations and responsibilities for child rearing and role modeling. The multiple family household framework provides family members with a strong sense of belonging along both vertical and horizontal extensions. The authority structure of the extended family system can be arranged in a variety of ways, with an administrative focus on the oldest man or woman. The extended family network fosters intense personal exchanges that have lasting effects upon a child's life and behavior (Speck & Attneave, 1974).

Traditionally, American Indians regard tribal spirituality as an integral part of tribal life (Hippler, 1974). A child's early introduction to the spiritual life of the tribe fosters in him or her a loving respect for nature and independence as well as self-discipline. Because the basic parental disciplinary role is shared among relatives of several generations, biological parents have the opportunity to engage in fun-oriented activities with their children. As infants, children experience intense, warm maternal care from the mother. This kind of extreme nurturance generates a strong sense of security in the children, who are egocentric and friendly but ambivalent about violence (Hippler, 1974).

Despite diverse tribal differences in family relations, children are of utmost importance for all because they represent the renewal of life. Indian children are not seen as entirely dependent beings, but rather as individuals who can, within a short time after birth, make the most important decision regarding the identity they will assume. American Indian children are not taught to feel guilt, for custom advocates no control over others or their own environment (Attneave, 1982).

Mental Health Issues and Problems

Epidemiological Data

Epidemiological studies concerning American Indian children are plagued by many problems. Methodologies and instruments employed by researchers may be culturally biased. American Indians' cultural beliefs in endurance, fatalism, individuality and noninterference make mental problems difficult to discern. LaFramboise and Plake (1983) also indicate the logistical and political difficulty in conducting research studies in isolated Indian communities. Nevertheless, there are several major studies that provide important information pertaining to the mental health problems and status of American Indian children and youth.

Meshane's (1982) study considers *otitis media* (middle ear infection) the most frequently identified disease of Indian children. Its special significance for adolescent mental health lies in the learning and developmental consequences that may follow from subsequent mild to moderate hearing loss. The negative effects of otitis media range from delays in cognitive and psycholinguistic development (Katz, 1978) and lowered educational achievement (DiSarno & Barringer, 1978) to reading problems and emotional difficulties (F. Bennett et al., 1980). Katz (1978) estimates that as many as 75% of all Indian children experience otitis media, that 13,000 Indians are in need of hearing aids, and that as many as 22,000 may need otologic surgery.

Fetal Alcohol Syndrome (FAS) and Fetal Alcohol Effects (FAE) and their potential for engendering neurosensory and developmental disabilities also are prevalent among American Indian children. In a detailed comparative analysis of selected Indian Health Service (IHS) units and reservations on which there were documented case findings, P. May and Hymbaugh (1983) found that one group of Indians had a higher incidence of FAS than any that had been reported previously. Of all the fetal alcohol children, 73% had been adopted or placed in foster homes due to abandonment or neglect by their natural mothers. Twenty-three percent of the biological mothers had died, almost always from an accident, cirrhosis of the liver, or other alcohol-related trauma and illness.

The National Technical Information Service (1986) reported a high rate of deaths among young Indians due to causes related to substance use, particularly alcohol. Beauvais et al. (1989) recently found high rates of alcohol and drug experimentation among Indian adolescents relative to non-Indian adolescents. For example, in 1976-1987, an average of 81% of Indian students in grades 7 to 12 used alcohol at some time; 61% had used marijuana; 24% had used inhalants; 25% had used stimulants; 8% had used cocaine; 10% had used hallucinogens; 11% had used sedatives; and 5% had used heroin. American Indian youth also have been found to begin abusing various substances at a younger age than their White counterparts (Weibel, 1984).

Developmental disabilities are another serious problem among Indian children and adolescents. O'Connell (1987) reports that nationally among public school students, the frequency of learning disabilities was greatest for American Indians: 5.28% of all Indian students, compared to 4% for all minorities on the average and slightly more than 4% for Anglo students. Indian students were second only to Blacks in the proportion of educable and trainable mentally retarded.

Diagnostic Categories

Two studies (Krush et al., 1966; Whitaker, 1989) comparing the level of depression among Indian adolescents with a sample of non-Indians reported more depression among Indian adolescents. This data is more evident when self-report screening methods are used (Kleinfeld et al., 1977).

Beiser and Attneave (1982) reported that anxiety was the fourth most common mental health problem for youth seen through the IHS mental health program. Eight percent of all boys and girls between the ages of 15 and 19 years were identified as suffering from anxiety. Another study (P. May & Hymbaugh, 1983) also revealed that in 1981 and 1982, about 18% of all males and nearly 10% of all females seen for anxiety in the Albuquerque Area Office mental health program were between 10 and 19 years of age.

Suicide is the second leading cause of death for American Indian and Alaskan native adolescents. In 1986, the age-specific mortality rate for suicide for 15- to 19-year-old Indians was an estimated 26.3 deaths per 100,000 (U.S. Congress, 1986). In comparison, the figure for the same age group overall in the United States was 10.0 per 100,000. Suicide deaths for 10- to 14-year old American Indians are approximately four times higher than for the general population. In 1986, the death rate for adolescent Indian males (10 to 19) was approximately 10 times higher than for females of the same age. The suicide rate also is higher among Indian adolescents who have previously attempted suicide, who have frequent encounters with the criminal justice system, or who have experienced multiple home placements (Berlin, 1986).

Many studies reveal that Indian students drop out of school at rates substantially higher than the general population (Development Associates, 1983; Grant, 1975; Thompson et al., 1963). The frequency of dropout in the general population ranges from 5% to 30%, whereas Indian students' dropout rate ranges from 15% to 60%. Indian students' high dropout rate may be related to their need to care for younger siblings and older family members, high mobility of the parents due to employment opportunities, and/or family conflicts and parental alcoholism (E. Brown, 1973).

Juvenile delinquency among American Indian youth is generally high. P. May and Hymbaugh's (1983) analyses of Bureau of Indian Affairs (BIA) law enforcement data from the Albuquerque area are consistent with earlier findings from the Wind River Reservation. In 1982 the most frequent causes for arrest were disorderly conduct (25.9%), liquor law violations (11.2%), curfew violations (9.8%), drunkenness (9.6%), and running away from home (6.6%). Of all juvenile arrests, 58% were for alcohol use: 63% for males and 37% for females.

Due to racism, discrimination practices against them and difficulty in functioning in a bicultural world, it is to be expected that Indian youth tend to score low on (culturally-biased) standardized tests. Since Indian youth still hold their cultural group in high regard (Development Associates, 1983), they consider friendliness, happiness, and helpfulness to be more important than academic success and material achievement.

Problems Associated with Relocation

The breakdown of American Indian cultural traditions and family customs began as early as the 1800s. In 1815 tribal leaders were coerced by the U.S. government into signing treaties they could not read and thus could not understand (Costo & Henry, 1977, p. 209). These treaties opened the doors for a greater influx of European homesteaders and miners. Many illegal treaties were subsequently signed, including the Sacred Black Hills Treaty. The buffalo were destroyed, and Indian languages and religious practices were forbidden by the missionary schools (Merian, 1977, p. 14). Many Indian children were taken away from their parents so the children could be educated in the White man's mold. These children's placements later included boarding schools, religious institutions, foster care, and adoption. These practices severed the links of the support system that centered on children and thus encouraged the destruction of the basic tenets of tribal life.

The unemployment rate for Indians returning to their reservations following World War II soared. In 1952, American Indian men and women who left the reservations experienced great difficulty in finding employment in urban cities (Stuart, 1971). In the next sixteen years, the BIA (1971) stepped in to relieve such high unemployment crisis through (by) relocating some 67,522 (American) Indians who were the head of households. Families and individuals were immersed in urban environments that were distant from native homelands and traditional kin systems. The relocations necessitated adaptations in personal lifestyle, aspirations, and behavior. The statistics for income, education, mental health, and crime among urban Indians present a bleak picture. Urban Indians are the poorest, least educated, and most highly unemployed (Chadwick & Strauss, 1975) and have the highest crime rate related to drunkenness (Fogleman, 1972). The children of these families are being raised with fewer contacts with traditional life. Their peers are often non-Indians, diluting further their Indian heritage (Price, 1981).

Western educational and social services often pull Indian children further from their own community and tribal life. In this new environment, not only is the community compartmentalized, but it becomes a major destructive force to tribal life and to the Indian youth. Pervasive and intense relocation experiences create a world of confusion whose impact has been, and will continue to be, felt for many generations.

Ecological Approach to Assessment

The Personal System

Level of Acculturation

Just as tribes represent a wide range of characteristics, so do American Indian children, insofar as their degree of acculturation to mainstream societal lifestyle. Level of acculturation clearly is related to a child's reservation or urban residence. The social and cultural influences that come to bear on a child's acculturation are very different. Whereas a child growing up on a reservation may benefit from a number of federally supplied services, such as health care, the urban Indian child is often deprived of these services. In addition, an Indian child growing up on a reservation continues to have regular access to traditional customs; those who grow up in urban areas are generally cut off from many Indian influences. However, opportunities for employment and higher education are often greater for Indian children living in urban areas.

Although it is generally recognized that an Indian child living away from the reservation must be acculturated and acquire essential skills for survival, Western educational values such as acquisitiveness, mercantilism, competition, and individualism are antithetical to Indian values (Red Horse, 1980). Tribal leaders now generally agree that Western values should be learned by Indian children as social and economic skills and not as values to be internalized. The traditional Indian values of concern for the group and generosity and disdain for material possessions are reinforced constantly in tribal ceremonies.

Two studies investigated the level of acculturation of urban Indian families. Miller and Schoenfield (1975) discretely classified Indian families according to whether they were urban or traditionally oriented. An assumption was made that urban-oriented families would be inclined to adhere to mainstream standards of child rearing. The study reported that irrespective of their traditional identity status, the majority of Indian families failed to use high degrees of White childrearing techniques. Another study by Red Horse (1976) explored the impact of familiar imprints and injunctions upon attitudes of Indian adolescents regarding expectations surrounding early childhood development. Findings indicated that Indian adolescents had expectations that varied considerably from mainstream, non-

Indian expectations. In addition, an Indian child's upward social class movement does not necessarily assure that he or she will adopt adult White middle-class values as a standard for living.

Although many changes are occuring within Indian cultures and many Indian children are being acculturated into the mainstream value system and living style, there is a strong resistance to assimilation among both Indians on reservations and in urban areas (Chadwick & Strauss, 1975). This resistance attests to the strength of Indian culture and traditions.

Physical Appearance

The American Indian is often portrayed by media as an individual with black hair, brown skin, high cheekbones, and most often dressed in clothing typical of Plains Indian life (Trimble, 1976). However, the idea that there is an "Indian" stereotype that could fit all or even most American Indians today is naive and simplistic. The fact is American Indians represent a wide range of phenotypic characteristics with respect to body size, skin, hair color, and facial features. Deloria (1969) summed up the frustration among Indian people of having others stereotype them: "People can tell just by looking at us what we want, what should be done to help us, how we feel, and what a 'real' Indian is like" (p. 9).

The physical appearance of an American Indian child is further negatively affected by the concept of *quantum blood* imposed by the U.S. government on Indian people. Quantum blood—or biological "Indianness"—refers to the degree of Indian ancestry an individual possesses. The arbitrary blood requirement of the government is a dominant culture policy that has resulted in divisiveness and dissension among Indians who have had to fight for limited funds and services. The traditional Indian physical stereotype and the concept of quantum blood have created confusion and conflict especially among those American Indian children who do not fit such descriptions. As a result, many of those children encounter prejudice and rejection from both Indians and non-Indians.

Speech and Language

There is a difference between the construction of the American Indian languages and English. Appropriate use of the Indian languages requires a knowledge of and sensitivity to the relational patterns of the individual's community. The exact manner in which certain communication is sent is directly related to the status of the speaker, the status of the person spoken to, the sexes of the people, and their relationship to each other. Indian linguistic structures are entirely different from those of English. Some concepts that are important in some of the Indian languages have no counterpart in English, and vice versa (Zimiles et al., 1976).

The learning patterns of observation and participation of American Indian students do not require that verbal instruction be the major transmitter of knowledge. Many important lessons regarding all spheres of life are learned through nonverbal communication. Research in regard to the learning style of American Indians indicates that American Indian children learn visually rather than linguistically (Gold, 1977). These researchers reported that Pueblo children, in listening to legends, learn to represent them visually because they are not allowed to ask questions or reflect verbally on what they hear.

Indian children's facility in the English language is among the poorest of any group in the United States. This is still the case even among those Indian children who grew up in homes where English is spoken as their first or only language (Zimiles et al., 1976). Indian children rarely receive stimulation from books written in English. American Indian parents find some English books biased and irrelevant to Indian life. Additionally, some Indian parents' proficiency in English may not be much better than the child's, and consequently the parents and children cannot share in the reading experience.

Interpersonal Relations

American Indian children from an early age learn important lessons regarding all areas of life through keen observation, nonverbal communication, and participation. They are encouraged to be sensitive to what others think. Hence, they are vulnerable to criticism and to external influences. Bentz (1977) attributes Indian childrens' interpersonal vulnerability to the lack of development of the kinds of defense mechanisms and habitual patterns that are required by other societies. Additionally, American Indian children are taught to respect the individuality of others. They come from an environment where people gain their status according to a particular competence. Every individual has and is allowed competent status, including an emotionally retarded individual who might be thought to have unusual or special powers.

In mainstream institutional systems, competition and individualism are required of children to succeed. Neither the expectation nor the means to achieve it are made clear to Indian children. They see little relevance to previous tribal values. When an Indian child is required to learn the nature of competitiveness in White institutions, the child may become confused, withdrawn, and ineffectual in interpersonal relations (A. Ortiz, 1969).

Attitude Toward Self

G. Bryde (1971) reported that Indian children show a significantly high incidence of feelings of rejection, depression, anxiety, and alienation from both Indian and the majority societies. An Indian child learns that in order for him to make a decent living for his future family, he must eventually leave his Indian home and go into the non-Indian world to learn other skills. He learns that he may not measure up to the norms of the dominant culture, which judges a worthy person by material achievement. He also learns that outside groups *expect* Indians to be no good, undependable, lazy, and to get drunk every chance they get. Eventually, he begins to view himself in this same way. Although Indian students test at lower than normative levels with respect to their personal self-concept, they consistently hold their own cultural group in high regard (Development Associates, 1983). They may characterize themselves as being friendly, helpful, easygoing, and more interested in happiness than in success, but not as being particularly smart, strong, good-looking, or at ease in front of groups.

Issues of Sexuality

Because most American Indian children were instructed to learn by observation and participation, they grow up with minimal direct sexual education and verbal exchange with parents and other elders regarding sex. They may be encouraged to participate in sex-related activities with their brothers, sisters, and cousins. Contact between boys and girls is controlled by the clan mores and systems. Partly due to the extended family system households and partly due to the male's traditional role as a hunter whose work took him outside of the home, open display of emotions and affection between males and females is rare even after they become husband and wife, although the mutual bond may in fact be close, affectionate, and satisfying. Males from some tribes have traditionally treated females as inferior and have been reluctant to have close interpersonal contacts (Hippler, 1974). Mixed-sex couples rarely visit together or entertain

friends together. Nonkin social gatherings are usually of the same
sex only. Traditionally, as a sign of respect within the Navajo tribe,
the sons-in-law were not permitted to speak to or to look at their
mothers-in-law (E. Brown & Shaughnessy, 1982, p. 7). Adolescent
girls, independent for the most part, played a submissive, supportive
role to the boys (Hanson, 1980). Heavily influenced by media, most
Indian youth did not view themselves as good-looking or sexually
desirable (Development Associates, 1983).

The Family System

Immigration History and Level of Acculturation

There are numerous theories and explanations of how Indians got
to America, but each tribe has its own explanation of how it came to
be a people (the Indian names of the tribes invariably translate as
"the people"). Tribes also derive their differences from their origins
and the geographic areas they emerged from as a people. The first
people of any tribe brought with them the character and strength of
being from the place of origin. This played a deciding role in the philosophical interpretations that the people developed about their life
and its meaning. Such interpretations then formed the basis of the
specific art and material as well as the spiritual culture of the tribes.
All tribes are intertwined in a philosophical mosaic and adhere to the
presence of a Creator. Each tribe has its specific belief system developed from tribal and family history.

As a result of the Dawes Act of 1887 (Merian, 1977, p. 22), Indian
men and women were forced to become farmers and ranchers on
their alloted reservation lands. With the shift of occupational skills
and requirements, Indian men were no longer recognized as brave
warriors or hunters and Indian women were traumatized by the experience of witnessing their children being taken away.

In 1952, the BIA sought to relieve the high unemployment problem
of Indians by finding jobs for them in urban areas (Stuart, 1977). Between 1952 and 1968, some 67,522 Indians who were the heads of
households were relocated through this direct employment program
(BIA, 1971). This program was considered as yet another attempt by
the government to destroy the Indian culture and family structure by
encouraging assimilation into the urban environment, rather than an
attempt to strengthen Indian ways of life by developing more work
opportunities on reservations (Farris, 1973, p. 84). Today, there are

more Indians living in urban areas than on reservations (U.S. Bureau of the Census, 1980a).

Family Structure and Life Patterns

Contemporary American Indian family structures and life patterns can be classified into four types (Red Horse, 1980).

1. *Traditional families* overtly adheres to culturally defined styles of living. The parents and grandparents speak the native language. Elders assume respected roles because their accumulated wisdom is necessary to interpret lives and relationships in a sacred context. Methods of social control among traditional families have changed with contemporary times, but modal behaviors influenced through early village structure remain reasonably constant. These families interpret life events in sacred terms. Relationships are expressed through ritual ceremonies, and depending on tribal custom, these families are articulate with sacred bonds such as ritual names, clans, and namesakes.

2. *Nontraditional or bicultural families* appears to have adopted many aspects of nontraditional styles of living. Typically, these families do not transmit specific traditional knowledge across generations. Parents often may understand their native language but prefer to speak English at home. Parents may be acquainted with ritual custom but have converted to non-Indian religions. Most children in bicultural families do not have ritual names, are not familiar with their clans, and do not have namesakes. Despite acquiring many characteristics of American society, bicultural families are not integrated socially. They prefer relationships with other American Indians and have introduced important adaptations that contribute to a construction of generalized American Indian values. These families often replicate traditional extended kin systems through fictive structures that incorporate nonkin into roles normally found in extended families. To compensate for geographic isolation, the bicultural families attend powwows in urban areas or on nearby reservations.

3. *Acculturated families* are characterized by their modal behavior similar to the general American population. Parents speak English and use mainstream cultural child rearing practices. They have non-Indian religions and no linkages to land or kin and maintain a nuclear family structure.

4. *Pantraditional families* are characterized by their overt struggles to redefine and reconfirm previously lost cultural lifestyles. They speak both English and their native language and they practice a

modified tribal belief system and struggle to maintain a traditional extended family network, as well as cultural activities.

The different family lifestyle patterns among American Indians do not imply an ongoing erosion of cultural values. Regardless of family lifestyle patterns, American Indian *core values* are retained and remain as a constant (Native American Research Group, 1979).

Because of different parenting styles, as described previously, ordering and physical punishment to force a behavior on Indian children are discouraged (Morey & Gilliam, 1974). Because parents believe they have no control over others or their own environment, American Indian children are not taught to have guilt (Attneave, 1982). Finally, Indian children are seldom told directly what to do and are often left to their own devices and decisions. This freedom to exercise freedom is in concert with the felt expectations from many significant adults including the grandparents (Red Horse, 1980).

Attitudes About Mental Health

Mental illness was considered among traditional Indians as an imbalance in the natural order of things. When an individual's imbalance caused hardship for another person, the recipient had the responsibility to assist in the return to balance. This could be done through the recipient sponsoring a ceremony, such as a giveaway, for the person who was experiencing the imbalance. American Indians' view of imbalance or disorders also can be extended to the disruptions in human relationships or undesirable influences from within or outside the tribe. Such human disorders allowed people to understand and appreciate the nature of the world, humankind's relationship to it, and the balance of life. Hence, imbalance of any sort, including mental health problems, assumes the character of the natural order of things.

Help-Seeking Behavioral Patterns

American Indians have underutilized mental health, health, and social services provided by public agencies (Wise, 1979). There are seven reasons why these services are not utilized.

1. Many Indian parents are simply not aware of the services available.
2. Policies and procedures to acquire these services are often confusing and highly impersonal, requiring a great deal of motivation and knowledge in filling out complicated forms.

3. Such services are inconveniently located, requiring reliable transportation that many American Indians do not have.

4. Past experiences cause many American Indians to mistrust the dominant culture and its institutions.

5. Many Indians are resentful of the dependent and often powerless positions they find themselves in with respect to federal and state services.

6. By utilizing these public services, they fear that they may lose their traditional culture, ethnic identity, and spiritual identity.

7. The value systems and therapeutic approaches employed by these agencies are frequently inappropriate and conflict with an Indian's view of the world.

In an attempt to schematize American Indian's help-seeking patterns, Lewis (1984) further confirms the extended network helping behavior characteristic of American Indian families. When personal or family problems arise, American Indians often exhaust all primary resources before considering taking their problems to a stranger. The extended family network is the first source to be contacted. Second, a religious leader may be consulted to resolve personal or family problems. Third, if the problem remains unresolved, then the family will contact the tribal community elders. Last, when all these fail, the family may seek help from the mainstream society health care system.

The School System

Racial/Ethnic Composition

Early reports on Indian education in 1969 and later education reports of the American Indian Policy Review Commission (Association on American Indian Affairs, 1976) revealed that education of Indian children still was deplorable. Western education of Indian children was first accomplished in 1850 by removing them when they were quite young from their tribes and forcing them to attend boarding schools established by the U.S. government. They were required to discard their language, dress, and food and to spend 8 continuous years away from their families and tribes. Neither the parents nor the tribe had a voice in the educational program of these children.

Today, many American Indian children have great difficulty in adjusting in a mainstream school system that is so foreign to their world view. Literature reveals that Indian students drop out of school at rates substantially higher than the general population. The frequency of dropout rate in the general population ranges from 5% to 30%, but for Indian students it ranges from 15% to 60% (J. Bryde, 1967; U.S. Commission on Civil Rights, 1978). The schools' historical failure to address Indian cultural values and ideals and the lack of parental participation in the school system have led many Indian people to perceive school as irrelevant. For many Indians, family needs assume priority over personal desires. It is no accident, then, that Indian dropouts have frequently cited being needed at home to care for younger siblings and older family members as a reason for leaving school (Hanks, 1973). Indian children also are more likely than Anglo students to perceive public schools as a hostile environment infested with alcohol, drugs, property destruction, violent acts, and theft (Whitaker, 1989).

Attitudes of Teachers and Staff

The teachers' and staff's attitudes toward Indians are heavily influenced by television, movies, and popular literature that depict an Indian as a painted, feathered, warring savage with animal-like cunning who is always defeated by the superior strength of the White man. Indian religion and customs are portrayed as exotic, often barbaric and superstitious, and always futile in resisting the encroachment of civilization.

Schools are increasing on reservations, but they continue to be primarily run by Anglos who encourage such majority cultural values as competition, achievement, and motivation. Textbooks on American history reflect the stereotyped attitude of the dominant society toward Indians. Costo (1970), after reviewing more than 300 American history textbooks, concluded that most of the books contained inadequate and unreliable facts about the history and culture of the Indian people. Many books also had derogatory remarks about the Indian people.

Indian children are aware of the ways they are perceived by some of the teachers and staff, and though they may know that the stereotypes are false, they become sensitive to negative expectations and attitudes. Their distrust of non-Indian teachers can be detrimental to their academic achievement, a source of anxiety, and a cause of other mental health disturbances.

Societal Issues

Considering the complex interactional effects of changing family values, cultural conflicts with the mainstream society, poverty, educational conflicts, and negative stereotypes portrayed in the media and literature, the mental health outlook for American Indian children appears to be bleak. American Indians living in urban areas are the poorest, least educated, most highly unemployed, and have the highest crime rate related to drunkenness (Chadwick & Strauss, 1975). Living with such societal stresses and daily survival threats, the life of an Indian family is certain to deteriorate, and the mental health of an Indian child will be at great risk. Additionally, the children of these families are being raised with fewer contacts with traditional life. Their peers are often non-Indian, and they increasingly grow up to marry non-Indians, further diluting their Indian heritage (Price, 1981).

Despite the many conflicts and obstacles facing Indian children today, the reality is that increasing numbers of Indians are becoming educated and working with their own people to preserve their culture. Moreover, the Indian population is increasing and Indians are becoming a potent political force in our society, as well as better realizing their goal of self-determination. Their political force is having an impact. The U.S. Senate Select Committee on Indian Affairs is considering legislation to enhance and improve mental health services to Indians (U.S. Department of Health and Human Services, 1990).

4

Black American Children and Adolescents

Historical Background

Demographic Data

Presently, Blacks constitute about 12% of the population of the United States. Since 1900, the proportion of Blacks in comparison to Whites has been in the 10% to 12% range. Their proportion is expected to increase to 13.3%, or a total of over 35 million by the year 2000. The contemporary Black population is younger than the White. The median age for Blacks is 26.9 years, compared with a White median age of 32.7 (U.S. Bureau of the Census, 1987b). In 1983 there were 5,463,000 Black youth in the 10- to 19-year age bracket—2,831,000 in the 15- to 19-year bracket—and another 2,961,000 in the 20- to 24-year age bracket. It is also projected that by the year 2000, 32% of Blacks will be under 18 years of age, compared with 24% of Whites (U.S. Bureau of the Census, 1986).

In 1984 the Black population consisted of about 1.4 million more women than men. The structure of Black families has changed over the past 2 decades, with the number of female-headed households increasing, the number of children living with two parents decreasing, and the rate of poverty among Blacks increasing. In 1986 the median income for Black families was $17,604, or 57% of White family income. Nearly half (42.7%) of all Black youth under 18 lived in families below the poverty line, and more than two thirds (67.1%) of those in female-headed households were poor (U.S. Bureau of Census, 1987b).

In regard to educational attainment, there still is a discrepancy between Blacks and Whites. For Blacks aged 25 years and older, 40.2% had not attained a high school diploma, in contrast to 24.5% for Whites aged 25 and older. Only 11.1% of Blacks as compared to 20% of Whites had completed 4 years of college education.

With a low level of educational attainment, racism, and discrimination, the unemployment rate of Blacks has continued to be disproportionately higher than of Whites. For example, in 1986 the average unemployment rate was 14.5% for Blacks and 6.0% for Whites. The unemployment rate for Black teenagers was 39.3%; for White teenagers, it was only 15.6% (Swinton, 1988).

The Black population has traditionally been concentrated in the south. They began to migrate to the north and west early in 1910. In early 1980 Blacks still formed the highest proportion of the total population of the south (18.4%) and the lowest in the west (5.1%), with intermediate proportions in the north central (9.0%) and northeastern (9.6%) regions of the country (U.S. Bureau of the Census, 1983a). A large proportion of Black youth live in deteriorating central-city neighborhoods, in substandard housing with poor sanitation, and have limited access to adequate health and mental health facilities (Children's Defense Fund, 1986).

Immigration Data

Blacks have emigrated to the United States from many different countries over the past four centuries. Today, the largest group of Blacks in the United States is of African origin whose ancestors were brought directly here as slaves (A. Brown & Forde, 1967). Not all Blacks were slaves. Lewis Bennett (1982), a noted historian, notes that in the late 1780s there were 697,000 Black slaves and 59,000 free Blacks. By 1860 there were about 500,000 free Blacks, most living in such southeastern states as Maryland, North Carolina, and Louisiana. Free Blacks were allowed to vote in some states (e.g., Maryland and New York), but in southern states free Blacks were not allowed to vote.

In addition to Afro-American Blacks, there have been a number of waves of immigration from the West Indies in the last century (Brice, 1982). There is a great deal of cultural diversity among the Blacks from the West Indies, which at one time were colonized by the French, the British, the Spanish, and the Dutch. The history of Black West Indians and their immigration patterns to the United States has not been well researched, along with many Blacks who have come to this country within the last 40 years from the countries of Africa. The Black population on which this book focuses is primarily Black Afro-American families whose ancestors were originally brought to this country from Africa as slaves.

Native Culture

Many Black cultural values are heavily influenced by three major sources: (a) residuals from Africa; (b) acculturation with mainstream America; and (c) adaptation and responses to the "victim" system that is a product of racism, poverty, and oppression (Pinderhughes, 1979). Hill (1972) has identified six cultural themes that he believes form the bases of survival for Blacks. Although these values are basically responses to the problems of the victim system, they are also themes that underlie the diversity of Black families and communities that give them coherence. These cultural themes are (a) strong kinship bonds; (b) role flexibility; (c) strong work, education, and achievement orientation; (d) strong commitment to religious values and church participation; (e) humanistic orientation; and (f) endurance of suffering. Each of these cultural themes is discussed below.

Strong Kinship Bonds. The strength of kinship bonds is attributable to the African tribal heritage of Black people, as well as to the importance of maintaining family and community cohesion in the face of the adversities connected with slavery and its residue. Strong kinship bonds can provide valuable functions and needed service to Black people. Stack (1974) has described how kinship ties and extended family problems may become an integral part of family life. As a result of these strong kinship bonds, many Black families have become extended families in which relatives of a variety of blood ties have been absorbed into a coherent network for mutual emotional and economic support.

Role Flexibility. Many Black husbands and fathers perform expressive (i.e., domestic and emotional) functions while wives and mothers perform instrumental (i.e., economic) functions. This pattern of functioning probably was developed as a response to economic necessities. Historically, the Black female had greater access to the economic opportunity structure of society than the Black male did. Hill (1972) also points out that the high percentage of women and adolescents who have had to work to help support the family has forced the typical Black family to be unusually versatile in assuming and fulfilling family roles. Older children sometimes need to stand in as parents and caretakers; mothers fill the shoes of both parents or trade traditional roles with fathers, and so on. If the roles in a particular family are flexible, then the family is more likely to be able to cope with changes in circumstances. Because of role flexibility and because the wife/mother may assume instrumental functions, therapists should not assume that Black families are matriarchal. Contrarily, most research supports the fact that an equalitarian pattern typifies most Black families (Scanzoni, 1975).

Strong Work, Education, and Achievement Orientation. The high unemployment rate among Blacks is a direct result of the victim system, and it should not be misconstrued as Blacks lacking a work incentive or work ethic. A study by Looney and Lewis (1983) indicated that the literature has tended to overlook stable Black families in which hard work is definitely an important cultural value. It was quite common for women to work in Black families long before this became the norm in the American population as a whole (McAdoo, 1981). Hill (1972, p. 19) also cited data that indicate that 60% of the Black poor work, as compared with about 50% of the White poor.

Education is seen as the way out of poverty for many Black families. Parents or older siblings frequently make sacrifices to enable the younger members of the family to secure a good education. This "reciprocal obligation" process explains why some older children drop out of school (McAdoo, 1978). Studies have also indicated that a majority of low-income Black parents aspire to a college education for their children and that an overwhelming majority of Black college students come from lower- and working-class families (Hill, 1972, p. 13). The strong achievement orientation among Blacks also is reflected by a study (Looney & Lewis, 1983) that discusses the working-class Black families who give their children the message that they would "make it" despite discrimination and racism.

Strong Commitment to Religious Values and Church Participation. Knox (1985) states that spirituality is deeply embedded in the Black psyche. The Black sense of spirituality has its roots in the tradition of African religions (Nobles, 1980). According to Nobles, religion permeated every aspect of the African's life and was an integral part of man's existence, accompanying the individual from conception to long after death (p. 25). Mitchell and Lewter (1986) also point out that people who grew up in a traditional Black community are spontaneously equipped with a system of core beliefs, particularly spiritual ones (p. 2). The Black church has served a nurturing function for Black people for many years. It played a vital role in the escape of Blacks from the oppression of slavery. Today, in times of crisis, religion and the social services provided by the church have been supportive elements in revitalizing hope for the Black people. The churches were, and often still are, one of the few places where Black men and women could feel that they were respected for their own talents and abilities. The community church also became one of the most important sources of leadership experience and development in the Black community. Many Blacks have used this as a major coping mechanism in handling the often overwhelming pain of racism and discrimination.

Humanistic Orientation. Showing concern for each other and dealing with each other in a spontaneous, natural, and authentic way also are highly valued among Blacks. Soloman (1976) has referred to this value dimension of Blacks as "more humanistic and [Blacks] have greater validity than the hollow values of middle-class American society" (p. 169). This humanistic attitude that forms an interactive pattern is connected to a strong religious orientation, but without the Puritan influences such as task-centerness and materialistic achievement that are characteristic of White middle-class American values.

Endurance of Suffering. In adjusting to the victim system and adversity, Black Americans have developed great tolerance for conflict, stress, ambiguity, and ambivalence. They also have developed a "healthy cultural paranoia" (Grier & Cobbs, 1968) that makes them highly suspicious of others who differ from themselves in color, lifestyle, and values. Black peoples' endurance of suffering may be influenced by their strong religious or spiritual orientation, which views emotional difficulties as "the wages of sin" and interpersonal conflicts as not following "the Lord's teachings." To seek help from a therapist rather than through prayer may signify an absence of trust in God.

Family Tradition

The Black family has played a significant role in screening and protecting its members from the dehumanizing features of American society. The extended family has been most instrumental in ensuring the stability and well-being of the family through providing services that would ensure the survival of the family. Relatives, friends, and members of the community often assist with childcare responsibilities, contribute to the financial security of the family, care for the elderly, absorb young children of parents who cannot provide for them and children without parents, and provide emotional support to members of the family.

In financially secure families, family roles are relatively traditional, with the father acting as head of the household and the mother assuming the child rearing and household responsibilities. Although a Black father's involvement with his children sometimes is hindered by economic restrictions, a Black mother is generally recognized for her devotion and care of her children. The role of Black mothers is often misunderstood and criticized because they do not conform to middle-class modes of child rearing. Billingsley (1968) has pointed out that child rearing or "socialization is doubly challenging, for the family must teach its young members how to be human, but also how to be Black in a White society" (p. 28).

In disciplining the children, Black parents may use physical measures, but this is done with love and care. The frequent absence of the father or male figure has long been considered a negative factor in the psychological and emotional development of a Black child (Rainwater, 1966). However, studies indicate that the fatherless child does not significantly suffer from the absence of the father (Hare, 1975; Rubin, 1974). This, in part, may be corrected by the Black child's opportunity to have male models among the male kinsmen in his extended family network.

Mental Health Issues and Problems

Epidemiological Data

The physical and psychological disorders among Black children and youth are greatly affected by risk factors such as poverty and racial oppression (Rickel & Allen, 1987). When Black parents are economically insecure, the child in utero may encounter potential hazards. The end result is a child born "at risk." The high incidence of hypertension and toxemia in pregnant Black women puts in jeopardy the lives of both mother and infant. Reports of the Children's Defense Fund (1985) indicate that Black children in two-parent homes are more than twice as likely as White children to have no employed parent and five times more likely to have an adolescent or single mother. Further, more than 56% of all Black babies in the reports were born to women out of wedlock. The extreme youthfulness of a great many Black mothers, their malnutrition, and their inadequate prenatal care often result in premature births and babies of low birth weight. Sickle cell disease is known to be the major genetic disorder in Blacks (Squires, 1987).

Poor urban Black children have been found to exhibit the highest rates of childhood psychopathology and psychiatric impairment (Gould & Canino, 1981) in comparison to other ethnic groups. Psychiatric referrals of Black children are most often for help with behavioral problems (Myers, 1976). These range from aggressive defiance at home and/or disruptive, destructive, aggressive behavior to overt acts of delinquency. The formal diagnosis attached to such children has usually been phrased as adjustment reaction, or some version of personality disorder. Many of these children are given diagnostic labels without the benefit of a complete diagnostic evaluation that employs culturally unbiased instruments.

Many of these Black childrens' overt behaviors may actually reflect significant levels of depression. A recent study by Vincenzi (1987) indicates that at least 36% of an urban sixth-grade class at one school were at least mildly depressed as evidenced by scores on the Child Depression Inventory. Black juvenile delinquents also have higher rates than White juvenile delinquents of depression and of other psychological and neurological symptoms that are often undetected and misdiagnosed (Dembo, 1988). The next section presents various diagnostic categories that Black youth frequently encounter.

Diagnostic Categories

A strong relationship between stressful life events and psychiatric symptomatology has been established by a recent study of 1,347 Black female adolescent medical patients (Pryor Brown & Peters, 1989). Hypertension, a stress-related chronic illness, is one of the five leading causes of mortality among Black youth (U.S. Department of Health and Human Services, 1986). Asthma, another stress-related chronic childhood illness, is also most common among Black children. Morbidity and mortality rates from asthma are higher among Black children, ages 1 to 19, who have an annual age-adjusted death rate nearly six times higher than the rate for Whites (National Center for Health Statistics, 1986).

There were only 16 cases (14 females and 2 males) of eating disorders, such as anorexia nervosa or bulimia, reported among Black youth in the literature through 1985 (Robinson & Andersen, 1985). Suicide is the third leading cause of death among Black youth aged 15 to 24, after homicides and accidents (Gibbs, 1988). The suicide rate for this age group for Black males and for Black females doubled from 1960 to 1979 (Gibbs, 1988). The highest rates occur in urban areas, such as New York City, where the suicide rate among Black males and females aged 15 to 30 is higher than among Whites of the same age group (Henkin, 1987). The leading cause of death among Black males aged 15 to 19 in 1986 was homicide. This phenomenon was related to the rapid rise of drug wars and violent crimes in the Black community.

The school dropout rates for inner-city Black youth range from 40% to 60%, with higher rates for males than females. Functional illiteracy has contributed to the Black male's high dropout rate (Reed, 1988). Black youth numbered less than one fifth of the total youth population under the jurisdiction of the juvenile courts in 1985, but Black youth accounted for 23.2% of all juvenile arrests in the United States (Krisberg, 1986).

Studies of substance abuse consistently report that Black youth have a lower rate of alcohol use (Barnes & Welte, 1986; Rachal et al., 1980) and overall drug use (Skager, 1986) than White youth. However, rates of cocaine and heroin use are generally reported to be higher among older Black youth than among their White counterparts (Brunswick, 1979). The current epidemic of AIDS (acquired immunodeficiency syndrome) is especially alarming to Black youth who use drugs and frequently share unsterilized needles. The Centers for Disease

Control reported that there were 300 cases of AIDS among 13- to 19-year-old Black youth as of September, 1988. Due to Black youth's high-risk drug and sexual behaviors, the incidence of AIDS in this group is expected to increase (Children's Defense Fund, 1988).

Nearly 50% of Black females are pregnant by the age of 20. According to the Children's Defense Fund (1988), Black youth under 15 are particularly at risk for early childbearing, and almost 60% of all births to teenagers younger than age 15 were to Black adolescents. Moreover, close to 90% of all Black teenage parents are not married (Stengel, 1985). Only one in five girls under the age of 15 will receive prenatal care during the first few months of pregnancy. Infants born to these mothers are almost twice as likely to die than infants born to White teenage mothers (Taborn, 1987). Further, Black teenage mothers had high rates of school dropout, welfare dependency, and unemployment (Children's Defense Fund, 1986).

Problems Associated with Relocation

Like every other ethnic minority group, Black Americans are forced to adapt to the American mainstream and victim systems. Although some Blacks exhibit unusual strength, flexibility, and tolerance for ambiguity and creativity in their relationship with the systems, other Blacks consistently experience difficulty in value conflict and identity confusion. Although legal segregation was eliminated by a series of Supreme Court decisions, discriminatory practices are still pervasive and pernicious, depriving Blacks of equal access to housing, jobs, schools, health care, public recreation, and public facilities (Omi & Winant, 1986). The mass migration of Blacks from the rural South to northern industrial centers between World War I and World War II resulted in the development of urban ghettos with further social and cultural isolation from the dominant society (Wilson, 1987).

In an attempt to survive the oppressive victim system and problems associated with relocation, some Black Americans adopt a value orientation that emphasizes cooperation to resist powerlessness; strict obedience to authority in the context of felt oppression; toughness of character and creative activities in the form of art, music, and sports. This value orientation, when translated behaviorally, can lead an individual to free emotional expression, immediate gratification, manipulative relationships, and passive-aggressive rebellions, or aggressive characteristics. Such behaviors may be essential in adapting to powerlessness, but they can be destructive to a person's mental health and interpersonal relationships (Pinderhughes, 1982).

Ecological Approach to Assessment

The Personal System

Level of Acculturation

Black youths' level of acculturation to mainstream culture has great implications in the assessment and treatment phases of therapy. If a Black youth was born in this country, his or her level of exposure to integrated schools and neighborhoods also will dictate the level of acculturation. Given the pace of racial integration, surprisingly few Blacks have become assimilated into the mainstream mode of behavior. Scanzoni (1971) shows that even though middle-class Black Americans have opted to function by removing barriers to assimilation, they realize that the process itself is costly and tends to generate cultural value and familial relational conflict. They continue to socialize in the inner cities after moving to the suburbs and maintain solidarity with extended family ties and with the Black community (Staples, 1978).

If the Black youth's birthplace was outside of this country, cultural specific information relevant to each child's life experience must be ascertained. Personal data such as language and dialect spoken, physical health and medical history, help-seeking behavior patterns, and other significant demographic information (years in the United States, country of origin, immigration status, and so on) are helpful in assessment.

Physical Appearance

Early studies (Johnson, 1941; Warner, Lawrence, & Devore, 1978) have suggested that children with darker skin and children who have fewer "White" characteristics are likely to view themselves more negatively than those who are more "White-like." Color has many different levels of symbolism for Black youth. Many Black youth view their color proudly, as a badge of pride and honor; others are negative, or at best ambivalent, and view their blackness as a "mark of oppression" (Kardiner & Ovesey, 1951). At the other end of the spectrum there have been light-skinned Blacks who have denied their blackness and have "passed" for White. A child's skin color can also help to explain why that child has been singled out for the family projection process. The darkest or lightest child in these families may be seen as strange and, therefore, targeted as the family scapegoat at an early age.

Preferences for lighter skin and straighter hair texture have gradually been altered. In the 1960s the label of inferiority was ripped from the characteristic of Blackness and replaced with the concept that "Black is beautiful." Hence, some Black youth may view their light skin as a liability because they resent being mistaken as White by their Black peers and the exclusion that can result.

Hence, the Black child's phenotypic characteristics (i.e., coloring) and physical features (i.e., eye color, shape of nose and mouth) are all important in assessing racial self-perceptions and self-concept. The congruence or incongruence between his or her physical appearance and racial self-identification and self-concept may suggest whether there may be issues related to racial identity. A young Black youth with a medium-brown complexion and curly hair who indicates that her racial identity is part White may actually have one White birth parent but may also be uncomfortable with acknowledging her visible Black heritage. This may suggest to the therapist that further sensitive exploration regarding the client's racial identity issues is needed.

Speech and Language

The degree of acculturation to mainstream lifestyles affects the language characteristics of Blacks. Some Black youth may use *Ebonics,* or Black English (Dillard, 1983), whereas others may use mainstream Standard American English. Ebonics is an oral communication consisting of phonology, syntax, morphology, semantics, lexicon, rate, rhythm, stress, and nonverbal communication (Wofford, 1979). Ebonics is "nonstandard" English differing from Standard English in the following ways: (a) a pattern of dropping final consonants, (b) the omission of the verb "to be" in the present tense (*is*), and (c) the use of the singular noun for plural objects. Houston (1971) suggests that this form of English is not the total of the child's linguistic performance nor in any way representative of the child's linguistic competence. Others like Kochman (1972) and Lobov (1972) also assert that Black youth usually have good verbal skills even if they express themselves in "Black English." Many youth are skilled in the use of both standard and Black English and vary their communication styles depending upon the situation. A therapist would not experience a communication barrier in therapy if he or she understands and appreciates that language not only serves symbolic functions for Black youth as a form of artistic expression and confrontation but can also represent a source of conflict in school or at work where their native linguistic style is devalued (Mancini, 1980).

Interpersonal Relations

The quality and intensity of a Black youth's interpersonal relations can be evaluated according to four different interpersonal styles within his or her social and cultural environment (Bell & Evans, 1981):

1. The *traditional* interpersonal style includes youth who have limited contact outside the Black community. Being Black is an innate part of the person, so the person does not actively accept or reject his or her Black identity.
2. The *culturally immersed* interpersonal style is characterized by a rejection of White values, norms, and culture. Individuals adopting to this style are often inner-city youth from poverty backgrounds. They form same-sex peer groups for social identity and mutual protection. The intense emotional bonds among these group members can foster involvement in antisocial or self-destructive activities, such as joining gangs, dropping out of school, and engaging in frequent premarital sexual activities (Felner & Franklin, 1985; Mancini, 1980).
3. The *acculturated* interpersonal style is characterized by Black youth who have chosen to assimilate into the White mainstream culture and have rejected Black identity as inferior to the dominant culture's norms. These youth do not feel comfortable with other Black youth, who in turn reject them. This style becomes problematic only when the rejection of one's culture also means rejection of one's self, or self-hatred.
4. Black youth having a *bicultural* interpersonal style have a great deal of pride in their racial identity but also tend to seek out diversity. Those youth can have both intense and quality relationships with Black or other ethnic groups. Generally, they are middle class and live in integrated neighborhoods, and they may be involved in interracial friendships and dating. An assessment of youths' perceptions of their own racial identity and how Blacks and Whites view them yields much useful information when working with youths and their problems.

Attitude Toward Self

Much of the pre-1960s literature (Clark, 1952; Goodman, 1952) emphasized the self-hate and self-rejection behavior of Black children and suggested that Black children had poor self-concepts because they belonged to a racial group that was perceived negatively in American society. More recent research suggest that Blacks, especially Black school children, have relatively high levels of self-esteem (McRoy & Zurcher, 1983; Simmons, 1978). The Black pride movement of the late 1960s and more relevant theories of self-concept development and research methodologies may be responsible for altering the Black children's perception of self. Further, McAdoo (1978) indicates that geographical and social environment affect a Black child's perception of self. Southern Black children felt better about themselves and had a greater sense of security than their northern counterparts. Because of their all-Black environment, southern Black children were not placed in a position of being reminded of the ethnic group's lowered status position by contact with non-Blacks, and they also may not have been placed in a defensive posture of protecting themselves from subtle and overt antagonism that is predicted by the general attitudinal preferences for non-Blacks.

A Black youth's attitude toward self is also contingent upon gender and peer group differences. Although athletic ability is a major source of esteem for Black male adolescents, physical attractiveness and social skills are very important assets for Black females (Cauce, 1986). Similarly, academic achievement may be valued by some Black youth in some settings; in other settings, it is demeaned and ridiculed as acting "just like Whites." Hence, accurate assessment of a Black youth's attitude toward self must take into consideration of his or her subjective view along with the social context in which the adolescent is a member of the majority or minority.

Anxiety and Patterns of Defense

According to statistics from the Federal Bureau of Investigation, more than half of the teenagers arrested in 1983 for violent crimes were Black, yet less than 15% of the population aged 14 to 17 was Black (Flanagan & McGarrell, 1985). Black youth, especially males, also appear to suffer disproportionately high rates of incarceration. In 1985, 37% of the juveniles in public correctional facilities were Black (U.S. Department of Justice, 1987). Judging by these data, it appears that Black youth are having great difficulties in coping with

insurmountable psychological and environmental stress. External-
ization of anxiety is a culturally acceptable childrearing practice
among Blacks. Also, harsh environmental stressors, continuous discriminatory practices, and other anxiety provoking situations at
school, at work, in the family, and in the community reduce the Black
youth's defense. Whereas older youth adopt psychosomatic complaints as a means to mask their anxiety (National Center for Health
Statistics, 1986), younger Black youth may manifest their anxiety and
depression in hyperactivity, acting out, substance abuse, and suicide
(Sturkie & Flanzer, 1987).

Issues of Sexuality

Moore (1986) reports that in 1979, 89% of Black males and females
in the United States under age 19 had had sexual intercourse. The
incidence of high birth rate to Black teenage mothers indicates the
failure to prevent conception. In 1980, among mothers 15 to 19 years
of age, 87% of the Black and 33% of the White births were outside
of marriage (Moore, 1986). In 1986 the birth rates (per 1,000 population for the specified group) for unmarried Black women between
the ages of 15 and 19 years were 89.9% (U.S. Bureau of the Census,
1987b). Having a child at such an early age has been found to interfere with sexuality and opportunities for a more productive, satisfying life for Black mothers (Furstenberg & Gellas, 1987). In counseling
Black youth regarding sexuality issues, it is important for a therapist
to be sensitive to the client's cultural conception about sexuality
and teenage parenthood. Franklin (1982) suggests that for many low-
income Black teenagers, early parenthood is viewed as a rite of pas-
sage to adulthood. Hence, a Black teenage parent may not experience
the same degree of anxiety, shame, and social stigma normally experienced by middle-class White adolescents.

The Family System

Immigration History and Level of Acculturation

The experience of Blacks is a grim one: 200 years of slavery, 20 brief
years of civil rights, and another century of struggling to regain
equal rights, opportunities, and protection under the law that is
guaranteed to all U.S. citizens. The extent of America's ambiguous
feelings of accepting Blacks as equals is briefly presented in the
chronological history traced below.

In 1619 the first Blacks were brought to Jamestown, Virginia, by a Dutch man-of-war. Not until January 1, 1808, was the importation and other participation in the slave trade outlawed in the United States. On March 4, 1861, seven slave states seceded and the Confederate States of America was organized. The next year, the Emancipation Proclamation was signed by President Lincoln proclaiming emancipation for slaves in those states that were in rebellion with the Federation. Three years later, the Thirteenth Amendment abolished slavery everywhere in the United States. Civil rights bills of 1872, 1873, and 1875 provided that all persons, regardless of race, color, or previous conditions of servitude, were entitled to equal treatment before the law. On May 31, 1955, *Brown v. the Board of Education* resulted in the Supreme Court acknowledging that segregated public schools were not equal and could not be made equal and, therefore, deprived Black citizens of equal protection of the law. On July 2, 1964, the Civil Rights Act declared discriminatory employment practices illegal, and it also outlawed racial discrimination in all federally assisted programs, including housing, child care, medical care, and so on. The Voting Rights Act of 1965, which provided greater protection and enforcement of the voting rights of Blacks, was a direct result of Dr. Martin Luther King's march to Montgomery, Alabama, protesting racial discrimination in registration and voting. However, beginning from the mid-1970s until recently, a gradual but steady return to the conservatism of the past has been observed. For example, in *Regent v. Bakke*, the Supreme Court ruled in favor of Bakke, a White medical school applicant who was denied admission because of the quota system.

Like every other ethnic minority group, Black Americans are forced to adapt to American mainstream and victim systems. Some families exhibit unusual strengths, flexibility, and tolerance for ambiguity and creativity in their relationship with the system. Other families consistently experience difficulty in value conflicts and identity confusion. There are four possible ways in which a Black family can adapt to discrimination and biculturality (D. Young, 1969). A Black family can (a) attempt to meet crises as they arise, (b) physically remove themselves from any stresses caused by a racist society, (c) willfully maintain externally imposed or self-imposed segregation, or (d) remove major barriers to acculturation into the opportunity structure. The path to acculturation is costly in terms of generation of cultural and familial relational conflicts. Middle-class Blacks, despite being assimilated into the mainstream mode of behavior, continue socializing in the inner cities and maintain solidarity with extended family ties and with the Black community (Staples, 1978).

Family Structure and Life Patterns

Contemporary studies on Black family structure indicate viable functional systems (Gary & Glasgrow, 1983; McAdoo, 1977). However, this observation is by no means a denial that the Black family is presently experiencing a great deal of internal (family conflicts) and external (victim systems) stress. Such stress has helped to shape the diversified changing Black family systems and structures.

As a result of responding adaptively to daily stressors, three types of Black families have emerged (Billingsley, 1987): nuclear, extended, and augmented families. The nuclear family consists of spouses and children and no other person living with them. Such a nuclear household can be *incipient* when there are no children, *simple* if composed of husband and wife and their children, or *attenuated* if there is a single parent with no other parent figure present.

Extended families refer to those families in which other relatives or in-laws of the husband and wife share the same household with the nuclear family. Extended families also may be incipient, simple, or attenuated, depending upon whether children are present or whether there is only one parent. Augmented families include nonrelatives in the household.

These three types of Black family structures have changed significantly in the past 2 decades. For example, in 1960 married couple families constituted 78% of all Black families. In 1980 the percentage of married couple families had decreased to 53%. This decline parallels an increase in female-headed families from 22% in 1960 to 44% in 1987. A high rate of unemployment, separation and divorce, unmarried parenthood, and early deaths of Black men have contributed to this dramatic increase in single-parent families (Billingsley, 1987). Single-parent families may be described as the fastest-growing structure among Black families (Moore, 1986).

Economic and social conditions frequently make it necessary for Black women to contribute to the income of the household, even in two-parent homes. Although Black women historically have contributed to the financial well-being of the family, their ability to easily assume head-of-household responsibilities has unjustifiably earned them the stigma of strong matriarchs. This matriarchal image is further

reinforced by society's refusal to recognize Black males as authority figures. Studies have indicated that equalitarian patterns of
shared decision making and household responsibilities often exist,
even in households where the women may be the primary provider
(J. Jackson, 1973; Scanzoni, 1971).

Attitudes About Mental Health

Black youth and their families still view mental health service as
strange and think of it as a process for "strange" or "crazy" people
only. Neighbors and Taylor's (1985) study found that the majority of
Blacks did not use mental health services, and that the majority of
those who did (14.4%) had incomes of less than $10,000 and con-
tacted mental health services regardless of their problem. Contact
with mental health services is usually precipitated by a crisis and
happens when other sources of help have been depleted. The
Black's underutilization of psychological services also is related to
their general mistrust of the therapist, especially the White therapist
(J. Jackson, 1973). Blacks' negative attitudes toward mental health
and mental health providers may explain, to some extent, why Blacks
have been found to drop out of therapy earlier and more frequently
than Whites (S. Sue, Sue, & Sue, 1974).

Help-Seeking Behavioral Patterns

Blacks rely heavily upon extended family ties and church organizations during times of crisis. During times of need Blacks seek help
from mutual aid and informal helping networks, such as the Black
extended family and kin networks (Martin & Martin, 1985). McAdoo
(1978) found that neither socioeconomic status nor upward mobility
decreased the amount of this informal support received by urban
Blacks. Similarly, Taylor's (1976) study of Black family support among
a sample of Blacks revealed that the majority received support from
extended family members. Reliance on natural support systems produces fewer feelings of defeat, humiliation, and powerlessness. The
mutual aid system operates on the twin premises that families
should seek security and independence, but that where family integrity is threatened, sharing resources and exchanging services across
households are crucial and acceptable.

However, the helping tradition that formerly appeared institution-
alized in the Black community now seems to be waning. The racial
consciousness of the 1960s and the mutual aid system have taken a

backseat to the desire of some Blacks to obtain material goods, gain social status, and escape the stigma of being poor (Martin & Martin, 1985).

There is evidence that Blacks are utilizing psychological services in increasing numbers and at much higher rates than expected (S. Sue et al., 1974). Although Blacks do prefer Black therapists over White therapists, they also prefer competent therapists over less competent Black therapists (Sattler, 1977).

The School System

A Black youth's success or failure depends upon many factors, including the nature of his or her relationship with the school system. The facts provided by the National Coalition (1985) indicate that Black youth in general do not fare well in school. According to the same report, the school achievement of Black children tends to drop below expectations in elementary school and to fall further behind as the children get older. Disciplinary action toward Black students is disproportionately higher than that against White students. Black students constituted 16% of the American school population in 1980, but they constituted 28% of all expelled, suspended, and corporally punished students (Ploski & Williams, 1983). Black children are placed in classes for the educable mentally retarded at three times the rate of White children. In addition, Black children are only half as likely to be placed in a class for gifted and talented students.

Racial/Ethnic Composition

Race and others' perceptions of race may play a role in the self-appraisal process and, thus, may affect Black children's achievement at school. A study by Rosenfeld, Chess, and Wilson (1981) demonstrates that the ethnic composition of the classroom affects the behavior and school performance of Black children. Their findings indicated that (a) the higher the percentage of Blacks in a class, the more Black friends the White students had; (b) the greater the number of Blacks in a class displaying hostility towards Whites, the more negative were the Whites' attitudes toward Blacks; and (c) the more equal the social class and achievement levels of the Whites and Blacks in a class, the more White students indicated having minority friends. Hence, the learning environment of the school sometimes is contingent upon ethnic composition and the students attitudes toward each other. If the child's school environment is safe, it facilitates learning and personal growth. Conversely, if the school milieu consists of ethnic hostility and unrest, a Black child's learning and social development will be hampered.

Attitudes of Teachers and Staff

A Black child's performance and academic achievements also are related to the attitudes of teachers and staffs. Roscoe and Peterson (1982) suggest that the educational experience and academically beneficial nature of schooling are facilitated by teachers who interact with students in a genuinely accepting manner. Unfortunately, research findings reveal that facilitative teaching and learning are lacking in desegregated schools (Washington, 1980). Further, unfavorable attitudes, unfavorable perceptions, and unfavorable classroom behavior were directed more often toward Black children. Irrespective of a teacher's race, teachers have biased perceptions of Black children. Black teachers, more so than the White teachers, viewed desegregation and cultural diversity in a positive manner. Female students were perceived more positively than male students by both Black and White teachers, but Black female students were perceived as less favorable than White female students (Washington, 1982).

Societal Issues

Racism continues to contribute to school failure among Black children. The negative result is shared by the dropout's family, community, and society as a whole. Initially, the greatest concern of this country was for educating those who would run the country, mainly White males (Ploski & Williams, 1983). When public education was seen as possibly enabling Black people to improve their personal status and to take full advantage of their freedom, new laws were enacted to keep White schools from including Black students and to otherwise make public facilities and funds unavailable for Black children. Legislation and informal agreements have been employed by some public schools to block the full access of funds and facilities for Black children. For example, enrollment in neighborhood schools has been controlled by informal arrangements in the business community about which racial and ethnic groups will or will not be permitted to rent or buy homes in the community.

The U.S. Supreme Court ruling of 1954 that racially separate schools were inherently unequal was met with minimal effort toward desegregation. This led to another Supreme Court ruling in 1969 that dual school systems were to end immediately. The ruling was resisted by new tactics ranging from closing public schools to repealing the compulsory education laws and discriminatory class assignments that kept Black children segregated by classroom (Allen-Meares, Gibbs, & Arkoff, 1986). Despite all legal and voluntary efforts, in 1982 over 63% of Black students still attended predominantly Black schools (National Coalition, 1985). Within this societal context of overt and covert racism, Black families and children continue to experience a sense of exclusion, devaluation, alienation, and powerlessness with regard to public school education and their overall well-being. Assessment of Black youth referred for antisocial or self-destructive behavior requires therapist sensitivity regarding their underlying feelings of alienation, depression, and rage (Franklin, 1982).

5

Hispanic American Children and Adolescents

Historical Background

Demographic Data

The Hispanic population of the United States constitutes the second largest minority group and the fastest growing ethnic group in the country. If present trends continue, this group will someday replace Blacks as the nation's largest minority group (C. Davis, Padilla, & Paz, 1983). The 1980 census figures showed the Hispanic population to number over 12 million (U.S. Bureau of the Census, 1980b). The census breakdown of Hispanic groups reports the following population figures: Mexican American, 7.2 million; Puerto Rican, 1.8 million; and Spanish, 3 million. The latter category includes persons of Central or South American, Cuban, and "other" Spanish origins.

Over 60% of the Hispanics in the United States reside in just three states: California, Texas, and New York (U.S. Bureau of the Census, 1982). Hispanics represent 10% or more of the total population in five states: New Mexico (37%), Texas (21%), California (19%), Arizona (16%), and Colorado (12%). The southwestern states—including Arizona, California, Colorado, New Mexico, and Texas—account for 60% of all Hispanics, most of whom are Mexican. Fifteen percent of all Hispanics (primarily Puerto Ricans but also people of Caribbean and Latin American origin) live in New York and in New Jersey. The Cuban population is concentrated in Florida, where 6% of all Hispanics live. Eighty-eight percent of Hispanics reside in urban areas; this percentage is second only to the Asian population (91%) and is 13 points higher than the national figure (75%) representing all urban residents.

The median income of the Hispanic household is $6,000 below the national average. The majority of Hispanic Americans live at a low socioeconomic level. They are also severely underrepresented in higher levels of education and in occupational and professional jobs (U.S. Bureau of the Census, 1980b). The educational levels of Hispanics, who make up the largest proportion of people without a high school degree and the smallest proportion of those with at least a college degree, remain among the lowest in the nation (U.S. Bureau of the Census, 1981). Although data indicate that Hispanics have clearly made gains in education during this period, they continue to earn 70% of the income earned by non-Hispanics (C. Davis et al., 1983).

Hispanic families are more likely than either Black or White families to have children under age 18. One out of every five Hispanic households is headed by a female whose spouse is not present. Hispanic households that are headed by women are more likely to include children than are those headed by Black and White women. Mexican Americans are the youngest among Hispanic groups, with a median age of 23.3 years, compared with 24.3 years for Puerto Ricans, 39.1 for Cuban Americans, and 31.9 for non-Hispanics.

Immigration Data

The Hispanic immigrational experience to the United States has not been as widely reported as for other ethnic groups. This is partly due to the geographic isolation of Mexicans in the Southwest and because there was little legislative action aimed at the discrimination against Mexicans as a group. Not until after World War II, when the United States' relationship with Mexico and Cuba began to break down, was new legislation enacted that restricted the immigration of Mexican workers. Laws once were passed to facilitate Hispanic settlement in New Mexico, which was sparsely populated. In Texas, where anti-Mexican sentiments have existed since the Alamo, Mexicans have experienced discrimination making it difficult for them to advance politically, economically, and socially. Following is a synopsis of significant historical dates of Hispanic immigration patterns and U.S. policies and legation that depicts the Hispanic experience in this country (Mindel et al., 1988).

In 1821, Mexico gained independence from Spain and there was limited immigration from Mexico to the United States. In 1845 Texas was annexed by the United States, and there were strong anti-Mexican sentiments. The treaty of Guadalupe Hidalgo (Mexican-American War) was signed in 1849, which resulted in the United States gaining the rest of the Southwestern Territory and granting citizenship to Mexican and Spanish residents of the territory. The signing of the Treaty of Paris after the Spanish-American War in 1898 granted the United States four former Spanish territories: Cuba, Guam, the Philippines, and Puerto Rico. In 1917 Puerto Rico's status changed from territory to commonwealth and its residents were finally granted U.S. citizenship. Prior to the depression years of the 1930s, the U.S. government encouraged immigration of Mexican workers to supplement the American work force. As the Depression set in and jobs became scarce, "illegal workers" caused problems. After World War II the great economic distress in Puerto Rico resulted in many Puerto Ricans immigrating to the United States in search of jobs. During the 1950s there was a resurgence of "undocumented workers." This accelerated in the mid-1960s after the cancellation of bilateral agreements, which had allowed Mexican workers permits to work in the United States for short periods and protected their rights to the extent of their permits. During the 1960s there was also a flood of Cuban refugees who were largely White middle-class Cubans fleeing Fidel Castro's regime. The 1970s brought a large number of South and Central Americans (some refugees and some illegals) to the United States for political as well as economic reasons. The 1980 influx of Cuban immigrants was found to consist of 40% poorly educated non-Whites and their sociopolitical descendants (Spencer, Keefe, & Carlos, 1981).

From 1961 to 1980, approximately 2.3 million legal immigrants from Latin America and Mexico entered the United States. Some chose to return to their native countries, but the majority are now permanent residents of the United States (Bean et al., 1984). Although there is no reliable method to estimate the number of undocumented Hispanic immigrants in the United States, there is agreement that the majority are from Mexico and from Latin America (Passel & Woodrow, 1984).

Native Culture

Although Mexican Americans, Puerto Ricans, Cubans, and other Spanish-speaking minorities in the United States share a Hispanic cultural background, there are important differences among them. In Mexico, native Indian populations had achieved a high degree of civilization but still were highly subjugated by the Spaniards. Mexican culture became a blend of the Indian and the Spanish (Padilla & Ruiz, 1973). In Puerto Rico, the indigenous Indians were virtually eradicated by the Spaniards, who replaced them with African slaves (Fitzpatrick, 1981). Today's Puerto Rican culture reflects that blend. The Cuban culture is a blending of Spanish and African culture (Bustamante Santa Cruz, 1975; C. Ortiz, 1973). Cuba's unique historical connection to powerful nations such as Spain, the United States, and the Soviet Union further distinguishes Cubans from other Latin countries.

The heritage and native culture of Hispanic Americans is rich and diverse. However, some commonalities do exist, such as shared lineage with both Spanish and local indigenous Indian groups. Certain unifying cultural concepts also distinguish them from the dominant society. These culture concepts include familism, personalism, hierarchy, spiritualism, and fatalism. Each of these is described below.

Familism. The Hispanic American places a great deal of value and pride on this membership in the family. The importance of family membership and belonging cuts across caste lines and socioeconomic conditions. Individuals' relationships to other family members influence their self-confidence, worth, security, self-identity, and ethnic identity. The significant importance of family is evident in the Hispanic's use of family names (Fitzpatrick, 1981). The man generally uses both his father's and mother's name together with his given name, for example, Jose Garcia Rivera. Garcia is his father's family name and Rivera is his mother's family name. To reflect the patriarchal pattern of the Hispanic family, the father's family name is used if the man is to be addressed by only one name.

Family obligation plays a vital part in the Hispanic cultural concept of familism. The needs of the family collectively often supersede the individual's needs. During good times or during crisis, the family's name and family members' welfare always come first. The family is the strongest area of life activities from which all members derive status and esteem (Ulibarri, 1970, p. 31).

Personalism. Along with the concept of familism, Hispanics define self-worth in terms of those inner qualities that give them self-respect and earn the respect of others. They feel an inner dignity (*dignidad*) and expect others to show respect (*respecto*) for that dignidad. A person automatically possesses dignidad, which is a belief in the innate worth and inner importance of each individual. The spirit and goal are more important than the body. The focus is on the person's qualities, uniqueness, goodness, and integrity (Mintz, 1973).

Closely related to the concept of personalism is the quality *machismo*, literally maleness. Machismo is referred to as a quality of personal magnetism that impresses and influences others. It is a style of personal daring by which one faces challenge, danger, and threats with calmness and self-possession. Machismo ideally encompasses a strong sense of personal honor, family, loyalty, and care for the children; however, machismo may also connote exaggerated masculinity, virility, and aggressiveness (Trankina, 1983).

Sense of Hierarchy. This concept of sense of hierarchy probably emanated from the caste system that existed in most Latin American countries. The rich and poor were fixed in their socioeconomic status, with limited opportunities for mobility. A person's social position was as fixed and natural as the parts of his or her body. The Hispanic sense of hierarchy is further manifested in the leadership structure of the family, where the father occupies the role of superior authority and the mother's role is to follow. In addition to gender hierarchy, there is also generational hierarchy in which parents expect to be obeyed when they advise their children. Younger children are expected to obey older children, who serve as role models.

Spiritualism. Hispanics emphasize spiritual values and are willing to sacrifice material satisfaction for spiritual goals. A significant part of the Hispanic population, especially the Puerto Ricans, believes the visible world is surrounded by an invisible world inhabited by good and evil spirits who influence human behavior (Delgado, 1978). Thus spirits can either protect or harm and can prevent or cause illness. In order to be protected by good spirits, an individual is expected to produce good and charitable deeds in a secular world. Catholicism is the predominant religion for Hispanic Americans (Grebler, Moore, & Guzman, 1973). However, the Roman Catholic ways of worship practiced by Hispanics differ from other ethnic groups, such as the Irish. Hispanics believe they can make direct contact with God and the supernatural without the assistance or intervention of clergy.

Folklore that combines the heritage of Spanish Catholic medical and religious practices with African and Indian belief systems is common among Hispanics. For example, the practice of *santeria*, which combines Catholicism with *Yorubans*, an African belief, and the practice of *espiritsismo* (exorcising evil spirits) are prevalent throughout Hispanic communities (Gonzales-Wippler, 1975).

Fatalism. Hispanics are not preoccupied with mastering the world; instead, they tend to think in terms of transcendent qualities such as justice, loyalty, or love. They have a keen sense of destiny and a sense of divine providence governing the world. The popular songs, "Que Será Será" (whatever will be, will be) and "Si Dios quiere" (If God wills it), reflect the Hispanics' expression of fatalism.

These common cultural Hispanic values of familism, personalism, hierarchy, spiritualism, and fatalism significantly influence Hispanic family tradition and practice.

Family Tradition

The family tradition of the Hispanics is characterized by an extended family network that includes such relatives as grandparents, uncles, aunts, and cousins (Madsen, 1964). The extended family encompasses not only those related by blood and marriage, but also those tied to it by custom in reciprocal bonds of obligation and feeling. Important parts of the Hispanic family systems are the *Compradazgo* and *hijos de Crianza* (Fitzpatrick, 1971).

The Compradazgo is the institution of *compadres* (companion parents), a network of ritual kinship whose members have a deep sense of obligation to each other. Such obligations include economic assistance, emotional support, and even personal correction. The institution of Compradazgo is often created through a Catholic baptismal ceremony. The child, by this process, acquires a godmother (*madrina*) and godfather (*padrino*) who directly share responsibility for the child's welfare and thus form coparent bonds with the child's parents. The two most important types of godparents are those selected at baptism and marriage. The godparents of baptism assume responsibility for the child if birth parents become unable to fulfill their duties. Godparents of marriage contribute to the expenses of the wedding and may function as mediators between the couple in case of quarrels or separations (Abad, Ramos, & Boyce, 1974).

Hijos de Crianza ("children of the upbringing") is the Hispanic cultural practice of accepting responsibility for another child, without the necessity of blood or even friendship ties. This child is raised as if it were one's own. Neither the biological parent nor the child is stigmatized for the relinquishment. There is also no stigma attached to an illegitimate child. Such institutional practices serve as an economic and emotional safety value for the family and often make it possible for the child to enjoy a better life. The "adoptive" family, in all likelihood, may not be able to produce legal documents for the child.

Mental Health Issues and Problems

Epidemiological Data

There is considerable controversy about the level of psychological distress among Hispanic children, with much evidence suggesting mental health problems produced by response style (Krause & Carr, 1978). Many of the reports pointing to increased distress of Hispanics are a consequence of the scales used and the Hispanic's alleged tendency to somatize problems. Escobar and Karrer (1986) and Angel and Guarnaccia (1989) have emphasized the high prevalence of somatization problems among Mexican American and Puerto Rican youth. Their study concluded that Hispanic youth, perhaps preferentially those of lower social class, express and show distress and maladaptation in a phenomenologically different mode than Anglo's. M. Garcia and Marks (1989) reported on the prevalence of depression among Mexican Americans in Los Angeles. A higher level of endorsement of certain items that indicate depression was observed among Mexican Americans than among Anglos in Los Angeles, but the meaning of this is unclear because matters involving semantics and culture could be an explanation.

Because the field of psychiatric and psychological epidemiology is anchored in establishment paradigms, it tends to constrain and shape the nature of the psychopathology it encounters. Despite this bias, important differences in the structure and interpretation of symptoms among Hispanic youth are still manifest in the studies cited.

Aside from systematic epidemiological studies, clinic-based research data also shed some light on the psychological disorders of Hispanic children. Ethnic differences in the expression of behavior problems and psychopathology were found in Stoker and Meadow's (1974) study, which reported that Mexican American boys were more frequently described as aggressive and acting out, whereas Anglo-American boys were more frequently reported as neurotic. Mexican American girls were also found to be overall more depressive than Mexican American boys.

Diagnostic Categories

A review of the literature on the use of alcohol and marijuana by Hispanic adolescents indicates that Hispanic adolescents have a higher percentage of abstainers than the general student population and that Puerto Rican and Mexican American adolescent females are predominantly nondrinkers (U.S. Department of Health and Human Services, 1981). However, as Hispanic adolescents got older, there was an increase in alcohol and/or drug use. Padilla, Carlos, and Keefe (1979), for example, noted that for Hispanic males aged 14 to 16 years, the percentage that had ever used alcohol increased from 52.7% to 71%, whereas for Hispanic females aged 14 to 16, the percentage increased from 46.1% to 55.5%.

Although a study by Guinn (1978) found no evidence of a clear-cut relationship between socioeconomic status and alcohol use, poor academic performance and lowered academic aspirations have been positively associated with increased alcohol consumption among Hispanic adolescents. Another study, by Menon, Burrett, and Simpson (1990), focused on school and peer influences on inhalant use in a sample of 599 Mexican American youths admitted to a drug abuse program in Texas. Data showed that problems in school performance, school conduct, peer associations, and attitudes of the school-based peer group were significantly related to inhalant use. Specifically, the odds of using inhalant regularly were significantly lower among Hispanic youths with better academic backgrounds.

Those without a history of school suspension were less likely to be regular users of inhalants.

Urban gangs have become a problem for many Hispanic youth. Of the 300 to 500 gangs in Los Angeles, approximately two thirds are Hispanic (200 to 332 gangs) and most of these are conflict-type gangs (Attorney General's Youth Gang Task Force, 1988, p. 17). Conflict gangs are very turf oriented and will engage in violent battle with individuals or rival groups that invade their neighborhood or commit acts that they consider insulting or degrading. Spergel (1984) identified 55 conflict gangs in Chicago, 33 of them involving Hispanic youth. The number of Hispanic female gangs also has increased, estimated at 10% (about 20 to 30 gangs) in Los Angeles.

Along with gang activities, the homicide rate for Hispanic youth also is increasing. According to the Centers for Disease Control (1988) study of the southwestern states for 1976 to 1980, the Hispanic homicide rate was almost three times higher than the rate for non-Hispanic Whites, specifically 21.6 per 100,000 to 7.7 per 100,000. However, rape homicide was virtually unknown among Hispanics. Lower homicide rates in Hispanic families have also been found in California, perhaps indicating a traditional Hispanic cultural norm in which the family is valued and protected.

In other psychological disorder categories, Hispanic youth exhibited a high representation in the symptoms of morbid depression, fears and phobias, anxiety and panic, school refusal, and disturbances of relationships with other children (Canino et al., 1986). During the period of June 1981 to November 1987, 23% of the nationally reported AIDS cases in children under age 13 were Hispanic. Of the adolescent cases with the single risk factor of intravenous drug abuse, 35% were Hispanic, compared with 5% who were White non-Hispanics (Centers for Disease Control, 1987).

Problems Associated with Relocation

Immigration and relocation can cause many problems and stress for any family, including the children. Family members are often faced with learning a new language and new social and political ways of life. To ascertain the impact of relocation, it is important to realize the heterogeneous nature of Hispanics. For example, many

Mexican Americans who reside in the southwestern United States were born in the United States. Due to a political agreement between the United States and Mexico and Puerto Rico, immigrants usually enjoy freedom of travel back and forth to visit relatives. On the other hand, Cuban immigrants until just recently were not allowed to visit their relatives in Cuba. An immigrant's inability to visit with relatives at home intensifies the emotional cutoff normally associated with relocation.

The timing of relocation is another factor affecting the adjustment problem of Hispanics (Casal et al., 1979). For example, the Cuban migration of the 1960s was overrepresented by Whites, disproportionately composed of the upper and middle class, and heavily aided by major U.S. federal programs. Conversely, the 1980 influx of Cuban immigrants was found to consist of 40% non-Whites who were poorly educated, sociopolitical dissidents (Spenser et al., 1981). The new arrivals are destined to encounter more severe adjustment problems than the 1960 group of immigrants.

Although there were, and continue to be, different immigration and relocation experiences, immigrants also share many common patterns and problems. First is the uprooting from friends, family, and culture, the emotional sacrifices needed to establish a new life, and the hardship on family members left behind. The second phase is the transition process of the family from one country to the other. This process may last for months or years. The final phase is the adaptation process, which usually is quite lengthy. Immigration and relocation is an endemic cultural process, which produces a profound impact on the family and the entire community. Although some immigrants find family networks of support, others find themselves socially isolated and facing radical changes in their lifestyles. The absence of the street life that typifies Latin countries becomes a depressing part of the relocation experience for many.

The Hispanic immigrant is usually a victim of economic and cultural marginality. Poor economic conditions and the frustration and stress inherent in the acculturation process result in various mental health problems (Ruiz, 1977). Isolation from their ethnic groups also has been associated with an increased rate of mental illness in Hispanics (Rabkin & Struening, 1976).

Ecological Approach to Assessment

The Personal System

Level of Acculturation

Acculturation refers to a process whereby behavioral and psychological responses occur in Hispanics when in contact with the American culture. Often cognitions, values, and behaviors of the Hispanics do not equip them to respond in ways appropriate to the host culture, and psychological stress ensues. Berry (1980) refers to this stress as "acculturative stress" to distinguish it from stress caused by other factors, such as crisis situations or unemployment. Acculturative stress results from behaviors and experiences generated during acculturation that are mildly pathological and disruptive to an individual and his group (e.g., deviant behaviors, psychosomatic symptoms, and feelings of marginality). Acculturative stress of Hispanics generally is caused by three factors (Berry & Annis, 1974): (a) a great disparity in behaviors and attitudes between Hispanics and the host culture, (b) strong pressures for the Hispanics to acculturate (e.g., migration to an "assimilating" society or "melting pot" society), and (c) a Hispanic culture that promotes less independence (i.e., less psychologically differentiated or more field dependent).

Literature strongly indicates that there is a direct correlation between a Hispanic child's level of acculturation and his or her psychological and behavioral adjustment. Knight et al. (1978) investigated field independence, school achievement, and self-esteem in second- and third-generation Mexican American grade school children. From second to third generation, field independence, reading achievement, and math achievement converged to Anglo-American norms, whereas third-generation children had lower self-esteem scores than did second-generation children. Buriel et al. (1982) examined the relationship between educational aspirations, delinquency, and acculturation in male Mexican American adolescents. More disparity between educational aspirations and expected fulfillment, and significantly higher rates of self-reported delinquency were observed in third-generation than in second-generation children. The above studies implied that strong identification with the Anglo-American culture was accompanied by more psychological distress than maintenance of a bicultural identity.

Bicultural identity, or identification with and adoption of both the Anglo-American and Hispanic cultures, seems to promote a healthier adjustment for Hispanic children than does complete assimilation. Buriel et al. (1982) explained that acculturating Hispanic children who maintain a footing in their traditional culture are better able to "inoculate" themselves against the generally negative image of Hispanic Americans held by White Americans and against the development of unrealistic expectations. Such a bicultural proposition is further supported by two other studies with Cuban American children. In one study (Szapocznik & Kurtines, 1980a), Cuban American teachers were asked to rate Cuban American students as to their level of adjustment in school. Bicultural Cuban American students were rated significantly more adjusted than less bicultural Cuban American students. Results of another study by Szapocznik and Kurtines (1980b) showed psychopathology scores of highly acculturated Cuban American adolescents to be significantly higher than those of bicultural Cuban Americans.

Physical Appearance

Hispanic children at preschool age have developed race awareness and preferences. Even before entering the public school system, Hispanic children have a concrete conception of what society favors or decrees as appropriate in the way of skin color. A sizable number of Hispanic children prefer light skin color as opposed to their own (Cota-Robles de Suarez, 1973). Some Hispanic parents are grateful that they have a child who is born light-skinned rather than darkskinned. They even use nicknames: *Hueda* (light one) or "chocolate," "Inky," or *Prieta* (dark one) to describe their preference.

The preference of light skin color is an outcome of both American racism and racism inherited from the European colonization of Mexico and other Latin American countries. For example, in Mexico, racism is directed against the Indian. If one looks and acts European, one is more acceptable. G. Gibson and Vasquez (1982) have observed this phenomenon among Chicano families: "One of the first questions usually asked immediately after a child is born is 'A quien se parece,' whom does he/she resemble or look like? Darker children, those with obvious Negroid or Indian features, often become the scapegoats in the family or the objects of pity" (p. 10).

This racism created for the individual and for the family by its measurement of worth in terms of color is vividly portrayed in *Down*

These Mean Streets, a Puerto Rican autobiography by P. Thomas (1967). He describes how his painful identity problem and destructive relationships with his siblings and father were related to the differences in color between him and his siblings and to feelings about himself and others tied to these color differences: "You and James [his brothers] are like houses painted white outside and blacker'n mother inside. An I'm close to being like Poppa—trying to be White on both sides" (p. 8).

Upon realizing society's preference toward lighter skin and European features, a Hispanic child's acceptance of such preference can lead him or her to a self-identity conflict and other self-denying behavior.

Speech and Language

According to information obtained from the 1976 Survey of Income and Education Data (U.S. Bureau of the Census, 1980b), 80% of Hispanic Americans lived in households where Spanish was spoken. Among Hispanics born in their native lands, about two thirds spoke Spanish as their primary language. Among those of corresponding heritage who were born in the United States, less than 20% usually spoke Spanish. Second-generation Hispanics usually are bilingual but are only functional in English. Quite often, the second generation is taught Spanish as a first language in the home, with the school emphasizing English. This process of Spanish-language dislocation results in a second generation that understands Spanish but has quite limited linguistic versatility. The impact of this socialization quite often provokes conflicts between children and parents. Generally, there appears to be an inverse relationship between educational attainment and English-language fluency. Cummins (1981) also has found that learning of literacy-related skills or knowledge in the first (native) language predicted learning and transfer of these skills in the second language.

As to the question of whether bilingualism is really a handicap for learning and for educational attainment, Padilla et al. (1979) concluded that cognitive development may be facilitated in bilingual Hispanic children in the following ways: (a) Bilinguals outperformed monolingual children on tests involving language comprehension and production; and (b) bilinguals demonstrated diversification of mental abilities, mental flexibility, and superiority in concept formation.

Hispanic children's language also affects their conception of psychological problems. LeVine and Padilla (1980) stated that concepts of mental illness vary among Hispanics depending on whether Spanish or English is spoken. Spanish-speaking adolescents more often viewed mental illness as inherited. Furthermore, expectations about not being understood by therapists could make Spanish-speaking adolescents more reluctant to utilize mental health services. Bilingual Hispanic adolescents may not have acquired parallel vocabularies or may not know various meanings of words. Sometimes, they need to use their native language to describe personal, intimate, or gut-level issues. Language difficulties can also make adolescents feel very defensive.

Affective Behavior

A Hispanic child's affective behavior is heavily influenced by the belief that a person, regardless of his or her social status, is entitled to be treated in this life with *respeto* (respect). Respecto connotes hierarchal relationships. Elders and superiors of one form or another are to be accorded respect. The superior, in turn, must always be cordial. Hispanic adolescents are very sensitive to affronts that would violate their *dignidad*. People who have been insulted or who experience interpersonal conflicts must always handle themselves in an honest, dignified, and upright manner. An attempt is made to settle the conflict *a la buena* (in a nice way). Direct confrontation is generally avoided and *pelea monga* (passive resistance) often is employed. When a man's machismo is threatened, aggression is permitted.

Hispanic adolescents have also been found to be field dependent—that is, with emphasis on group identity, respect for family, and religious authority—and displaying shared-function family and group characteristics (Ramirez & Price-Williams, 1974). Further, Hispanic female adolescents were found to be more field dependent than their male counterparts.

Interpersonal Relations

The concept of interpersonal relations is closely tied to the Hispanic idea of *una persona bien educada* (an educated person). Una persona bien educada is a person who has become knowledgeable and skilled in human interpersonal relationships. Such an individual understands the importance of interacting and relating to other humans with respect and dignity. Meaningful interaction and involvement with others should be the first priority and major concern of a person (Iuniga, 1987). In Hispanic culture, a person could be illiterate and still be considered una persona bien educada. Individuals who possess education are those who have training in human understanding and interpersonal relationships (Wahab, 1973).

Interpersonal relations are taught mainly through the family medium and strengthened through ethnic community circles. Values that emphasize a humanistic view often clash with modern and worldly values that stress materialism and prestige. A Hispanic child's belief that he lacks interpersonal skills can be an important stressor that impairs his psychological functioning and academic achievement.

Attitude Toward Self

Research studies indicate that there is a positive relationship between a child's perception and attitude toward self with school achievement and social functioning (Knight et al., 1978; Ramirez, 1969). Muller and Leonetti (1974) compared low-income Hispanic American and White children's self-concepts in kindergarten through fourth grade. Differences between the groups were found in kindergarten, where White students were described as having significantly higher self-concepts. B. Garcia's (1973) study also indicated Hispanic American children usually experience greater disillusionment, and, as a consequence, a drop in self-concept measurement with increasing age. The contention that Hispanic youth who strongly identify with the Hispanic culture would be expected to experience more stress and, in turn, manifest less self-esteem than those Hispanic youth who identity more with the Anglo-American culture was found invalid (Buriel et al., 1982). Contrarily, Hispanic youth who possess bicultural identity or identification with and adoption of both the Anglo-American and Hispanic cultures score higher in measurement of positive self-esteem (Szapocznik & Kurtines, 1980a).

The process of biculturation is so arduous that some Hispanic youth find themselves in the midst of "social schizophrenia." Such youth are represented by school dropouts who have learned that their position in society is clearly lower than that of Anglos (U.S. Commission on Civil Rights, 1976). This newly acquired consciousness of societal rejection was in violent opposition to their internalized sense of respeto and dignided. The easiest way out was to dissociate themselves from school, a major establishment symbol.

Some students joined gangs, which provided an environment where they could find recognition, new respect, and leadership roles.

Issues of Sexuality

Physical modesty is an important norm implicit in dignidad and respecto. Nudity is discouraged except for the very young, and great value is attached to physical integrity (Lawrence & Lurie, 1972). The topics of sex and reproduction are rarely discussed between parents and children (Boulette, 1980). Evidence of sexual behavior, especially among adolescent females, is a form of disrespect for the family.

Cross-sex sibling companionship is curtailed at adolescence and is replaced by complementary functions such as girls doing household chores and boys chaperoning and protecting girls. A girl is afforded less freedom than her brothers. She begins to play the role of mother and homemaker by caring for younger brothers and sisters and by helping with the housework. A boy is encouraged to join with others of his age in informal social groups known as *palomillas* (Murillo, 1971), which aim to socialize a young boy to become an adult male.

The Family System

Immigration History and Level of Acculturation

There is some evidence suggesting a "differential" pattern of acculturation within Hispanic families (Sabogal, Padilla, & Mizio, 1987). These researchers investigated the relationship between acculturation and three dimensions of attitudinal familism and found that perceived family obligations and the family as referent decreased with acculturation, while perceived family support did not. Vega and Casas (1986) also found cohesion and adaptability for Mexican Americans to be differentially related to acculturation. The most recent study by Rueschenberg and Buriel (1989) also suggests that acculturation is not an all-or-none phenomenon and that adjustment to American society can take place with the basic integrity of the family remaining intact.

However, not all Hispanic families experiencing acculturation can retain the basic integrity of the family. Immigration usually produces a transitional crisis in the family with predictable stages (Sluzki, 1979). As the family experiences acculturation, membership changes within the family necessitate family restructuring of roles, functions, and transactions. The traditional hierarchical role structure may run into conflict when the husband/father becomes unemployed. If women must work outside of the home to help support the family, they frequently suffer role confusion and conflict. The wife's employable status and earning power may be essential for the economic survival of the family, but it threatens the superior role of the husband/father. The wife's long working hours outside the home can frustrate and negatively affect her satisfaction and self-image as a "good" wife and mother.

The acculturation rate of the children can also threaten authoritarian parents, especially fathers, who may have to depend on their children to translate for them when dealing with community agencies, immigration authorities, and health care services. The faster rate of acculturation for young Hispanics (Szapocznik & Kurtines, 1980b) has increased stresses and conflicts in many families. Lack of support outside the family system and fear of crime, drug addiction, and more accepting sexual morals often cause parents to be strict and overprotective with adolescents, especially daughters (Badillo-Ghadli, 1977).

Family Structure and Life Patterns

The hierarchical role of Hispanic male dominance and female submission rooted in Spanish customs defines the husband-wife relationship. The husband assumes the instrumental role of provider and protector of the family and the wife the expressive role of homemaker and caretaker. The Hispanic man is expected to be dignified, hardworking, and macho. Machismo (maleness, virility) to the Hispanic man is a desirable combination of virtue, courage, romanticism, and fearlessness (Abad et al., 1974). Machismo in its individualized expression can be viewed in the context of a society denying a male his manhood by societal castration. This situation has been responsible for panic, confusion, marital discord, and the breakdown of family ties among many Hispanics, especially among those who are unemployed (Giordano, 1976).

Because it is the wife's responsibility to care for the home and to keep the family together, the husband is not expected to assume household tasks or help care for the children. This role arrangement results in wives assuming power behind the scenes, while overtly supporting their husband's authority (Steven, 1973). Because it is the existence of children that validates and cements the marriage, motherly love (*elanor de madre*) is a much greater force than wifely love. In reality, the contemporary Hispanic families may include husbands who are domineering and patriarchal (Penalosa, 1968), who are submissive and dependent on their wives for major decisions, or who follow a more egalitarian power arrangement (Hawkes & Taylor, 1975).

The parental functions of Hispanics follow the cultural prescriptions for the husband-wife relationship. The Hispanic father disciplines and controls while the mother provides nurturance and support. Parents engender the respect of children through complementary transactions. They would not expect or want to be friends with their children.

The role of the mother is idealized and equated with self-denial and abnegation. The father protects the mother and demands that the children obey her. He usually is relaxed and playful with younger children and more stern and strict with older children, especially daughters (Fitzpatrick, 1981, p. 209).

Although Hispanic families today usually reside in single households (Mindel et al., 1988), extended family members, such as grandparents, uncles, aunts, and godparents, perform many parental functions. Although Hispanics regard the family as the most important unit in life, previous researchers have suggested that many of the characteristics of Hispanic families compare unfavorably with those of other groups, especially Anglos (Montiel, 1983; Panitz, Scopetta, & Tillman, 1983). The Schumm, Pearce, and Friedman (1988) study, based upon random samples of rural and urban intact families in 14 states, compared perceptions of parents and one adolescent family member in four categories (family life, marital, parent-child, and sibling) of family-life satisfaction. Hispanic family members reported higher satisfaction in most areas, with significant differences remaining even after considering controls for duration of residence in state, area of residence, education, income, and family size.

Attitudes About Mental Health

The argument that certain behaviors would be considered inappropriate and provoke a serious reaction in Anglo culture but not in Hispanic American culture seems plausible only within certain domains. It is generally known that expectations and sanctions for nonconformity to social roles within the family are probably more rigidly defined and controlled among Hispanic Americans than among their Anglo counterparts. Hispanic parents may perceive limitations on their ability to control their children's behavior outside the home. They may reproach, castigate, and even reject a family member who violates primary group norms. However, when their expectations are not fulfilled within the external domain, the degree of sanction is less severe.

Hispanic adolescents' attitudes about mental health are also related to their degree of acculturation and whether they speak English or not. Adolescents who speak only Spanish often viewed mental illness as inherited (LeVine & Padilla, 1980), whereas English-speaking Hispanic adolescents viewed mental illness as psychological and interpersonal. A study by Edgerton and Karno (1971) also pointed to the importance of language orientation in relation to attitudes and beliefs about psychiatric illness. In a report concentrating on attitudes toward the mentally ill, Para (1985) showed that age and gender of Hispanic Americans were influential but that in general few overall differences were obtained between Anglos and Hispanics.

Help-Seeking Behavioral Patterns

Decisions about mental health care and the treatment procedures required are not made by the Hispanic patient alone; they must also be supported by the human network that begins with the immediate family. Hispanic Americans often make use of mental health services or social agencies as a last resort; instead, they are more likely to seek assistance from family, friends, or people with some special expertise who are known informally through their social networks, not as institutional representatives (Ghali, 1977). Acosta et al. (1982, p. 64) gave the following reasons for Hispanics' underutilization of health and mental health services: (a) language barriers, (b) cultural and social class differences between therapist and patients, (c) insufficient number of mental health facilities, (d) overuse or misuse of physicians for psychological problems, (e) reluctance to recognize the urgency for help, and (f) lack of awareness of the existence of mental health clinics. Yamamoto et al. (1968) also noted that Hispanics are more likely to receive somatic and medication treatment and less individual or group psychotherapy. These experiences can and do result in premature termination.

Another recent study reported that although Hispanics were found to underutilize mental health facilities, they fully utilized the inpatient care of public general hospitals (Center for Health Education and Social Systems Studies, 1985). It appears that when Hispanics experience less than severe symptoms, they use the family or informal support network to resolve their problems. When symptoms are severe, Hispanics may use mental health facilities.

Hispanics also are known to use lay systems of care in resolving their mental illness. Alegia, Rivera, & Marina (1977) describe and analyze some of the properties of the lay treatment centers available to Mexican Americans of San Antonio, Texas. Kreisman (1975) also reports on the creative integration of folk and establishment traditions in the treatment of Hispanic psychotic patients. Because Catholicism plays a vital role in the life of Hispanic Americans, in times of stress and illness, priests, folk leaders, and religious leaders can be strong resources. It is not unusual for a Hispanic to equate the role of the therapist with that of a priest and to expect some immediate help from the therapist. At other times, the Hispanic individual may see the therapist as a physician to whom they traditionally seek help for emotional and psychological problems (Padilla et al., 1979).

The School System

Racial/Ethnic Composition

The school system contributes to the development of the self-concept of Hispanic children at an early age. Hispanic children aged $2\frac{1}{2}$ to 3 years entering preschool predominantly populated by Anglo children are confronted with the individual racism of their White peers. Research has indicated that children as young as 3 years may be able to differentiate color for self-designation (Kendale, 1983). Prejudices communicated to Hispanic children reflect the norms of the larger society, norms that include a disdain for and rejection of culturally and racially distinct people. Such racist norms exist in school systems that reflect a White middle-class orientation.

Banks (1984) identified the following practices in school systems that adversely affect Hispanic children. Such practices include the paucity of ethnic and racial school staff, the lack of a multicultural content in the formalized and hidden curricular, the lack of culturally pluralistic teaching strategies and materials, and lastly, testing and counseling programs that are culturally biased. The controversial funding of bilingual programs depicts the lack of concern with and awareness of the importance of language to a Hispanic child's identity. For the Hispanic children who are warned not to speak their native language on school premises, the unequivocal message is that their ethnic heritage is inferior and worthless (G. May, 1976). Racial composition or grouping in some classes also contributes to negative self-concepts and low performance on the part of Hispanic students. Rodriguez (1983) notes that twice as many White students are in high-ability classes than are Chicano students and twice as many Chicano students are in low-ability classes than are White students. The self-fulfilling-prophecy effect of being placed in a slow class can magnify the Hispanic child's sense of worthlessness (Menon et al., 1990).

Attitudes of Teachers and Staff

Teachers' and staffs' low expectations for Hispanic children are often embedded in teaching styles and classroom management practices (M. Gibson, 1988). In addition to poor or inappropriate teaching styles, such as giving only negative feedback, teachers' and staff's perceptions and attitudes of Hispanic students influence evaluations and grades. In a study by G. Jackson and Cosca (1974), teachers were recorded providing praise and encouragement to Anglo children 35% more often than to Hispanic American children; teachers used Anglo children's ideas 40% more often than those of Hispanic Americans, and teachers directed questions to Anglo children 21% more often than to Hispanic Americans. In another study by Stedman and Adams, (1973), teachers' behavioral ratings were higher for English, as opposed to Spanish, speakers.

Besides parents, classroom teachers are the next most important socializers for Hispanic children. Through their interaction with their teachers, Hispanic children are painfully aware of their teachers' perception and lower-status attitude toward them. This is explicitly evident from Gustafson and Owens' (1971) contrasts between teachers' perceptions and children's conceptions of "How I See Myself" and "How My Teacher Sees Me" and the teachers' checklist for third and sixth grades. In terms of the teacher checklist, a more positive relationship was shown between the Anglo children's self-esteem inventory and the teacher's evaluation. A positive correlation was also found for Anglo third graders relative to the child's evaluation of "How I See Myself" and "How My Teacher Sees Me." Results for sixth graders also displayed higher and more positive scores for the Anglo sample than for the Hispanic American sample. Unfortunately, teachers' behaviors and attitude contribute to lower self-esteem for Hispanic children and underscore their unequal educational opportunities. It is not coincidental that Hispanic youngsters have the highest school dropout rate in the nation (U.S. Bureau of the Census, 1983b). This dropout rate results from insensitive practices that are perpetrated by school policies (Banks, 1984). Research has also shown that the negative social labeling of "school dropout" can be a causal factor in subsequent deviant behavior such as drug use (Kaplan & Bloom, 1988).

Societal Issues

Racist practices, along with a highly technological, stratified, closed society, inhibit the upward mobility of Hispanics and relegate them to the lower social status. Minority in a racist society is synonymous with an outgroup whose worth, culture, values, and lifestyles are deprecated and stereotyped. Minority also is synonymous with blocked access to the political and economically powerful ingroups and the full benefits of the American way of life. The prevalent American way of life is to standardize individuals and to be intolerant of cultural and racial differences. Many Hispanic adolescents will continue to be victimized by such racist practices.

The mid-1960s gave rise not only to the civil rights and Black movements, but also to the Hispanic, especially, Chicano, movement. It enabled Hispanic youth to focus on inequities in educational opportunities, the high rate of unemployment and low-wage occupational opportunities, and the general poverty status of the Hispanic population. It also enabled the Hispanic activists to press for the rights they had been guaranteed by the U.S. Constitution. Finally, this movement had the effect of generating a new ethnic pride in the Spanish, Mexican, and Indian heritages, as well as giving birth to many Hispanic American organizations that continue to press for equal rights in all arenas of society (Acuna, 1981).

In the late 1970s and early 1980s, the mainstream political power of Hispanics began to emerge. The continued rapid growth of the Hispanic population and the legacy of the Hispanic movement were mainly responsible for this political emergence. Such developing political strength may prove to empower the Hispanic American with a strong voice and base in the future society of the United States.

PART III

Intervention and Treatment with Ethnic Minority Children and Adolescents

In the intervention and treatment of ethnic minority children and adolescents, it is necessary, but not sufficient, to understand personality and sociocultural factors. The therapist must go beyond cultural and personality awareness to an understanding of how these factors translate into concrete therapeutic behaviors that are relevant to the minority child's needs and problems.

The increased acceptance of the ecological approach to work with ethnic minority children and youth has generated many treatment theories and modalities. The philosophical orientations and the techniques employed by some of these modalities, such as individual, family, and group treatment, may diametrically oppose the indigenous cultural values, individual preferences, and family structures of an ethnic minority child (Mizo & Delaney, 1981). Tseung and McDermott (1975) warn that the minority child's orientation to the process of help-seeking and the "fit" between traditional paradigms and those utilized by providers may be critical to successful process and outcome.

S. Sue and Zane (1987) further explain the dual therapeutic processes of credibility and giving that are essential to work successfully with minority children and youth. Credibility refers to the child's perception of the therapist as an effective and trustworthy helper; giving refers to the child's perception that something positive is occurring from the therapeutic encounter. A minority child's perception of a therapist's credibility is influenced by two factors: ascribed and achieved status. Ascribed status refers to the therapist's position or role assigned by others. Achieved status refers directly to therapist's skills. The lack of ascribed credibility may be the primary reason for underutilization of therapy by minority clients. The lack of achieved credibility may explain why minority clients terminate therapy prematurely (S. Sue, 1977).

Judging by the overwhelming underutilization of mental health services and high dropout rate of ethnic minority clients, a wide gap clearly exists between the unmet needs of ethnic minority children and families and the therapist's ability to provide for their needs successfully (Mokuau, 1987). It is also clear that therapy with ethnic minority children requires an organized, culturally sensitive, credible theoretical framework. From such a culturally credible framework, appropriate treatment modalities can be applied to meet the specific needs of individual ethnic minority children and youth.

Part III of this book focuses on the differential application of treatment modalities with a conceptual framework for therapy with minority children and youth. This conceptual framework considers the ethnic minority child's reality, culture, biculturalism, developmental stages, family tradition and structure, degree of acculturation, language, and help-seeking behavior. The principles of acquiring achieved credibility and "gift giving" by applying individual, family, and group modalities are introduced. Ethnic minorities' traditional responses to different treatment modalities will be discussed. The therapist's modification of traditional techniques and skills in the application of different treatment modalities with other minority children and youth will be illustrated by case examples.

6

Cultural-Specific Methods, Techniques, and Skills in Individual Therapy

Rationale and Criteria for Individual Therapy

When Individual Therapy Is Indicated or Contraindicated

It is generally recognized that effective service to ethnic minority children should be multidimensional, that is, directed at the various components of the child's environment. It also should be multidisciplinary, involving professionals and workers from a variety of disciplines, and multimodal, offering a combination of individual, family, and group treatments (Gibbs et al., 1989; Ho, 1990a).

Individual therapy involving one-to-one therapist-client contact is the most frequently used modality in work with ethnic children and their parents. It can be used with a wide spectrum of minority children and can be flexibly provided in a myriad of ways, including crisis intervention; short term or long term; ego-supportive, intensive, or ego-modifying; educative; and cognitive behavioral. Individual treatment is also useful in conjunction with a variety of other types of supportive and concrete services. Advantages of employing individual therapy include the provisions of optimal safety, support, privacy, and confidentiality for the client, and a corrective transferential growth process for the child.

Individual therapy with a minority child is indicated when the child's problem is a function of the following factors:

Stresses imposed by immigration and acculturation

Stresses imposed by developmental tasks or current life role as a child, or as a family member whose family is unwilling to participate in treatment due to cultural constraints, confidentiality, language difficulty, or family tradition or structure

Stresses imposed by past traumatic reaction caused by immigrational or intrafamilial conflict, such as physical neglect or emotional or sexual abuses

The child's idiosyncratic characteristic or problem that causes rigidity in behavioral patterns, such as denial, lying, depression, acting out, or antisocial behavior

The child's ethnic and self-identity problem that requires a secure, safe bonding and an intense noncompetitive relationship with a significant other, such as a therapist

Goals of Individual Therapy

Individual therapy can help an ethnic minority child to do the following:

Enhance ego functioning, particularly in the areas of impulse control and judgment

Acquire better coping skills to function in a bicultural world

Improve appropriate role functioning and interpersonal relationships

Compensate for early developmental arrests

Modify long-standing behavior patterns

In view of ethnicity differences and, in some cases, poverty-stricken backgrounds, many therapists inaccurately assume that clinically oriented one-to-one treatment will not benefit other minority children and youth. The opposite is true in that ethnic minority children and youth often are most in need of the privacy and safety provided only by this one-to-one therapeutic encounter and trusting relationship with a therapist. Following is a discussion of some of the various types of individual therapy that an ethnic minority child can benefit from.

Types of Individual Therapy

Ego-Supportive Therapy

Short-term ego-supportive psychotherapy is the model of individual treatment recommended for ethnic minority children with non-psychotic disorders, who are usually seen in outpatient settings. This approach is especially suited for minority youth because it focuses on problem solving, strengthens coping skills, and is time-limited (Goldstein, 1984; Norman, 1980). Ego-supportive treatment can also be long-term and employs both psychological and environmental interventions. The focus of this approach generally is on here-and-now behavior, reality pressures, current relationships, conscious thoughts and feelings, and states of need and vulnerability. There may be some selective focus on past experiences as they directly relate to the present. Because the focus of this approach is on the support of the child's ego, the child-therapist relationship is critical in order to foster credibility and acceptance, sustain the child, increase motivation to change, develop empathy and self-esteem, permit functional role modeling, and promote corrective experiences. Techniques and skills employed by this approach include information giving, advice, and culturally relevant direction that aims to assist the child to gain a greater understanding of his or her own needs and to better manage his or her own impulses. Ego-supportive therapy is also useful for a wide range of minority children and youth problems, ranging from anxiety and depression to identify conflicts and acting-out behaviors.

In the following case example, the therapist directed his efforts to relieving Julie's anxiety and to restoring her ability to cope effectively at home and at school. The therapist focused on the client's here-and-now experiences and on her conscious thoughts and feelings. He used himself to provide an empathic, accepting, and safe relationship in which Julie could ventilate her fear and concern, identify new ways of coping with stress, and identify some of her dysfunctional responses at home and at school. The therapist primarily used the techniques of cultural joining, sustainment, and ventilation, along with some person-situation reflection. Important to Julie's improvement was the sense of mastery and reinforcement she experienced in being better able to cope at home with her mother. This, in turn, led to diminished pressures at school and diminished the frequency of complaints of physical symptoms.

✿ CASE STUDY
Julie—13-Year-Old Black Female

Julie, a 13-year-old Black female, was referred by her junior high school counselor due to frequent somatic complaints, excessive absences, impulsive behavior, and a poor relationship with peers. The counselor also indicated that Julie's present behavior was uncharacteristic, for she was known as a well-behaved student who liked school and seldom missed classes.

Julie was fearful and responded reluctantly to the therapist's effort to establish a therapeutic relationship with her. The therapist empathized by stating how much he understood the discomfort she must be experiencing upon being told that she needed to see a therapist. The therapist further reminded Julie of his previous knowledge of her as a good student. When Julie was asked how her family was doing, she burst into tears, uttering, "What family?!"

After a few moments, Julie volunteered that her younger brother was sent to a group home for behavioral problems after her parents divorced less than a year ago. Her mother's new boyfriend did not like Julie, who also feared that if her mother chose to remarry, she would have to live somewhere else—away from her mother. To ensure that her mother would not replace her with this boyfriend, Julie became excessively compliant at home. In addition to having nightmares, Julie also developed physical symptoms that "kept" her at home and away from school. Once she returned to school, she was unable to manage her schoolwork and it added to her already overwhelming anxiety.

Julie also explained that if her mother remarried, she might be sent to live with her aunt, whom Julie distrusted and disliked. The therapist sympathized by stating how fearful her situation was and that he understood how much she did not want to be separated from her mother. As one of the short-term goals, Julie agreed that clearing her concern with her mother might alleviate her apprehension and anxiety and, subsequently, improve her functioning in school and her relationship with her peers.

Ego-Modifying Therapy

Ego-modifying therapy aims for some reconstruction of the personality. This approach is essential for the treatment of minority children and youth who display repetitive rigid behavior and inner conflict that is both self-destructive and disturbing to others. This approach requires intensive and close examination of inner conflicts to understand what has gone awry. For this approach to succeed, a youth needs to possess the following characteristics: introspection and psychological open-mindedness, a long-term commitment, a high level of motivation, an ability to verbalize rather than act on intense feelings, a strong enough ego to tolerate the upheaval that results from stirring up highly-charged issues, and an absence of unusual or severe environmental pressure. These characteristics generally are not in evidence in ethnic minority children and youth, especially in the early stages of treatment. Because environmental pressure is usually a major factor, this approach is more successful in an inpatient or residential treatment facility.

✿ CASE STUDY
Rolando—Mexican American 17-Year-Old

Rolando, a Mexican American 17-year-old high school dropout and a former street gangster, was referred to a group home for treatment. He had stolen two cars and repeatedly run away from his relative's home and two foster homes. Soon after he entered the group home, he was identified as a natural leader. Rolando was very streetwise, manipulative, and defensive with the therapist. Despite his unusual intellectual ability, Rolando refused to apply himself and avoided discussion of his failures in a succession of schools. Rolando's other talent was art. Through his organizational skills in fundraising, Rolando helped the therapist establish a small art studio in the group home.

Despite his artistic skills, Rolando refused to take art lessons, considering that a direct insult to his talent. His arrogant and disdainful attitude isolated him from the staff and the residents of the group home. At times, Rolando became morose, hopeless, and bitter, and refused to go to school and to practice the artwork that brought him recognition. At a low ebb, he sought therapeutic help, claiming that he felt like "climbing the wall."

Rolando only vaguely remembered his father, who divorced his mother when he was 4 years old. He felt bitter that his father was unavailable to him when he was growing up. Rolando's mother lavished attention and material possessions on him but was emotionally cold toward him. Rolando was used to getting his own way, was disciplined rarely, and was able to control and manipulate his mother. He also recalled feeling extremely lonely and isolated. Although initially smooth and sociable, he became extremely competitive with others and was negligent of their needs.

After spending three sessions with Rolando, the therapist hypothesized that the client's difficulties were related to a lifelong defensive pattern involving grandiosity as protection against profound feelings of lack of worth. Rolando also showed feelings of entitlement, devaluation of others, difficulties in assuming responsibility for his own behavior, and low frustration tolerance. His difficulties appeared to have developed as a response to a childhood in which he did not derive a realistic sense of being valued and cared for, while at the same time he was treated like a "Latin prince." Rolando had never developed an integrated identity, although his grandiosity gave him the appearance of someone whose identity was based on a sense of superiority.

The therapist's twice-weekly meeting with Rolando had been difficult. The therapist's efforts to help Rolando reflect on how he was causing his own difficulties threatened his inflated ego, stimulated anxiety and underlying feelings of unworthiness, and produced resistance. At times Rolando resisted, accusing the therapist of failing to understand him because of their differences in age and race. At many points, Rolando exhibited all the feelings toward the therapist that he did toward others in life: disdain, contempt, possessiveness, boredom, and being demanding. Through the therapist's objective use of professional self, empathic understanding, and repeated clarification, Rolando was able to restrain his rage at the therapist and not terminate their contact.

After 5 months of twice-weekly individual sessions, Rolando began to relinquish his tenacious hold on his characteristic patterns. As his defenses lessened, Rolando underwent a depressive reaction but was able to work this through with therapeutic support and an increased understanding of its developmental and dynamic components. During this time, Rolando's functioning with peers at the home improved, along with his educational achievement and artwork.

Cognitive Behavioral Therapy

Cognitive behavioral therapy assumes that maladaptive behaviors are learned because they have been reinforced in the child's cultural and social environment. Its sensitivity to and emphasis on ecological factors make it relevant to work with minority children (Bandura,

1977). In contrast to the disease model of psychopathology, the theory behind cognitive behavioral therapy holds that most psychological problems are learned within the social milieu and maintained through cognitive reinforcement (Meichenbaum, 1977). Cognitive behavioral therapy also recognizes the impact of culture on personal and environmental variables and allows each culture to define its own appropriate behaviors or targets for intervention (LaFromboise & Rowe, 1983).

Prior to assessment of what constitutes the child's faulty or "irrational" cognitions, a therapist working with minority children, especially Asian American, American Indian, Black, or Hispanic American children, must be highly sensitive to the fact that self-depreciating beliefs, hesitancy, and some degree of paranoia may actually reflect an internalization of the mainstream culture's attitude toward them as ethnic minorities. Likewise, other cultural beliefs and practices, such as close extended family ties and intense mother-child relationships, which may be considered "irrational" or "enmeshed" by the dominant culture, may be perfectly reasonable in light of their cultural background and upbringing.

Once a therapist has identified dysfunctional thoughts or behavior in a cultural context, therapy can focus on the current determinants of behavior. It should involve the cultural assessment of that components of the belief or behavior and the modification of these components according to specific goals. The case example below illustrates the advantages of using cognitive behavioral therapy with an Asian American child.

The cognitive behavioral therapy was particularly helpful in this case for the following reasons. First, clear therapeutic structure was provided for clients who were involved in identifying the antecedents and consequences of their son's problem. Second, the therapeutic session focused directly on the problem defined by the clients. Such a focus adhered to the family's traditional interactive style, and it helped to ease the parents' discomfort and alleviated their sense of hopelessness. Third, the therapist comfortably assumed the role of an expert who satisfied the clients' need for receiving a gift that, in turn, reduced their original thinking and feelings of hopelessness about their son's problem. Fourth, active involvement with the parents by asking them to record and monitor observable and measurable behaviors satisfied their cultural needs for responsibility, mutuality, and concreteness.

Play Therapy

Playing is a natural part of a child's life and development. Through play, children release tension, express forbidden impulses, and assign to dolls and other figures their own fears and fantasies. In therapy with ethnic minority children whose cultures do not endorse open expression of feelings, especially to a nonkin member,

---

✿ CASE STUDY
Ming-Wah—American-Born Chinese Boy

Ming-Wah, a 6-year-old American-born Chinese boy, was referred by the school counselor, who claimed that the boy's parents had consulted with her about the boy's unmanageable tantrums at home. If not corrected, the tantrums could interfere with the boy's academic achievement.

When Ming-Wah's parents arrived at the agency, they appeared to be extremely polite and self-depreciating. The father apologized for the inconvenience the family had caused the therapist, who reciprocated that he was honored by their visit and was impressed by their efforts to provide the best help for their son's school performance and future success (problem reframing). After a few social exchanges for relationship building and for the establishment of credibility (S. Sue & Zane, 1987), the parents (who are immigrants from Hong Kong) explained their inability to "control" their son, who employed temper tantrums to avoid doing his homework. The father complained that he did not wish to use physical force, as many Chinese parents in Hong Kong do, to discipline his son. He also was frustrated when his wife did not support his ways of disciplining their son.

After a thorough behavioral assessment was conducted, the parents were instructed in the use of reinforcements and contingencies to reduce the frequency of Ming-Wah's tantrum behavior. Charts were used to monitor progress as the treatment progressed. Due to the parents' willingness to carry out the treatment plan and strategies, Ming-Wah's tantrum behavior decreased. The entire treatment period lasted for only five weekly sessions. To satisfy the clients' need for being helped or receiving a "gift" (S. Sue & Zane, 1987), the first session lasted 2 hours.

play sometimes can be a child's only form of communication. Playing in therapy permits children to verbalize conscious material and associated feelings safely and to act out unconscious conflicts and fantasies. They can communicate about past and current daily events. Therapeutic play differs from the play of ordinary life because the therapist accepts a role in a make-believe game. The child may assign the therapist the role, and the therapist can play out that role as the child expects. The following case example illustrates how play therapy was used to help an Asian American child relieve anxiety and tension.

Kung-Sa's first play activity vividly reflected her feeling of ethnic and self-identity that she was not as good as the rest of the light-haired (Caucasian) girls. This explained her feelings of isolation and withdrawal. Her second play activity reflected her ambivalence and hostility toward her parents, who took her out of her familiar home

---

✿ CASE STUDY
Kung-Sa—Korean American Girl

Kung-Sa, an 8-year-old Korean American girl, was referred by the teacher for therapy. The teacher reported that Kung-Sa was extremely shy and withdrawn and that her underachievement in school concerned her parents greatly. Kung-Sa and her parents immigrated to the United States 2 years ago from Seoul, Korea. Despite having limited difficulty with the English language, Kung-Sa did not interact with the rest of the class. Occasionally the teacher found Kung-Sa daydreaming, and she gradually fell behind in her classwork.

When Kung-Sa was introduced to the playroom, her spirits lifted. The therapist encouraged her to freely play with toys she liked. Kung-Sa spent a great deal of time during the first session exploring different toys. Her conversation with the therapist was limited to identifying the utilities of different toys. At the beginning of the second session, Kung-Sa immediately picked up several light-haired dolls and one dark-haired doll. The light-haired dolls joined a circle and would not allow the dark-haired doll to be a part of the circle. Once in a while, one light-haired doll would physically knock down the dark-haired doll. After such play actions were repeated several times, Kung-Sa changed her play by placing two adult dolls in a house and asked if the therapist would roll an object to demolish the house. Sensing the therapist's hesitancy, Kung-Sa abruptly said, "Never mind, I do it myself."

environment (Korea) and made her become an "outcast" in a mainstream societal group. To protect Kung-Sa's need for anonymity and loyalty toward her parents, no attempt was made to encourage her to reveal her real identity (e.g., she was the dark-haired girl in the play). However, Kung-Sa was encouraged to express for the dark-haired girl her true feelings about being cast in such a situation. The therapist's empathic and accepting attitude enabled Kung-Sa to personalize her feelings during the later part of the therapy, which lasted eight sessions.

When playing therapeutically with minority children, a therapist must accept the fantasies and feelings that arise and explore them to understand (rather than enforce) society's standards and ideals. Play therapy with ethnic minority children must consider the minority culture's attitude toward play. The Asian American cultural work ethic may view play as a frivolous activity. Asian parents may not consider play as productive to solving their children's problems, which they think often center around too much play and not enough serious work. Similarly Asian children, especially teenagers, can experience ambivalence about play activities that may have contributed to their inadequate or poor performance. It is important that a therapist explain to the parents and older children the value of therapeutic play.

Diagnostic understanding of the dynamics of a minority child's personality and therapeutic need will determine the therapist's approach, techniques, and skills, and the kinds of materials selected for a specific child. Play materials should be as simple as possible but diverse in color and ethnicity so as to facilitate identification and imagination. The basic equipment for play therapy includes a fixed or portable blackboard, a work surface, a variety of ethnic posters, building blocks, dolls of different colors, and human figures that represent family members of different ages, animals, clay, a few dishes, crayons, paints, paper, a toy telephone, and some games that have simple rules.

Music Therapy

By capitalizing on the attraction music has for children and youth, a therapist can use music to augment the traditional tools of her practice. Listening to popular music, the lyrics of which are often personally meaningful, can stimulate ethnic adolescents to discuss personal and interpersonal conflicts and distressing situations that they might not otherwise bring forward. There is a wide range of popular music available from which the therapist can choose that is applicable to both typical and unusual concerns encountered by ethnic adolescents. In addition, therapists working with minority adolescents can encourage the latter to choose their own ethnic music to aid in identifying and expressing inner feelings that are encountered at a particular moment. Popular music can serve as a useful diagnostic tool in pinpointing a minority child's struggle for ethnic and self-identity. The case study on Peter (on p. 130) illustrates this point.

Music can also help inarticulate and nonexpressive minority youth focus attention on their feelings (See Kelly, Case Study, p. 131).

Use of Testing

Standardized objective tests may have limited utility in the assessment of ethnic minority children. The major argument against the use of psychological tests, particularly intelligence tests, with ethnic minority children is that these tests tend to be standardized for White middle-class children and are insensitive to ethnic cultural differences (Sattler, 1988). In addition to ethnic group differences, social-class differences also can render inaccurate test results. Nichols and Anderson (1973) reported that the often-publicized 15-point differences in IQ in favor of Whites over Blacks is reduced to 5 points when social class is controlled between the two groups. Other factors that affect the interpretation of a psychological standardized test with ethnic minority children include the following (Irvine & Carroll, 1980):

Distinction between constructs and criteria
Establishment of equivalence
Nature of the test stimuli, including verbal as well as nonverbal material
Exporting of norms
Response sets
Tendency to infer deficits from test score differences
Cultural isomorphism of Western-based tests and the motives for taking them

If a standardized psychological test is to be used, it is important that the therapist be aware that the use of national norms can only yield information about relative performance among children. Such data should not be considered a source of information about the absolute abilities of any child.

✿ CASE STUDY
Peter—Korean-Born Asian American Boy

Peter, a 14-year-old Korean-born Asian American boy, was referred by the school counselor who was concerned about Peter's
withdrawn attitude toward school and his peers. Peter did fine
academic work, but he was isolated from his peers and gradually
became a recluse. Peter was born in Seoul, Korea. Three months
after he was born, he was adopted by a Caucasian couple who
lived in a small midwestern town in the United States. Peter's
adjustment in the adoptive home has been smooth. However, despite his fluency in the English language, Peter was constantly
treated by his classmates and teachers as a foreigner. In addition
to feeling ambivalent about others' mistaken identification of
him, Peter was embarrassed by the fact that despite his Asian
physical appearance, he knew nothing about the Korean culture
and language. Peter's ambivalence turned into stress, particularly when he reached his 14th birthday, and there were more
informal gatherings between girls and boys.

During the first two therapy sessions, Peter was guarded in his
interaction with the therapist. He claimed that there was nothing
wrong with wanting to be by himself. The therapist supported
Peter's right and discretion in choosing to be alone. However, the
therapist inquired about the nature of his thoughts while he was
alone. Peter answered that he thought a lot while alone, but
could offer no specific thought patterns or subject matter that he
wanted to disclose to the therapist. Peter then volunteered that
he listened to music a lot while he was alone. The therapist inquired if Peter would bring his favorite music tape to the next
therapy session. Peter replied, "I guess."

During the next session, Peter reluctantly played his favorite
song by Garth Brooks, titled "I Got Friends in Low Places." The
therapist listened with great interest. He asked Peter what particular aspect of the song he liked best. Peter answered that the
song represented his feelings that he just "didn't fit into" the
circle of friends he liked, and that regardless of where he was,
he just felt "out of place." Upon empathizing with Peter's ambivalence and distress, the therapist engaged him in discussions
about the importance of self-acceptance and his unique biculturalism. Instead of being forced to choose between two races,
Peter was helped to accept and take advantage of his Asian appearance and American culture and lifestyle.

✿ CASE STUDY
Kelly—American Indian Student

Kelly, a 17-year-old American Indian student, was experiencing a wide range of physical complaints. Her boyfriend had left her for another girl about 2 months prior to her seeking therapy. Kelly blamed her situation on her inability to communicate as she should. During therapy sessions, she seldom volunteered any information beyond this: "I am not good with words."

As a means of stimulating her to express her anger toward her boyfriend and distrust toward boys in general, the therapist invited her to listen to "I'll Never Fall in Love Again" by the Carpenters. After listening to the song, Kelly commented that the lies, pain, and sorrow described in the song expressed exactly how she felt. She vented her anger toward her boyfriend, labeling him "disloyal," "ungrateful," and "stupid." She also pointed out some good feelings about him that she still had. "Thinking about him is no good now; life has to continue: I have to go on with my life," she commented. The therapist then played another song: "Tomorrow" by Barbara Streisand. As Kelly listened quietly to the song, she cried and said, "Thank God, there is always tomorrow."

Many minority children mistrust standardized tests and lack test-taking skills. It is advisable that the tester establish rapport with the children before testing begins. Careful explanation of the task of testing and thorough test-taking rehearsal exercises may also help minority children achieve more accurate and optimum results.

Several intelligence assessment tests have established cross-cultural validity and reliability. These tests include the Cattell Culture-Fair Intelligence Test (Brislin et al., 1973), the Kohs-Blocks spatial- perceptual test (Witkin & Goodenough, 1981), the California Psychological Inventory (CPI; Megargee, 1972), and the State-Trait Anxiety Inventory (STAI; Spielberger, 1975). The Kinetic Family Drawing (KFD; Burns & Kaufmen, 1972) also is a useful culturally adapted test that allows minority children to provide subjective impressionistic data about themselves and about their family relationships.

Therapists should also be aware of the manner in which different ethnic minority families or children respond to their evaluation results. Given that all ethnic minority cultures encourage deference to authority, parents may passively accept test results without asking for clarification. Hence, therapists should make every effort to elicit questions or concerns from minority children and families when evaluation results are presented.

Ethnicity and the Therapeutic Relationship

This section explains the entry phase of therapy with ethnic minority children and youth. This phase of therapy is particularly important because it dictates the final outcome of therapy. Whether this beginning phase is successful or not depends on the therapist's ability to establish a therapeutic relationship with the minority child. A therapeutic relationship refers to a condition in which a child and therapist with some common interest between them, long term or temporary, interact with feeling. When only one has feeling invested, the other must recognize, receive, and respond to that feeling; when that reception and response are understanding and accepting, the sense of relationship has a positive quality. As the positive relationship is used consciously by the therapist as both climate and catalyst to problem solving, it will be seen to have some special elements that are essential in any professional therapeutic relationship.

Establishing a therapeutic relationship with an ethnic minority youth is no simple and easy task. Unlike White youth, most minority youth do not have knowledge or experience about therapy. Many minority youth may have been negatively warned by their families and friends that mainstream helping professionals are not truly helpful in terms of meeting their needs. Because mental health problems are still stigmatized as being "abnormal" or "crazy," and a source of shame and embarrassment among some minority families, many minority youth do not wish to be seen by a therapist. A minority youth's level of acculturation will directly affect how he or she talks to adults or authority figures. His or her English proficiency also influences the therapist's ability to establish a therapeutic relationship.

This section will detail the ethnicity-related issues a therapist must consider in the initial encounter with minority children and youth. Further suggestions will focus on how a therapist should overcome and capitalize on ethnicity issues such as gender and age credibility, communication styles, use of empathy and authority, use of an interpreter, transference and countertransference, and collaboration work with parents.

Gender, Age, and Credibility

Credibility refers to the minority client's perception of the therapist as an effective and trustworthy helper (S. Sue & Zane, 1987). It is essential in the establishment of a therapeutic relationship with minority children and youth. When a therapist first encounters a minority child, the therapist is assigned (by the client) *ascribed credibility* on the basis of gender, age, and expertise. If the therapist fails to recognize this ascribed credibility and fails to apply culturally relevant techniques and skills in problem solving, the first interview may be the last encounter.

In view of the hierarchical family structure of Hispanic, Asian American, and some American Indian tribes, women are subordinate to men and youths are subordinate to elders. Hence, a young female therapist would have a low ascribed status in contrast to an elderly male therapist. Preferences for same-sex therapists also have been found among American Indian high school students (Haviland, Horswill, O'Connell, & Dynneson, 1983).

In encountering Asian American, Hispanic American, and some American Indian children and families, a young female therapist may need to inform the family of her credentials (expertise) as a means of establishing ascribed credibility. If the therapist's race and gender are different from the client, she should discuss this with the family or the client. The therapist's approach will be deemed as culturally sensitive and will go a long way toward establishing ascribed credibility with minority children and families.

Communication Style

In view of the collectivist orientation of ethnic minority culture, minority children and youth will be more favorably disposed toward a therapist who demonstrates interpersonal competence (Acosta et al., 1982; Gibbs, 1987). S. Sue and Zane (1987) also agree that an active exchange rather than a passive therapist style works best with most Asian American clients. Avoidance of eye contact can be a sign of deference to authority figures in many cultures. The Western behavior of intense eye contact, physical gestures, and repeated direct questioning may be interpreted as intrusive by many minority clients, especially American Asians (Henkin, 1987) and American Indians (Lewis & Ho, 1976).

With regard to client self-disclosure, Danphinais and Rowe (1981) warn that Indian youth are looking for someone who understands the practical aspects of their culture and can give them sound advice about their lives. They do not want a therapist who reflects and re-states their feelings for purposes of analysis. Ridley (1984) also cautions that Black youth tend to be less comfortable with self-disclosure than White adolescents, partly reflecting the Black culture pattern of masking their true feelings and concerns from Whites and authority figures. In facilitating self-disclosure with Hispanic youth, a therapist needs to transmit her personal interest in the client rather than focusing on procedures. Self-disclosure among Hispanic youth can be greatly facilitated when the therapist becomes a philosopher of life through storytelling, anecdotes, humor, analogies, and proverbs (Falicov, 1982).

❁ CASE STUDY
Ron—American Indian Boy

Ron, a 13-year-old American Indian boy, was referred to the therapist by a school counselor who claimed that Ron had been a quiet, "well-behaved" student until recently. He now attended school irregularly, wore dirty clothes, exhibited destructive behavior in class, and refused to speak to anybody.

When Ron showed up in the office, the therapist immediately told him that he had wanted to come by his school to visit with him but changed his mind, because he did not want Ron's classmates to think that he was in trouble (convey interest and respect). Ron glanced at the therapist and said nothing. He then glanced at some Indian art and craftwork in the office (create comfortable environment for clients). These had been given to the therapist by his former clients. The therapist asked him to feel free to take time to look at them (convey Indian time orientation). Ron was also interested in the wall poster with pictures of Navajo Indians. The therapist asked Ron to explain to him what the symbols on the picture meant (to shift power position and to help client feel relaxed). Ron smiled and said that he wished he knew. Then, hesitantly, Ron asked if the therapist was Indian (client showed beginning trust). The therapist replied smilingly, "No, but I feel we are cousins, for history tells us that thousands of years ago, Indians migrated from China" (to establish mutuality and ties). Ron was very interested in the therapist's explanation and his ethnic background.

Early in therapy, the therapist's demonstration of interpersonal competence may include self-disclosure, which is interpreted as a desire for reciprocity (LaFromboise & Rowe, 1983). The preceding case study of Ron illustrates this point.

Use of Empathy and Authority

Empathizing with the client's feelings, regardless of the destructiveness of his or her behavior, is important in all phases of therapy with minority children and youth but is crucial to a successful engagement phase. The therapeutic alliance results both from the youth's readiness to accept help and from the therapist's ability to mobilize the youth's hope, trust, and willingness to work on different problems. Empathy is the feeling that emerges, enabling therapists to sense their clients' emotions and penetrate "their screen of defenses," which often hides their real feelings (Olden, 1953).

It is no easy task to empathize with adolescents who are unruly, belligerent, and abusive because of their fear and anger. Some minority youth's resistive moods, different styles, and explosive outbursts can bewilder a therapist. The key to empathy with such a client is to understand their ecological world and their physically and emotionally deprived past. This requires that therapists work in a kind of bicultural world: the past and the present, the real and unreal, their own and the youths'. An empathic understanding of youth evolves as the therapist enters into their stressed, frightening, and sometimes racist world of today, while simultaneously entering into their past oppressive and distrustful childhood experiences. Hence, a link is made between the dynamic social and psychological suffering they commonly endure and the symptoms and misbehavior they now demonstrate against themselves and others.

In many situations, minority youth will not seek help unless forced to do so. The use of authority to motivate them to seek help must be followed by empathic understanding and firm but sensitive intervention by the therapist in order to get the youth to comply with real motivation and engagement. The following case study of Maria illustrates these delicate processes.

✿ CASE STUDY
Maria—Cuban Student

Maria, a 15-year-old Cuban student, was referred to the therapist after she assaulted a White female student. Maria was warned by the principal in a predominantly White school that unless she sought counseling help for her emotional and physical outburst, she would not be allowed to return to school.

When Maria first met the therapist, she presented herself as resistant, sullen, and hostile. The therapist commented how difficult it must be for her to come for therapy. Maria remained quiet. The therapist continued that if he was in her place, he would not have chosen to come for therapy either. The therapist then commended Maria for coming for therapy and said that her presence reflected her willingness and eagerness to return to school. "I don't want to be kicked out of school—that's why I am here," echoed Maria.

The therapist then shifted focus and complemented her for good school work and for being a conscientious student. Maria responded that if other students, especially the White students, would just leave her alone, she would do okay. The therapist realized that Maria's defensiveness had been lessened, so he engaged her to relate the fighting incident that caused her suspension. Maria complained that other than her curly hair, she was as White as other girls. She just could not understand why White girls would not accept her and instead would spread malicious rumors to ruin her reputation. "I am as pretty as they [the White girls] are, and I could date White boys too," added Maria.

The therapist then empathized with her feelings of oppression and loneliness. He reframed the White female students' dislike of her, explaining perhaps it was due to her personality and physical attractiveness and that the White girls saw it as a great threat to them. Maria was assured and comforted by the therapist's new suggestions, and she was also willing to learn alternative ways to channel her aggression and hostility toward those who disliked her.

Transference and Countertransference

Transference refers to children's projections onto the therapist of feelings and attitudes that stem from past relationships with significant others. Transference, whether positive or negative, is an unconscious form of resistance to therapy goals. When the therapist is a member of the majority group and the client is a minority child, transference occurs often because a minority child may bring to the therapeutic relationship intense emotions derived from past experiences with the majority group (Carter & Haizlip, 1972). These emotions are usually negative and controlling in nature. The therapist may remind the child of past unpleasant experiences with majority group members and can cause the child to be suspicious of the therapist. In contrast, if the therapist and the child are of the same race, color, or ethnicity, positive transference usually takes place. Comas-Diaz and Jacobsen (1987) note that minority clients often attribute ethnocultural qualities to their therapists. For example, a dark-skinned Brazilian boy suffering from depression says to his Black male therapist "You can understand my predicament because we Black people always have had bad luck."

Countertransference refers to those reactions of the therapist that are unprovoked by the minority client. They are displacements onto the client of feelings and attitudes from the therapist's past significant relationships. A therapist's countertransference, especially in working with cross-racial children, can stem from the therapist's own discomfort with his or her own ethnicity and feelings of discomfort or guilt toward the minority child's ethnicity. Such a therapist will convey a sense of uncertainty in dealing with minority children and families. They can even convey a sense of admiration toward a minority child's "streetsense" and thus fail to set necessary limits for the child. Moreover, the same therapist may have a tendency to expect immediate success in working with minority clients and thereby overlook the "healthy cultural paranoia" many minority children adopt in the beginning phase of therapy.

If the therapist and the client are of the same minority race or ethnicity, a therapist's countertransference is more likely to stem from the therapist feeling guilt over having "made it" while leaving his or her own people "behind." Rather than working toward developing ethnically appropriate treatment strategies, the therapist overprotects the client and avoids addressing important issues. She may engage her client and family in an "us against the world" type of discussion, which will probably confuse the child or family. More-over, the same therapist may assume the role of a "moralizer" who is going to "raise the consciousness of her own people" (Hunt, 1987). Instead of using therapy to empower the child or family, the thera-pist adopts a "preacher/teacher" model and delivers impromptu lec-tures to her unsuspecting minority client (Hunt, 1987, p. 117). The therapist's "rescuer" role may even create a new dependency on the part of a minority child, and it may quickly "burn out" the therapist.

Regardless of the racial identity of the therapist, there is a direct relationship between the degree to which a therapist is comfortable with herself, her own racial and ethnic identity, and her ability to work with minority children. Varghese (1983) states that the essential task in psychotherapy with minority clients is to be aware of the client's feeling toward the therapist, sometimes by monitoring one's own feelings, reflecting back to the client, and thus gaining an em-pathic understanding of the client.

Working Relationship with Parents

A therapist should familiarize himself with the child's relationship with the family and the family's health and mental health systems, different help-seeking patterns, and English-language ability. Work-ing with minority children without involving their parents or other family members will have limited success. The following case study of Mei-Li illustrates the importance of a therapist's collaboration with a minority youth's parents.

Unless parents of minority children collaborate in treatment, little can be done to help the child. The therapists' failure to involve mi-nority parents is perhaps the primary cause of premature treatment termination of minority children. When minority parents are not asked to collaborate, they often experience a cultural paranoia that they have been judged and attacked. They do not trust the therapist. They want but do not know how to help the child. In some instances, when parents are uncertain of the outcome of the treatment, they ter-minate it, which of course ends any hope of helping their child.

Some minority parents come to the first interview armed with a ready-made, culturally prescribed solution to the child's problem. For instance, they may insist that the therapist tell the child what to do and interface with school or social agencies. The therapist needs to help the parents realize that despite their assessment and suggestions, which may be accurate, both the problem and the solution must be clarified and that their recommendations or conclusions must be reexamined. A therapist's skill in conveying respect for the parents' ideas, combined with the process of thinking rather than acting immediately, may help them modify their ideas. Acting quickly will only perpetuate impulsive behavior.

A minority child's problem may function to mask a parental conflict. The therapist should not tell the parents prematurely that they are the ones who need help or advice, for they may feel criticized and attacked. They will then become defensive, angry, and frightened, and will probably leave, taking their child with them. The therapist can involve the parents by supplying information about the child

---

✿ CASE STUDY
Mei-Li—Girl from Thailand

Mei-Li, a 17-year-old girl from Thailand, was referred to the therapist for outpatient treatment. Mei-Li immigrated to the United States 9 years ago. During the past 2 years, Mei-Li was in and out of an adolescent treatment center for inpatient therapy for paranoid schizophrenia. Mei-Li's parents are engineers. Although they were puzzled by Mei-Li's bizarre behavior, including hallucinations, they were supportive of her and of her therapy.

After Mei-Li's initial interview with the therapist, her parents were impressed that the therapist requested to see them. During the interview with both parents, the therapist first expressed appreciation for their presence and their input. The therapist then explained to the parents the etiology of paranoid schizophrenia, and included a cultural explanation of Mei-Li's hallucinations, which may be race related. The therapist then requested the parents' cooperation, especially in monitoring Mei-Li's regularity in taking her medication. Finally, the therapist gave the parents her telephone number in case they wished to contact her.

The parents were grateful that the therapist provided them with explanations about their daughter's mental condition. They were particularly thankful that the therapist actively solicited their help. With apparent trust toward the therapist, they began to vent how much they disliked their past experiences with two adolescent treatment hospitals who kept them "in the dark." They also attributed their daughter's prolonged hospitalization to the mental health staff's ignorance and disrespect of them as the patient's parents.

and even by complaining, so parents feel they are being asked to collaborate. By acknowledging that their job as parents is far more difficult than the therapist's and that they know more about their child then the therapist does, the therapist can enlist their cooperation.

Some parents come to the agency for help only because they have been forced to do so by some outside authority. This is often the case in neglect and abuse situations. The therapist must recognize this reality and try to assist them with this pressure. The therapist can empathize by respecting their belief that they have done all that they can and acknowledging how difficult their situation must be.

Some parents are so discouraged, depressed, and harried that they cannot see the usefulness of coming to the agency. They may, however, allow their children to come so that someone else will take over the burden. In these cases, the therapist should work with the children as long as the parents will send them. To respect the parents and to solicit their collaboration in the future whenever they are ready, the therapist should periodically send the parents a progress note outlining their child's improvement. Through indirect subtle activities, the therapist may evoke changes of attitude at home.

Use of Bilingualism and Interpreters

In working with minority children and families, a therapist may encounter clients who speak bidialectal or nonstandard English. In some instances, the children may be bilingual and the parents may speak no English at all. The therapist's use of standard English with a bidialectal or non-English-speaking child or family can itself affect the therapeutic relationship. Minority children and families are often conditioned to react to all English speakers in a similar manner and to expect similar behavior from them. Minority children, in fact, may stereotype standard-English speakers, including the therapist, and act in a socially distant or subservient manner. This presents problems in psychological therapy where an intimate working relationship is sought.

A therapist needs to be sensitive to behavior cues that language-based stereotypes evoke. These cues may include a minority client continually addressing the therapist by her surname and title while presenting themselves in a subservient and dependent manner. A minority child's overly subservient behavior should not be misconstrued as paying deference to an authority figure. Another cue is when the minority child insists on concrete answers and quick solutions. The therapist should realize that the child is simply behaving, in the therapeutic situation, in the same manner that he does with all formal interactions. The possibility always exists that the child's use of nonstandard English can lead to a misdiagnosis and a distorted conceptualization of the child's problem. When presented with a minority child or family who speaks nonstandard English, the therapist should automatically assume that her judgment and objectivity are going to be compromised. The only questions that remain are how much and in what manner.

To maximize the benefit of the therapy, the therapist needs to encourage the minority child to speak in the manner that he or she speaks to natural confidants, encouraging the child to become comfortable using the speech style he traditionally uses when sharing intimate information. One of the best ways for the therapist to communicate respect for nonstandard English is to plead ignorance and encourage the client to teach her the language. The therapist can also show acceptance of nonstandard-language forms by acknowledging that some forms of nonstandard language exist in every speech.

To maximize the subtleties and nuances in therapy with nonstandard-English-speaking minority children, the therapist may need to use reflective paraphrasing more liberally than usual. The following excerpt from an individual therapy session between a nonstandard-English-speaking 8-year-old Hispanic boy and a standard-English-speaking therapist demonstrates how paraphrasing and questioning can be used to prevent potential misunderstandings.

Hispanic Child:	*It be's that way . . . you know . . . don't nobody care nothin' about you except you them alike.*
Therapist:	*I hear you say nobody cares about you as a person?*
Hispanic Child:	*Yeah, I guess you could say it like that.*
Therapist:	*I like for you to help me explain "it be's that way."*
Hispanic Child:	*Well, I mean that way—it be's that way . . . ain't nobody cared about me, not boys or girls who are White . . . what's use.*
Therapist:	*So you mean nobody cares to be your friend or pay attention to you because you are not White.*
Hispanic Child:	*Yeah.*

To show respect for a client, it is important that the therapist use part of the child's own language and paraphrase in such a manner that he does not appear to be correcting the child.

Considering the large number of non-English-speaking minorities in the United States, it is essential that therapy with minority children and their families at times be conducted with the aid of an outside interpreter. For such therapy to take place effectively, the interpreter must be carefully selected and oriented (Glasser, 1983). Ideally, the culture of the interpreter and the minority child should be the same. The interpreter must understand his or her role in the therapeutic process. It is therapeutically more advantageous to have an interpreter experienced in psychological issues. The interpreter's role is to serve as a conduit linking the therapist with the child. Ideally, the interpreter is a neutral party who neither adds nor subtracts from what the primary parties communicate. The interpreter communicates not only with words but also with gestures, emotional expressions, and varying intonations. He or she must have the capacity to act exactly as the therapist acts and express the same feelings. It is important to use the same interpreter, if possible, and to reassure the client of confidentiality. It is also useful to schedule pretherapy sessions with the interpreter to establish a relationship, discuss the translation format, and allow the interpreter to raise questions.

Because children acculturate faster than their parents, children often learn the English language faster than their parents. To use children as interpreters may force the families, especially the Asian and Hispanic American families, to reverse their traditional hierarchical roles and render disrespect to the parents and a disservice to the family.

Ethnicity and Mutual Goal Formation

The techniques and process of mutual goal formation require that the therapist adhere to the value orientation of a specific ethnic minority child. Individual psychologically oriented goals will not fit well with an ethnic minority child's need for family protection and interdependence. Further, a minority child is often reluctant to formulate goals that benefit only himself or herself. The following case study of Twe illustrates the value conflict in mutual goal formation.

The process of mutual goal formation should always consider ethnic minority cultural traits of interdependence. Whenever possible, a therapist needs to involve all family members, even extended family members in the selection of a therapeutic goal. The process of involving all relevant family members can itself be so therapeutic that further intervention by the therapist may not be necessary.

✿ CASE STUDY
Twe—Vietnamese American Female Student

Twe, a 14-year-old Vietnamese American female student, was referred by the school counselor for depression. Throughout the interview session, Twe was extremely reluctant to talk about her depression. After confidentiality was assured, Twe mentioned the discomfort she experienced when her Anglo classmates teased her, saying that despite her being a teenager, she still was "tied to her parents' apron strings." Twe explained that she was born in this country one year after her parents escaped from Saigon. Her parents owned a restaurant. Being the oldest of four children, Twe was expected to help out daily in the restaurant after school. Because of her heavy work involvement and diligent study habits, Twe had practically no time for a social life. Her isolation from her friends bothered her more when she turned fourteen. For financial reasons, and in order to provide a good role example for her younger siblings, Twe deferred to her parents. She never complained, but she suffered quietly and became increasingly depressed.

The therapist's knowledge of Twe's culture, which emphasizes filial piety, self-control, and collectivism, helped him to be empathic toward Twe's dilemma. Instead of encouraging Twe to individuate and to do her own thing, the therapist commended her for fulfilling her dutiful obligations to her parents and her younger siblings. However, the therapist also empathized by letting Twe know he understood how much she wanted to be accepted and to be with her friends. Twe responded by saying that this was the dilemma that drove her "crazy" or "depressed."

When Twe was asked the possible solution for this dilemma, she replied "some compromises have to be made." She later suggested, "If I could just have Friday evening off from work and be with my friends, I would be very happy." The therapist asked Twe if she had ever approached her parents about this problem and her desire to have one evening off from work. Twe replied, "I dare not, and besides my parents will never let me for they themselves have to work all the time." The therapist encouraged her to relate her desire to her parents and at the same time reminded her that she could not honor her family if she was physically and mentally sick and "imbalanced."

Ethnic minority children tend to defer to authority figures and to view their emotional problems as physically based. Hence, they often approach the therapist like a patient seeking concrete medical advice from a physician (Tsui & Schutz, 1985). Therapy with minority children, therefore, needs to be more structured, especially in the initial sessions. Extensive diagnostic evaluations should be avoided. Instead, tangible, problem-focused goals should be established as soon as possible. Due to cognitive limitations, especially among younger minority children, plus linguistic complexities and deficiency in the English language, therapeutic goals mutually established with the child need to be structured, specific, realistic, concrete, practical, and readily achievable (Acosta et al., 1982; Edwards & Edwards, 1984). If they are, they can frequently produce immediate success in the child's life (Aponte, 1979).

Ethnicity, Problem Solving, and Termination

After a psychologically and culturally relevant understanding of the minority child's problem has been mutually formulated, the process of implementing a culturally sensitive intervention is in order. The line between understanding the minority child's problem and responding to it for the purpose of problem solving is characteristically a fine one. Generally, the minority child will have some definite ideas about what is conflictual and problematic in his behavior. Further, the child may have established patterns of stress responses that reflect his particular culture's life-adaptive strategies.

✿ CASE STUDY
Phillip—American Indian Probationer

Phillip, a 15-year-old American Indian probationer, was brought to the attention of a court-related worker who received a complaint that Phillip was running around from house to house visiting female friends without parental supervision. When the worker inquired about Phillip's family background, she discovered that he had several aunts and cousins. When the workers called all Phillip's aunts and cousins together for a family conference, she discovered that all his cousins were young females. The workers later learned that Phillip's behavior was very natural in the extended family system of his tribe.

By the time the problem-solving stage of therapy has been reached, the therapist has already demonstrated the capacity to be culturally adaptive and to relate in a variety of ways. This ensures that the minority child is afforded the opportunity to respond to his or her problematic experiences in new ways. Changes that take place in therapy are, in part, a shift or modification of the cultural life strategy of the child. This process requires that the child learn to restore, expand, or modify the traditional cultural stress response or problem-solving repertoire. The therapist introduces the change/modification process for the child by framing the change within a traditional framework or language. Basically, the minority child is validated in his problem-solving effort. This will form a foundation for adding something new. Affirming the foundation the child already has is a necessary precondition for assimilating and then accommodating a new response. This constitutes a key principle in therapy with a minority child during the problem-solving stage. The following case study of Van-Tran illustrates this practice principle.

Van-Tran's case indicates the therapist's ability to "frame" the change within the minority child's traditional, culturally acceptable language. The therapist's suggested change or new strategy was conceived by the client as an expansion of the "old" cultural problem-solving response. The therapist's suggested change also was consistent with the client's needs, degree of acculturation, motivation for change, and comfort in responding to the therapist's directives.

It is difficult to decide that the child has completed all the therapeutic work that should be accomplished. The question of when a minority child has finished is compounded by ethnicity issues that can cause premature termination. Many minority children are taught self-control, and they and their parents are reluctant to burden the therapist for long-term treatment and may initiate termination prematurely. Hence, termination evaluation that considers only the minority client's self-report may be inaccurate and inappropriate. Instead, the therapist needs to make home visits and engage in a variety of informal activities and rituals such as a tea party or festive celebrations within the client's own home environment and community. Through informal interaction with the client and the family, the therapist can obtain firsthand information pertaining to the overall functioning of the child.

Further, the usual therapeutic mentality of time-limited therapy with a clearcut, successful outcome may not be applicable in work with ethnic minority children. Rosen and Proctor's (1978) model for specifying and evaluating therapy outcome is relevant in work with

---

✿ CASE STUDY
Van-Tran—Vietnamese American Student

Van-Tran, a 13-year-old Vietnamese American, was a good student of Asian martial arts. He was a conscientious student, but Van-Tran repeatedly got into fights at school, which resulted in his being suspended by the school principal. Van-Tran's suspension was indefinite because he refused to promise the principle that he would not get into physical fights again. "Nobody can insult my mother; I will fight whether I win or lose," cried Van-Tran.

The therapist learned that Van-Tran's mother had recently died of cancer. Van-Tran was very close to his mother and had difficulty coping with her death. The therapist affirmed Van-Tran's love and loyalty for his mother. Van-Tran also volunteered that defending his mother's name was the least he could do, because this was clearly a traditional cultural practice in Vietnam. The therapist further affirmed Van-Tran of his cultural practice. He then inquired if Van-Tran's mother was honored by his fighting behavior. After a long pause, Van-Tran replied hesitantly that his mother would be proud of his defending her honor, but she would be displeased by his expulsion from school, for continued absences from school would jeopardize his chance of having a good life in the future.

Van-Tran still had difficulty reconciling the disgrace and cowardness of not defending his mother's honor. The therapist asked Van-Tran what his peers at school would say if he did not defend his mother's honor by resorting to violence. Van-Tran hesitated a moment and said "My Vietnamese peers will call me a coward or unfaithful son. I don't know what the others here will say, but I don't give a damn."

In order to be loyal to his mother and to bring honor to his family, the therapist asked Van-Tran what he felt his mother would want him to do. Van-Tran said tearfully, "She would like for me to go back to school." The therapist then taught Van-Tran some techniques, including cognitive restructuring, to cope and maintain self-control when his peers taunted him with name calling.

minority children. In evaluating therapy progress with ethnic minority children, three types of outcome goals should be considered. First are the *intermediate* outcomes that contribute to or create a climate for continued therapy. Some parents may only allow the therapist to help them with basic needs problems of their children. Such basic needs problems are subsumed under second or *instrumental* outcomes. When this is accomplished, therapy terminates. Third are the *ultimate* outcomes that constitute the reasons for which therapy was undertaken. Examples of these outcome goals include a child's adjustment problem in school or at home.

Some minority children are so psychologically isolated and emotionally deprived that the relationship with the therapist may represent the first stable, nurturing relationship they have ever experienced. They may interpret termination as a major loss in their lives. A therapist needs to be comfortable with this type of dependence and not view such behavior as deceptive manipulation.

Moreover, minority children should be actively involved in planning their termination. Their ambivalence, however, may bring back old symptoms, defenses against the pain of separation, and some denial that therapy or the therapist was important. It is difficult for children to grow up. This is especially true for minority children during the termination period, when they may fear that support will be left behind, that they will be on their own, and that all the good works and feelings they have experienced will be lost. Hence, sufficient time is needed to make the termination period as therapeutic as earlier therapy.

Some minority children may never want to end a good relationship. They learn to respect and love the therapist as a member of their family, and they may wish to maintain contact with the therapist even after the successful achievement of therapy goals. A therapist should learn to treasure such a natural relationship and not allow her "professionalism" to spoil a genuine human sharing. She should not hurriedly jeopardize the therapeutic benefits during the process of termination. Termination should be viewed as an invaluable time for evaluation, integration, and summing up what the child has accomplished and what the future may hold. The following case study of Cathy illustrates how these processes can take place.

The final session should be a sharing of the experiences the child and the therapist have had together. It can be a time to focus on the high spots and on the low ones, and then to look forward to a brighter future. Dwelling too much on what may go wrong in the future can leave the child with the feelings that the therapist is expecting this to happen. It is better for the therapist to emphasize the strengths the child has acquired during the course of the therapy, and how these will be safeguards against the recurrence of problems.

✿ CASE STUDY
Cathy—Puerto Rican Girl

Cathy, an 8-year-old Puerto Rican girl, was referred because of her explosive, bizarre, uncontrollable behavior at home. Cathy had been sexually abused by her stepfather since she was 6 years old. When therapy began, she lived with Puerto Rican foster parents who were very supportive of Cathy's therapy.

When Cathy was away from home, she became very frightened and refused to talk. Due to Cathy's unwillingness to talk, play therapy was the only individual therapeutic modality to which she would respond.

When Cathy began play therapy, her therapist gently showed her the toys that were available and allowed her to choose the ones she wanted. To facilitate a nonthreatening environment, the therapist avoided eye contact but followed the direction of Cathy's vision signifying the kinds of toys she wanted. As Cathy played, the therapist noticed the shapes of things that Cathy kneaded from clay, from long snakes to animals. Cathy indicated later that she wanted to fingerpaint, and the therapist set this up for her.

During the third session, the therapist began to make general comments that were pertinent to Cathy's play activity. Cathy did not respond but she did not object. At the end of each play session, the therapist carefully put Cathy's work away in a special place. Cathy began to help the therapist put away her work at the end of the fourth session. This indicated a trusting, positive rap-

---

port was developing. Cathy and the therapist never verbally communicated, but Cathy seemed to enjoy attending the play session and her behavior showed signs of improving, as reported by her foster parents during family therapy sessions.

Cathy continued her weekly therapy for 4 months. At the end of the third month, her foster parents had decided to move to another city and made preparations for Cathy to continue treatment there. The therapist then counted off the number of times they still had together and reassured Cathy that another therapist like her would continue therapy with her. Cathy had increased eye contact with the therapist, who always verbalized what seemed to be happening between both of them.

At the last meeting, the therapist told Cathy that it had been a pleasure working with her. Cathy took from the closet all the things she had made and looked them over. The therapist commented on her accomplishments, and the many new things she had learned, suggesting that perhaps now there were things Cathy wanted to do differently. Cathy responded with a big smile. The therapist then told Cathy that she could take home everything she had made. Cathy carefully selected some items and returned the rest to the closet. When the therapist thanked her for leaving part of what she had made, Cathy gave the therapist a goodbye hug.

7

Cultural-Specific Methods, Techniques, and Skills in Family Therapy

Rationale and Criteria for Family Therapy

This chapter presents the use of family as an intervention approach on behalf of minority children. Considering the ecological and ethnic reality of minority children and youth, their complex problems cannot be treated in isolation, independent of their parents and other family members. Young children are totally dependent on home and family, so resources or obstacles naturally lie within the family and must be regarded as most significant. As the child matures to young adulthood, the significance of the home decreases. When the entire family is seen as the unit of focus, there is a need to select therapeutic strategies that will address the family characteristics and interactions as a unit. Here, family therapy is defined as any psychotherapeutic endeavor that explicitly focuses on altering the interactions between or among family members and seeks to improve the functioning of the family as a unit, its subsystems, and/or the functioning of individual members of the family.

Family therapy as a treatment modality offers the following unique advantages, which individual and group therapy do not offer:

1. All ethnic minorities consider the family and extended family their primary source of support. Reliance on natural support systems produces fewer feelings of defeat, humiliation to self and to the family, and powerlessness (Ho, 1987).
2. It provides the therapist an opportunity to assess family interaction and the roles family members assume with one another.
3. It helps parents learn to communicate more directly, to problem solve jointly, to empathize with other family members, including the child who is identified as the client or patient, and to learn and experiment with more effective child management techniques.
4. It reduces the tendency of family members to polarize, split, blame, or scapegoat members of the family system.
5. Family therapy employs systems theory, which argues that the most helpful therapeutic interventions are those that enhance an individual's interaction with others or with the environment and, therefore, ensure lasting changes outside the context of the therapeutic relationship (Ivey, Ivey, & Simek-Downing, 1987).

When Family Therapy Is Indicated or Contraindicated

Family therapy with a minority child and family is most appropriate under the following conditions:

1. The child's problem or self-destructive behavior is symptomatic of a dysfunctional marital or family system.
2. The child serves as a scapegoat to parental frustrations or feelings of victimization or projection.
3. The child and the parents are experiencing generational, acculturational, and cultural conflicts.
4. The child and the parents are experiencing role conflicts and communication problems.
5. Parents need to know problem-solving skills and parenting skills.
6. The family members are sufficiently articulate and the level of anger in the family is not too high, and the family, especially the parents, shows sufficient motivation.

Family therapy with minority children and their families is contraindicated under the following conditions:

1. The parents suffer delusional psychosis.
2. The parents are emotionally explosive, aggressive sociopaths and violent individuals.

3. The parents are chronic substance abusers.
4. The parents are severely mentally retarded.
5. The therapist is not knowledgeable of the minority family's cultural value systems, family structure, and interactive style.

The following case study of Mrs. Martinez illustrates the misuse of family therapy in work with a Mexican American family.

This case clearly indicates the therapist's lack of knowledge and sensitivity of the Hispanic culture and hierarchical family structure, which does not allow a young female member (daughter) to be disrespectful to an older male family member (father), especially in front of a nonfamily member (therapist). The therapist's inactivity also reflected her insensitivity to the Hispanic sense of personalism. Mr. Martinez might have felt that his inner dignity (dignidad) was assaulted by his wife and daughter. The therapist's inactivity did little to convey to the father and other family members that revitalization of familism through the therapist's intervention was possible or could be expected.

✿ CASE STUDY
Mrs. Martinez

Mrs. Martinez requested therapy for her family because her 12-year-old daughter was getting "out of control." In addition to frequent emotional outbursts in the home, her daughter was failing in school. She also ran around with the "wrong crowd" after school.

Mrs. Martinez and her daughter attacked each other verbally during the first family session. The father sat quietly but experienced considerable discomfort. The therapist did not intervene but conveyed nonverbally to the family that she had lost control of the therapy session. After Mrs. Martinez and her daughter ran out of negative things to say to each other, they both turned to Mr. Martinez. Mrs. Martinez blamed her husband for his passivity, especially in disciplining their daughter. The daughter also complained that her father was totally inaccessible. Mr. Martinez remained silent during the entire therapy session. Before the family left, the therapist did express her newly gained understanding of the family conflict.

The family did not return for the next scheduled appointment. When the therapist called to inquire the reason why, Mrs. Martinez responded that she and her husband had decided to work on their family problem on their own.

Goals of Family Therapy

The use of family therapy as a treatment modality in therapy with minority children has the following major, somewhat overlapping goals: (a) support of adaptive functioning; (b) specific problem solving; (c) overt behavioral change; and (d) modification of systemic family processes, such as dysfunctional communication, dysfunctional family structure, and a defective parent-child relationship, couple relationship, or sibling relationship. These treatment goals, in turn, become the types of family therapy in the treatment of a minority child.

Types of Family Therapy

Support of Adaptive Functioning

All families experience some generational value conflicts between the child and parent. Such conflicts are often exacerbated in poor ethnic minority families that have many problems. Generational conflicts also intensify as children reach adolescence.

✿ CASE STUDY
Susan—Black Adolescent

Susan, a 15-year-old Black adolescent of Jamacan descent, was very angry at her mother's restrictions of her excessive interaction with her peers. During the conjoint family session with Susan and her mother, who was also a single parent, Susan repeatedly wanted her mother to "chill out" and to leave her alone. The mother, in turn, accused Susan of being "immature," "too Americanized," and caring only for herself and nobody else in the family.

In joining the family for therapy, the therapist utilized the technique of cultural reframing (Falicov & Karrer, 1984). By using this technique, the demands or expectations made by both Susan and her mother were analyzed in relation to the cultural values that constituted the background for the demands. Hence, the mother's demand that Susan interact less frequently with her peers and stay at home more was viewed as expressing a cultural value of familism that family takes priority over the individual. Susan's demand for greater freedom was viewed as expressing a value of individualism over family. Each value was understood to be functional, or adaptive, within its social context. The mother's definition of the situation was based upon the traditional value of the family over the individual, whereas the middle-class American value of the individual above the family is implicit in Susan's request.

Focusing on cultural differences allowed the mother-daughter conflict to shift from the individual blame of Susan or the mother to the acculturation process, which placed different demands on the adolescent and parent generations. After Susan and her mother were led to see the problem or conflict differently, from person to culture, an impartial model of the family life-cycle progression through the stages of adolescence was presented. As blaming and hostility disappeared, mother and daughter began to develop mutual trust, which in turn allowed the mother to openly share with the daughter her reluctance to see her grow up and leave her. A compromise was arranged whereby Susan would have a weekly preplanned outing with her friends and be at home at a time acceptable to her mother.

Help in Problem Solving

A minority child's behavioral problems are sometimes caused by unresolved parental conflict, which in turn is related to cultural prescriptions as to what is the proper role of a father or mother. Each culture has prohibitions prescribing the proper conduct and functioning of its members. When these prohibitions are violated, an individual and his family may suffer consequences, sometimes life-threatening ones.

✿ CASE STUDY
Ron Tiger—American Indian Boy

Ron Tiger, a 10-year-old American Indian boy, was experiencing increased difficulty both in school and at home. The most alarming incident, which brought the family to the clinic for help, was when Ron passed out from heavy glue sniffing.

Upon interviewing Ron's mother, who is Cherokee, the therapist learned that Ron had been a "normal" child until recently, when he became withdrawn. Mrs. Tiger apologetically attributed

Ron's withdrawal to her marital discord with her husband, who is a Hopi Indian. Mrs. Tiger also volunteered that a majority of her conflict with her husband centered around his passivity, especially in disciplining their son.

In the therapist's interview with Mr. Tiger, who was a kind, soft-spoken, mild-mannered man, Mr. Tiger explained that in the Hopi tribe, the husband moved into his wife's household. The wife, in this particular tribe, had primary responsibility for child rearing. The husband's responsibility was to raise his sister's children, especially the male children.

Mr. Tiger moved with his parents to a large city when he was 15. When he was 20, he married his present wife. During the couple's courtship, and until the couple had their first child, his wife was impressed with his interest and concern for young children, especially his sister's children. After the couple had their own child, Mrs. Tiger was disappointed with the apathy her husband showed toward the new baby. She rationalized her husband's apathetic behavior by saying he did not relate to infants well. She later discovered that Mr. Tiger's apathetic behavior, especially with discipline, did not change as their child grew older. This began to create problems in their marriage.

The therapist inquired what efforts the couple had attempted previously to rectify the discipline problem. Mrs. Tiger disappointedly related that the couple had gone to see a marriage counselor once but never returned. Mr. Tiger did not like that counselor and felt he sided with his wife and insisted that a father should discipline his child.

With the permission of Mr. Tiger, the therapist consulted with an elder from Mr. Tiger's tribe. This elder then privately advised Mr. Tiger that his previously learned taboo of shared parental responsibility for his child applied only to marriages within the same tribe. Because his wife was from a different tribe, the prohibition did not apply.

The above example involving problem solving with ethnic minority families occurs more frequently than most family therapists realize. When it happens, it should not be categorically labeled just another sign of client resistance. It should be carefully examined and respected. Often, the therapist may need to explore whether the clients have tried previously to resolve the problem and failed. If the client's unsuccessful attempt was caused by cultural taboos or rigid traditional practices, the therapist may need to seek help from tribal leaders, including the elders and the medicine man. Such timely consultation and collaboration with indigenous healers is consistent with the ecosystemic principles of equifinality, meaning that a number of different interventions may, owing to the complexity of systems, produce similar effects or outcomes.

Overt Behavioral Change

Minority children and their families often exhibit general distrust or "cultural paranoia," especially in dealing with White therapists. They sometimes exhibit unwillingness to express their feelings verbally and pragmatic differences in communication styles. A therapeutic technique solely dependent on verbal exchange may fall short in helping the minority client understand and alter his or her way of interacting with others. Therapeutic techniques focusing on a here-and-now transaction with other family members may achieve better results. The following case study of Mrs. Smith illustrates the use of an action-oriented technique in altering the mother's perceptions and behavior toward her son, who was originally labeled as having a bad behavioral and attitude problem.

✿ CASE STUDY
Mrs. Smith—Black, Single Parent

In an attempt to persuade her 8-year-old son Jamil to show more interest in school and to be more helpful at home, Mrs. Smith (who is Black and a single parent) accused her son of not wanting to do anything and of being plain "lazy." When her son finally explained how his effort was being constantly undermined and criticized by his mother, Mrs. Smith would repeatedly interrupt him before he could finish what he had to say. Mrs. Smith also complained that she was not going to raise her son to be "no lazy bum," like his father. As Mrs. Smith continued to berate her son, he regressed into a depressed state and stared at the floor.

The therapist's several attempts to block Mrs. Smith's interruptions and ventilation were unsuccessful. The therapist then explained he would sit next to Jamil and dramatize how Jamil might feel when he was interrupted whenever he tried to explain. Mrs. Smith and Jamil agreed to the plan. As Jamil continued to explain to his mother how much he disliked her treating him like his father because of his dark skin and physical appearance, Mrs. Smith got angry and said, "As far as I'm concerned, the way you have been acting, you are worse than your no-good father." The therapist immediately dropped down on the floor and said nothing. After Mrs. Smith got over her initial astonishment, she continued to berate Jamil about his immaturity. The therapist then crawled toward the door and started pounding. This finally got the mother's attention. Mrs. Smith then stopped and asked what the therapist's behavior was supposed to mean. The therapist redirected the question and asked if she could come up with an answer. After a short pause, Mrs. Smith reluctantly turned to Jamil and asked, "Did I really make you feel this bad?" Jamil nodded and said, "All the time!"

The therapist then empathized with Mrs. Smith's frustration at work and at home, as well as her high expectations for her son. Mrs. Smith replied that she did realize lately that she had been yelling instead of talking to Jamil who, in turn, responded by overt passive behavior at home and in school. As mother-son communication improved, Jamil became more responsible at home and his school work improved.

Modification of Systemic Family Process

✿ CASE STUDY
Kathy—Puerto Rican Student

Kathy, an 11-year-old Puerto Rican student, was late to school regularly. Sometimes she did not get to school until noon. Generally a good student academically, Kathy came to school appearing physically exhausted. Although she seemed to get along well with her peers, Kathy occasionally lost patience with the younger kids at school. Recently, she physically injured two of the first graders who would not "get out of her way." The school counselor referred her to the clinic for therapy.

During the first visit with Kathy, the therapist learned that Kathy lived in a poor neighborhood. Her father was in prison for dealing drugs. Her mother, who was an alcoholic, worked irregularly as a waitress at a restaurant. When her mother was at work, Kathy was left in charge of two sisters, ages 8 and 6, and one brother, age 4. Although Kathy's aunt, who was the oldest sister of her mother, lived with the family, her physical disability and general ill health had prevented her from helping the children.

Due to the mother's irregular work hours, alcoholism problem, and "tired of coming to therapy" attitude, the therapist concluded that the treatment unit of choice would have to be Kathy's siblings.

The first therapy session with the siblings was chaotic—while Kathy's two younger sisters were fighting over some toys, her 4-year-old brother was throwing a hard object at a cat, making the cat scream. After the cat ran out of the room, he would stare out the window. Realizing the physical and emotional unavailability of the parental role in this family, the therapist decided the first treatment goal for the siblings was to strengthen the hierarchies, so that some degree of order and stability could be developed for meaningful family interactions. Kathy broke up the fight between her two younger sisters, but the brother continued to stare out the window. The therapist asked the older children if they noticed what their brother was doing, and then encouraged Kathy to lead a discussion of how their little brother might be feeling. When the girls talked about the possibility of their brother feeling left out or lonely, Kathy began organizing activities that included him and told the girls to make sure to let the brother play with them.

Whenever one of the younger girls hit the other, Kathy would hit the aggressor or scream her. The therapist, working as a consultant to Kathy, offered suggestions such as "Instead of hitting your sister, tell her in a firm voice that she must not hit others in the family." The therapist would then support her with comments, such as, "Kathy just told you not to do that. She is your big sister, and you need to listen to her." Initially, Kathy's instructions were obeyed only because the therapist repeatedly reinforced them. By the third session, Kathy's voice was more convincing and she was getting more positive results.

In order to teach the children to appreciate Kathy's parenting efforts, the therapist began accentuating her caring. For example, when Kathy would play with one of the younger children, or offer to help one of them with homework, the therapist would say, "Have you thanked Kathy for helping you? Wasn't that nice of her to do that? You certainly look like you liked her playing with you."

To safeguard Kathy's normal adolescent developmental needs, the therapist commented to Kathy about the unfairness of her being the oldest and having to assume responsibility of the younger siblings. The therapist also talked to Kathy about her friends and conferred with the school and her mother about building in other peer activities. Once the chaotic family situation was stabilized and Kathy was receiving positive feedback and nurturance from her younger siblings, her mother, and her aunt, she had no difficulty attending school regularly and conducting herself appropriately while there.

In a 2-month period, the therapist saw Kathy and her siblings a total of nine sessions. The children's mother never attended the sessions but was kept informed of the progress through telephone calls. During the last telephone conversation, the mother expressed an interest in possibly consulting at a later date with the therapist regarding the children, as well as her own problem.

The above case illustrates how the systemic family process can be modified to help a child with problem solving and to insure continued developmental growth. Stereotypically, the parental child has been seen as an unhealthy role for the oldest child from large poor families. With the increase in single-parent and two-working-parent families, this role is currently becoming more prevalent (Morawetz & Walker, 1984), especially among ethnic minority families who face the doubly harsh reality of poverty, poor health, and unemployment (Levitan, 1988).

When the parents are unavailable to provide for their children physically and emotionally, working with the sibling group may be the only therapeutic modality whereby children can be protected from destruction. When the sibling hierarchy is clear and functioning well, the family runs smoothly. The younger children get their physical and emotional needs met, and the parental child develops a sense of responsibility and competence and establishes a special place in the family. The role of the parental child is only problematic when the child does not have a clear set of rules, when parents are inconsistent in allocating responsibility, and when the parental child mirrors negative parenting (Minuchin, 1974).

A minority child's problem can also be helped by modifying the systemic family process by involving the grandparents.

✿ CASE STUDY

Mei-Ling—Chinese American Girl

Mei-Ling, a 16-year-old Chinese American girl, was referred to the clinic for therapy because of poor academic performance and an attempted suicide. Mei-Ling lived with her adopted parents and grandmother, who on more than one occasion noticed Mei-Ling's suicidal thoughts. Mei-Ling's adopted father worked long hours in a family-owned import shop and had "no time" for therapy. During the first interview, both Mei-Ling and her mother, Mrs. Chan, wept openly but offered little information regarding Mei-Ling's unhappiness. The therapist requested that the grandmother come to the next therapy session.

At the second therapy session with Mei-Ling, her mother, and grandmother, an important family theme was discovered. Mei-Ling's mother volunteered that she too was an adopted child. Mei-Ling's grandmother immediately defended herself by saying, "I have never treated you as though you are not my own— since you are my only child, I don't know what it is like having my own [biological] child." Mrs. Chan, who has a degree in engineering, continued that even though she studied hard and made good grades in school, she felt that she and her mother were never close.

Mrs. Chan's mother was feeling uncomfortable and wanted to shift the focus from herself to her granddaughter, so she asked the therapist how her relationship with her daughter had anything to do with her granddaughter's problem. The therapist respected the grandmother's need for self-protection. He asked Mei-Ling how she felt about her mother's adopted status and relationship with her grandmother. Mei-Ling hesitantly replied that she was surprised that her mother was adopted. Because she and her mother shared the same status as "adopted child," this brought her closer to her mother. Mei-Ling continued that because of her poor academic performance in school, especially in math and in science, she felt that her mother was disappointed in her. Additionally, Mei-Ling felt disloyal to her mother, who had adopted her when she was only 3 years old. Because she saw no acceptable way to fulfill her obligation to the family, she often thought death would be a way to end her family's disappointment in her and a way to end her own misery.

Mrs. Chan wept uncontrollably and buried her face in her lap. The therapist thanked the family for sharing intimate painful information that he could use to help solve Mei-Ling's depression and suicidal problem. The therapist then invited Mrs. Chan and her mother to return next session to provide more information that could be used to help Mei-Ling.

In the next session with Mrs. Chan and her mother, Mrs. Chan described her anxiety and the pain of being an adopted child, wanting to be accepted by her mother. Before she finished telling her mother of her fear, loneliness, and insecurity, Mrs. Chan began to cry. Her mother reached out to comfort her, and Mrs. Chan wept in her arms. During the session, the two women achieved a level of intimacy they had never had before. After connecting with her mother in this meaningful way, Mrs. Chan realized more of her previous conditional affection for Mei-Ling. She also found it easier to attain a closer relationship with Mei-Ling, regardless of her interest and ability in math and science subjects. As Mrs. Chan's relationship with her daughter improved, Mei-Ling did better in school and thoughts of not wanting to live ceased to cross her mind.

Mei-Ling's case study illustrates that a minority child's dysfunctional behaviors and problems can be treated by modifying systemic family relationships, interactions, and processes. However, the therapeutic process used to modify the dysfunctional family relationships requires a therapist who is skilled in the various phases of family therapy. A skill refers to the unique fusion of ethnic-sensitive aptitudes and knowledge or capabilities essential to performing a professional task or activity. Unique aptitudes that are part of skill may include a therapist's warmth, sensitivity (to his or her own ethnic background, client's ethnic background and reality, and adaptation of skills in response to client's ethnic reality), flexibility, and positive regard and respect for the client/family. Capabilities that are part of skill include therapeutic procedures responsible for accomplishing a task. The following section presents cultural- and ethnic-specific skills needed in the engagement, problem-solving, and evaluation and termination phases of family therapy with ethnic minority clients.

Cultural- and Ethnic-Specific Skills
in the Engagement Phase of Family Therapy

The engagement phase of family therapy with ethnic minorities is most important, as well as very difficult (Aponte, 1990; Ho, 1990b.) If this beginning phase of therapy is not "properly" conducted, the first therapy session will most likely be the last time the therapist will have contact with the family. There are several reasons as to why the engagement phase with ethnic minority families is so critical and difficult. Minority families may have many contacts with public and private health care agencies, but they often have no prior knowledge of family therapy. They utilize family therapy only if all other traditional help-seeking attempts have failed. Many ethnic minority families have contact with family therapists only because they are referred by mainstream societal agencies, such as schools, mental health care agencies, the court, or social service agencies. Most ethnic minority clients distrust therapists, who represent the mainstream society that oppresses them and perpetuates their sense of powerlessness. Due to cultural value differences, it is especially difficult for Asian and Hispanic Americans to rely on an outside family therapist to resolve private family problems. It is antithetical to familial piety and a betrayal of ancestors. To American Indians and Blacks, family therapy is considered an unwelcome intrusion to self-determination and individuality. Most ethnic minority clients are extremely uncomfortable with "talk" therapy and are self-conscious of their English-language deficiency. Also, they often lack financial resources to seek long-term therapy.

In the initial engagement phase with an ethnic minority family, therapists should be aware of certain characteristics of verbal and nonverbal communication in their initial face-to-face meetings. The therapist should demonstrate personal interest in the family, for this is consistent with the ethnic minority families' orientation of personalism and collaterality. Hispanic Americans normally expect less physical distance in personal interactions and are accustomed to frequent physical contact (Levine & Padilla, 1980), whereas Asian Americans and American Indians are more reserved and formal in their initial encounters (Ho, 1987). Black American families are very sensitive to a sense of being condescended to and they usually consider it disrespectful if the therapist addresses older family members by their first names (Boyd-Franklin, 1989, p. 135). It is helpful to ask family members by what name they would like to be addressed. To achieve ascribed credibility with Asian American families, therapists should not hesitate to disclose his or her educational background and work experience. Asian American clients need to be assured that their therapist is more powerful than their family problem or illness and will "cure" them with competence and the necessary know-how.

To facilitate the development of a positive therapeutic alliance, the therapist needs to search for strengths within the family and to praise the family for its dignity and willingness to seek professional help. During this initial stage, a therapist is cautioned not to challenge the family's verbal statements about their lifestyle or culturally prescribed norms. For example, a Hispanic wife may say that her husband is the "boss" although the therapist and the rest of the family are all aware that she is dominating the therapy session and the family. The Hispanic wife's behavior needs to be observed within the family's cultural context and internally noted but not verbalized (Falicov, 1982, p. 151). Interpretations of interactional dysfuncton or direct confrontations at this stage of therapy tend to heighten the family's insecurity and may be perceived as disrespect and disapproval rather than an invitation for change.

Most ethnic minority clients perceive the role of a family therapist as that of a physician (Asians and Blacks), a medicine man (American Indians), or a folk healer (Hispanics). A brief orientation to the families on how to make use of family therapy is often helpful. The therapist should explore with the families information about setting therapy goals, the role of the therapist, and their own involvement in the therapeutic process. Because race is a major factor underlying the ethnic minority client's sense of powerlessness and cultural paranoia, openly sharing with families racial differences between the therapist and the family can convey to the families that the therapist is not "color blind" and that open and honest discussion is encouraged.

Older traditional minority clients often exhibit difficulty with the English language. A therapist is advised against using children as translators because this reverses the authority stance of the families and threatens older family members, particularly males. When there are no native-speaking therapists available, an adult interpreter is highly recommended (Kline, Austin, & Acosta, 1980).

Because the therapist is perceived by minority families as an authority figure, she or he needs to assume an active role in the beginning phase of the therapy process. The therapist will be accepted by these families more readily if he or she shows leadership (Minuchin, 1974, p. 174). To be respectful of the families and to minimize the unnaturalness of the initial therapist-family contact, Minuchin's maintenance technique "requires the therapist to be organized by the basic rules that regulate the transactional process in a specific family system" (p. 175). For instance, given that social interaction of the Asian and Hispanic American is governed by a hierarchical role structure, the therapist should address the grandfather or father first.

To engage an ethnic minority family in therapy, a therapist also needs to consider the nature of the referral, the motivational level of the client or potential client, and the most appropriate treatment modality, regardless of the nature of the problem. The following family case example illustrates the culturally sensitive engagement process and the application of an appropriate treatment modality.

✿ CASE STUDY
Mrs. Tran—Vietnamese American

One day after the interview, Mrs. Tran, a Vietnamese American, informed the therapist that her husband had physical fights with her son. Mrs. Tran called again to inform the therapist that her son Fan had returned home after being missing for 2 days and that her husband and Fan had gotten into another "big" physical fight. Mrs. Tran asked if the therapist would talk with her and her family before "something terrible" happened. The therapist indicated to Mrs. Tran that he would like to see her husband alone for the first meeting. The therapist also suggested to Mrs. Tran that he would telephone Mr. Tran for the appointment (therapist helped Mr. Tran to "save face" and to convey respect).

When the therapist telephoned Mr. Tran for an appointment the next day, he expressed appreciation of the therapist's willingness to help. However, he said he doubted he could get off work and that he didn't know where the therapist's agency was located (client's fear of conspicuousness and need for privacy). The therapist volunteered to meet with him at a Vietnamese restaurant two blocks from where he worked (therapist's respect of client's space). Mr. Tran accepted the invitation.

Mr. Tran, a frail but gentle-looking man, was early for the appointment and he graciously ushered the therapist to a quiet corner table. The therapist expressed to him regret that he couldn't speak Vietnamese (therapist showed humility and respect). Mr. Tran reciprocated by informing the therapist that despite his

Chinese/Vietnamese ancestry, he could speak only a few words of Chinese (perhaps his wife had informed him that the therapist was Chinese). As Mr. Tran was relating his background to the therapist, he avoided eye contact by helping the therapist with tea (client's attempt to hide shame).

The therapist asked Mr. Tran if his work at the store kept him busy (therapist's attempt to ease client anxiety). He immediately played down the importance of his present job. The therapist empathized by letting him know that he must feel frustrated at not being able to practice his profession. Mr. Tran sighed that, "my best years are over—they have been for quite some time." The therapist remained silent but at the same time helped Mr. Tran with tea (therapist's nonintrusive attempt to encourage client to disclose).

Mr. Tran continued to relate to the therapist his immigration experiences, his love for his lost home and country, his extended family members who were left in Vietnam, and finally his beloved vocation as a dentist in Vietnam.

"I am happy for you that you still have your immediate family with you," the therapist commented (therapist's attempt to help client focus on immediate problem). "That's my greatest problem now," complained Mr. Tran. Mr. Tran then proceeded to tell the difficulties he was experiencing with his son.

Understanding and respecting the ethnic minority family's cultural norms, the nature of the presenting problem, and the clients' social context are perhaps the most important skills in selecting and in engaging a subsystem unit for therapy. The family's need for privacy and the hierarchical and vertical structure of Asian American, Hispanic American, and some American Indian families discourage family members from showing their true thoughts and negative feelings. A separate session with the father in this case and at the beginning therapy phase helped the father to save "face" and perhaps was the only way by which the father could be engaged. Seeing the father alone initially is also relevant to working with underinvolved Black (Boyd-Franklin, 1989, p. 138) and American Indian fathers (Red Horse, 1988) who often experience role peripherality within the family.

Considering the intense involvement that ethnic minority families have with their extended family, some family problems can be resolved simply by involving these extended family members, especially the spokesperson, who normally is the grandfather (Asian and Hispanic) or grandmother (Black and Indian). The process of joining is part of a cyclical process; it does not occur at a single point in a linear progression. In the course of engaging the extended family members, the therapist will have to join and engage them at various points in the treatment process. At times, friends and neighbors who accompany the family for therapy can contribute greatly to the assessment and treatment of the family. This is particularly true in work with Black families (Boyd-Franklin, 1989, p. 139).

Due to the healthy cultural paranoia and action orientation of ethnic minority families, they are often resistant to approaches that collect massive amounts of cultural, historical family data in the first family-therapist encounter. The therapist needs to join the family and focus on the initial presenting problem in the first sessions. Extensive data collection and the reliability of the data are appropriate issues only after trust with the family has been developed. However, in work with "the child is to blame" cases, inquiries about the family's cultural background can temporarily shift the focus of the therapy session away from the "problem" or the "identified patient." It can also provide the family an opportunity to educate the therapist, who assumes the role of a researcher (Bowen, 1978). The technique of cultural mapping and genograms provides insight into family's intergenerational perspectives and levels of "differentiation" (Bowen, 1978). Many ethnic minorities practice informal adoption and consequently their genograms may not conform completely to bloodlines (Boyd-Franklin, 1989). Hence, to obtain accurate information, the therapist needs to inquire who is in the family, as well as who lives in the home. The therapist should look for a natural opening to gather the desired information rather than adhering to an inflexible schedule.

After the pertinent information about a family based upon the ecosystem framework (Ho, 1987, p. 19) has been collected, the next therapeutic process is to engage the family in mutual goal formation. The process of mutual goal formation requires that the therapist adhere to the value orientation of a specific ethnic minority family. The interdependent and collectivist nature of minority families indicates avoiding treatment goals that are individually and psychologically oriented. Because ethnic family structure places strong emphasis on the parent-child relationship, early therapeutic goals emphasizing only improvement of the husband-wife relationship will meet with disapproval. The minority families' "present" and "doing" orientation, plus linguistic complexity or limitations in speaking English, require that therapeutic goals be problem focused, structured, realistic, concrete, practical, and readily achievable. Minuchin (1974) affirms that when patterns of change in the family are out of phase with the realities of extrafamilial systems, therapy will fail.

Cultural- and Ethnic-Specific Skills in the Problem-Solving Phase of Family Therapy

By the time the problem-solving stage of therapy has been reached, the therapist has already demonstrated the capacity to be culturally adaptive and to relate in a variety of ways. This ensures that the minority family is afforded the opportunity to respond to their conflictual or problematic experiences in new ways. Changes that take place in family therapy are, in part, a shift or modification of the cultural life strategy of the entire family. This process requires that family members learn to restore, expand, or modify the traditional cultural stress response or problem-solving repertoire.

The therapist introduces the change/modification process for the family by framing the change within a traditional framework or language. Basically, the family is validated in the problem-solving effort. This will form a foundation for adding something new or trying something different in the name of assisting the family in adjusting to their "familial culture" that is in transition. The therapist's new suggestion(s) should be presented as an extension of the family's "old" cultural stress response. The importance of affirming the foundation of what the family already has as the necessary precondition for assimilating and then accommodating a new response constitutes a key principle in therapy with an ethnic minority family during the problem-solving stage.

Skills and techniques used in therapy with ethnic minority clients need to be guided by existing sound theories that are culturally relevant (Ho, 1987). Within the ecological systemic framework, problem-solving skills are derived from two major categories of family therapy theories: structural and communication (Levande, 1976). The Fundamental Interpersonal Relations Orientation (FIRO; Schutz, 1958) framework allows the problem-solving skills of the structural and communication theories of family therapy to be differentially applied to work with ethnic minority families (Ho, 1989).

The FIRO model conceptualizes three fundamental issues that are predominant in all human relatedness. These issues are inclusion, control, and affection (Schutz, 1958). *Inclusion* is defined as the "need to maintain a satisfactory relationship with respect to interaction and association" (p. 19). *Control* is defined as the "need to influence and to have power in relationships with people" (p. 20). *Affection* is defined as the need to "establish and maintain a satisfactory relation with others with respect to love and affection" (p. 20). Schutz concludes, "Generally speaking, inclusion is concerned with the problem of in or out, control with top or bottom, and affection with close or far" (p. 24).

By extending Schutz's FIRO model and theory of family group development, the inclusion issue has to be dealt with first, the control issue second, and affection or intimacy issues last. This order of treatment has great significance and application in working with ethnic minority families. Most ethnic minority Americans do not rely on social or psychological theories to account for behavioral or family difficulties (Lapuz, 1973). Recently arrived Asian, Hispanic, or Black immigrant families and American Indians who left the reservations direct most of their energy simply to adjusting to a completely new environment. Hence the inclusion issue, which centers around membership or family-community interfaces and family subsystem boundaries, generally is the area in which the family is willing to seek or receive help. Initial requests may be for information and referral, advocacy, and other such concrete service as legal aid, child care, or English-language instruction. Only after the inclusion issue has been successfully dealt with can the control and intimacy issues be openly discussed with the family.

Immigrant-American families, characterized by foreign-born parents and their American-born children, often experience cultural and power struggle conflicts. Younger family members are usually more acculturated, Americanized, assertive, individualistic, and independent. Subsystem members such as the wife and husband, parent and child, and siblings may share different values and goals that conflict with those set previously by parents or grandparents. These families usually require help in resolving generational conflicts, communication problems, role clarification, and renegotiation. The immigrant-descent families consisting of second-, third-, or fourth-generation

Table 7.1 Family Therapy Theories, FIRO Issues, Therapeutic Emphases, and Types of Ethnic Minority Families

	Structural Theory	*Communication Theory*	
Theories employed	Ecostructural (Germain/Aponte) Family structure (Minuchin/Bowen)	Strategic (Haley/Madanes)	Humanistic (Satir/Whitaker)
FIRO issues	Inclusion	Control	Affection (intimacy)
Therapeutic emphases	Family environment, membership, boundaries, family size shifts	Power, expectations, roles, rules, decision making	Intimacy, loyalty, friendship
Types of ethnic minority families	Recently arrived immigrant families	Immigrant/ American families	Immigrant/ descendant families

American-born parents and their children seek help more willingly with intimacy issues than the previous two groups.

It is important to stress that though all three FIRO issues are always present in families, the emphasis changes according to the family's degree of acculturation, the family life-cycle stage, and other circumstances. With minority families that experience major additions, the extent to which the control and the intimacy issues can be effectively dealt with depends on whether the inclusion issue has been successfully resolved. Furthermore, the trust that the therapist develops with the minority family will also dictate if the latter is willing to receive help with control or intimacy issues.

In analyzing the specific emphases of major contemporary schools (structure/communication) of family therapy, one finds that all of them tend to focus on one of the family FIRO issues of inclusion, control, or intimacy. Table 7.1 links the major school of family therapy with the FIRO issues with which they are most closely identified and their specific responsiveness to the types of ethnic minority families needing services.

As Table 7.1 indicates, ecostructural (Germain, 1973) and structural (Bowen, 1978; Minuchin, 1974) family therapy focus on issues of family inclusion. Family therapy with a minority family as guided by this conceptualization suggests two levels of intervention: strengthening the boundary-maintaining ability of the family for adaptive purposes, and intervention at the broader societal level to reduce destructive environmental influences upon families (Aponte, 1979; Minuchin, 1974). The communicative framework developed and advanced by Haley (1976) informs the therapist how to help the minority families to resolve control issues in communication, conflict resolution, and decision making. Whitaker's symbolic-experiential (Whitaker & Keith, 1981) and Satir's humanistic approach (Satir, 1972) both inform the therapist what techniques and skills to use to help minority families resolve intimacy issues. The application of techniques and skills derived from structural and communication theories focusing on the FIRO issues is illustrated in the following case study of Suzana.

❀ CASE STUDY
Suzana—Mexican American Student

Suzana, a 10-year-old Mexican American student, was given a final warning by the school principal that unless she improved her social attitude in the classroom and afterschool program, she would not be allowed to continue in school. Suzana and her parents had immigrated to the United States less than 2 years earlier. She spoke limited English and her parents spoke no English at all. When the family first arrived in the United States, they lived with Suzana's uncle, who was a computer programmer. One year later, the uncle got a promotion and moved to another city and had little contact with Suzana's family. Suzana's father was unemployed. Her mother was employed as a garment factory worker. Suzana's parents expressed great disappointment, shame, and resentment toward their daughter's school problem, and her father occasionally administered physical punishment to her. His discipline had been brought to the attention of a court-related agency. By being sympathetic with Suzana, her mother further angered the father who, in turn, displayed greater disapproval of Suzana (daughter-mother triangulation).

When the family was referred to a therapist on the staff of the Transcultural Family Institute, the therapist immediately supported the family by empathizing with them concerning the problems associated with immigration and acculturation (inclusion issue). The therapist's next intervention was to visit the school principal (ecosystem theory: therapist as advocate), who expressed frustration at not being able to communicate with the family, which he perceived as "resistive." The therapist reassured the principal that the parent's lack of response was due mainly to their inability to communicate in the English language and their unfamiliarity with the school system. Given some understanding of the family's inability to adjust to the new environment, the school principal was relieved that the therapist would serve as a liaison between the student, the school, and the family. The principal assured the therapist that he would not expel Suzana as long as this working arrangement continued.

The therapist then interviewed Suzana's father individually twice (individual session was used to affirm the family's hierarchical structure and to provide privacy and confidentiality). The focus of the interview was to assure the man that he was a good father and that he also needed support and help.

With the help of another Mexican American family, the father was able to obtain a part-time job as a gardener (concrete service, person-in-situation focus). The father also was helped to maintain a proper distance from the daughter. When the father asked what he could do to assist his daughter in school, the therapist suggested that he continue to be supportive, accepting, and positive with her. The therapist also worked on inclusion, repairing the parent-child subsystem (structural theory) by suggesting that the father consult with Suzana on matters that concerned her. The father commented, "I forget Suzana is no longer a baby" (control issue: communication theory, Haley).

The therapist also worked on repairing the parental subsystem (structural theory), suggesting to the father that he elicit help from his wife in dealing with their daughter. The intimacy issue (communication theory, Whitaker/Satir) emerged when the father replied that in the future he hoped to consult with the therapist regarding his feelings and relationship with his wife. The therapist responded positively, "Any time you [father] are ready."

The FIRO framework is a useful guide that can clearly help the therapist and the minority family set therapeutic goals and, accordingly, appropriate therapeutic techniques and skills can be selected to meet those goals. Due to the transitional nature and the ethnic background of the family in the preceding illustration, the inclusion issue centered around family-environment needs, then the control issue (father-daughter communication), and finally the intimacy issue (spousal relationship). If the control issue between father and daughter had been the first therapeutic goal, the therapist would have appeared insensitive to the family's ethnic background and acculturation process. It was important that the therapist first establish credibility and trust with the family by resolving the family's inclusion issue. Otherwise, in this case, the father would have resisted any attempt by the therapist to resolve the control issue between the father and the daughter. Likewise, had the therapist focussed on the inclusion issue between the parents at the expense of the family's adaptive immigrational need, the parents would have resisted or terminated therapy immediately. Moreover, if the spousal intimacy issue had been explored prior to resolving the inclusion and control issues, the parents probably would have terminated therapy.

Cultural- and Ethnic-Specific Skills in the Evaluation and Termination Phases of Family Therapy

The ecological framework consists of four major categories: family/environment interface, family structure, family processes, and individual symptoms and/or character traits. This framework is particularly helpful in determining if a specific goal has been accomplished through family therapy. A therapist needs to be cognizant of the unique perspectives of each ethnic minority culture when assessing therapeutic goals relating to dysfunctional patterns of cultural transition or transcultural dysfunctional patterns. The intense interactive subsystem relationship characteristic of a nuclear family in a White middle-class culture should not be used as a yardstick in evaluating the functional structure and transaction of an ethnic minority family. Contrarily, the inclusive extended family framework must be considered when evaluating an ethnic minority family's functioning.

Ethnic minority Americans may not verbally express the progress they make in therapy. They usually display strong feelings of obligation, interdependence, self-control, and fatalism. Their consideration of the therapist's time and effort often causes them hesitancy in engaging in long-term therapy. Hence the therapist may need to maximize his or her observational skills and use other ethnic-sensitive skills in evaluating the family's progress.

At present, evaluating goals and procedures in family therapy is frequently done using standardized terminology and criteria that may not be appropriate or relevant to the case at hand. The abstract terms *mutuality* or *tolerance,* for example, may have different meanings for different individuals and families. It is an internal state that has unique experiential correlates for different people of different ethnic backgrounds. Standardized tests, by their very nature, are not oriented to an individual or family's specific needs but rather are based on global concepts of mental health. Standardized tests do not take into account an individual's cultural and ethnic background or the present family situation and environment.

The major flaw in some current evaluation procedures is that the outcomes of family therapy are not determined by what the family thinks is important. Hence, evaluators who use objective judges or procedure may pronounce the therapy successful even though the client or family still feels dissatisfied or unchanged. The client's or family's own perception of positive change and the principle of accountability are vital factors. Outcome satisfaction is ultimately assessed by whether the family feels that they are a more functioning family system.

The Practice Outcome Inventory (POI; Ho, 1976a) as an evaluative instrument for family therapy is distinguished by the following features:

1. It considers the family's perceptions, subjectivity, and active involvement.
2. It considers the family's cultural and ethnic background, environmental and social conditions, current needs, and unique goals.
3. It uses terminology that is concrete and behaviorally anchored to ensure that ethnic minority families are clear about their cultural and experiential definitions.
4. It generally facilitates the family therapy process.

The procedure for administering the POI consists essentially of three parts: (a) the family's listing of descriptors (situational problems, disabling behavior, dysfunctional family interactions, environmental circumstances) that they consider important; (b) the family's ranking of the relative importance of such descriptors; and (c) the family's rating of how characteristic these descriptors are of themselves. The following steps can serve as a guide for therapists to follow when using the POI, which is illustrated in Table 7.2.

1. Family Specification of Descriptors. This usually takes place during the first few sessions. A family's identification of characteristics that they deem most important begins the process of mutual goal formation. Completion of the POI early in the therapeutic process provides a baseline from which to make comparisons later in the therapy. Obviously, the ability of the family to name descriptors openly and honestly depends on the trusting rapport created by the therapist. To help the family list important characteristics, the therapist might say, for example, "Please tell me what you would like to see changed in your family. Share with me those family relationship qualities that matter most to you, whether or not your family possesses them now." Should a family experience reluctance or difficulty in making the list, the therapist may encourage the family to complete the initial list at home and then discuss and expand on it during the next therapy session.

2. Therapist's Specification of Behavioral Anchors for Each Descriptor. If the family says that harmony in the family is important, for example, the therapist asks what this means in terms of actual behavior. The family might say that it is a means of resolving differences without yelling or hitting. Such behavioral anchors provide both the family and the therapist with clear goals and also serve as points of reference at later evaluation periods.

3. Family Ranking of Each Descriptor. If a family's descriptors list consists of ten items, the item which the family considers most important ranks 10 and that of least importance ranks 1. This method of scoring is used so that the total score is a reflection of the most important items.

4. Family Self-Rating on Each of the Descriptors. The possible ratings are –5 (totally dissatisfied with level of functioning on this dimension (e.g., physical violence), –4, –3, –2, –1, 0, 1, 2, 3, 4, and 5 (completely satisfied with level of functioning on this dimension, e.g., reaching consensus).

5. Scoring. For each of the ten items, the rank ordering is multiplied by the family self-rating to obtain scores that reflect the family's perceptions. For instance, if open communication is ranked 8 and the self-rating is –5, then the score on that item is –40 ($8 \times -5 = -40$). The scores are then added to yield one total score indicating the family's present overall self-evaluation. Items of most importance carry the most weight. For a 10-item list, the total score can range from –275 to 275. Accordingly, for a 9-item list, the total score will range from –225 to 225.

6. *A Working Contract.* The therapist requests the family to choose the item or items on which they will work. Then expectations, including responsibilities and functions on the part of both the family and the therapist, are explicated in a contract. Agreement on a target time for the completion of each item will also expedite the treatment as well as future evaluations. The following case example illustrating the use of POI in therapy with a Black family.

✿ CASE STUDY
Jimmy—Afro-American Boy

Jimmy, a 13-year-old Afro-American boy, was brought to the Youth Service Agency after he had vandalized several candy machines in the neighborhood laundromat. Jimmy is an only child whose parents were divorced 1 year ago. His father remarried recently and visits him regularly on weekends. His mother remarried 6 months ago but had to divorce her second husband, who was an alcoholic. In order to supplement the family income, his mother reluctantly took a job as a waitress in a neighborhood fast-food restaurant.

The therapist interviewed Jimmy and his mother separately at the first meeting, then together thereafter. They began the POI at the second interview and continued it at the third to give Jimmy and his mother time to arrive at some consensus on the POI items. They decided to use only five descriptors because they felt that more behavioral anchors for certain descriptors were necessary to accurately monitor their progress.

The second (middle therapy phase) inventory took place 5 weeks later, and substantial change was noted (see Table 7.2).

However, only limited progress was made regarding their desire to "get along better with Jimmy's father." Upon mutual exploration of the reasons for such limited progress, the family accepted the therapist's suggestion to include Jimmy's father in the next three sessions. During these sessions, both the nurturing role and the discipline role of Jimmy's mother were better defined. In the presence of Jimmy's father, a great deal of ambivalence and role confusion emerged and were discussed and clarified. These three sessions were directly responsible for Jimmy "getting along" and "communicating better" with his mother (end phase measurement). The total treatment period covered 13 sessions on a weekly basis.

Finally, the termination process with ethnic minority families should consider the ethnic minority family's concept of time and space in a relationship. Some families may never want to end a good relationship and they learn to respect and love the therapist as a member of their family. It is important that a therapist be comfortable with this element of cultural and human inclusiveness and make termination a natural and gradual process.

Table 7.2 Use of the Practice Outcome Inventory with Family

| | | | Treatment Phases | | | | | | | | |
| | | | Pre | | Middle | | End | | Follow-Up | | |
Descriptor	Behavioral Anchor	Rank	Rating	Score	Rating	Score	Rating	Score	New Rank	Rating	Score
Stop vandalism	No vandalism	10	-5	-50	5	50	5	50	1	5	50
Get along with each other	Mother spends more time with J	9	-4	-36	1	9	-2	18	2	2	18
	Mother and J do more together	8	-4	-32	1	8	2	16	7	3	24
	J does more household chores	7	-4	-28	2	14	2	14	6	1	7
	J acts less rebellious toward mother	6	-5	-30	-1	-6	2	12	8	1	6
Better communication	More honest discussions	5	-4	-20	1	5	2	10	9	2	10
	Make decisions together	4	-5	-20	1	4	1	4	10	1	4
Get along with J's father	Have discussions together	3	-5	-15	-3	-9	1	3	5	2	6
Progress in school	Raise grades	2	-5	-8	-3	-6	1	2	3	3	6
	Decrease absences	1	-4	-4	-1	-1	-1	-1	4	0	0
Total score				-245		+68		+128			+131

8

Cultural-Specific Methods, Techniques, and Skills in Group Therapy

Group Therapy and Ethnic Minority Cultures

Ethnic minority culture traditionally has relied on a variety of group activities to bring families, clans, and tribal groups together for social, cultural, and religious activities. Minority children's growth and developmental milestones are often celebrated with group activities involving the extended family and clan. Special seasons of the year or events related to planting and harvesting also are group celebrations with games, dances, music, contests, and socializing. In view of the minority culture's collectivist or "groupism" orientation (Spiegel, 1971), minority children are probably more capable of becoming cohesive in a group than White children who come from an individualistic culture (Yamaguchi, 1986). Minority clients may, however, initially experience difficulty in talking about personal and family problems in a group setting and in front of a stranger who is the group therapist. However, group interaction and group therapy, if properly provided, may have advantages that individual and family therapy do not.

Ethnic minority children who value interdependence and cooperation can gain much from the power and strength of collective group feedback. In a cohesive group atmosphere, members can be very supportive of one another in patterns resembling the family situation. Like family members, they will work together to solve one another's problems. If the group consists of diverse racial and ethnic memberships, group members can learn additional communication styles and skills for expressiveness and problem solving (McKinley, 1991). Seeing other lifestyles can teach an ethnic minority child the flexibility offered by different norms, therefore providing more ways of solving a problem.

The group atmosphere can sometimes be less threatening than that of individual therapy. Rather than being constantly pressured to talk, as in individual therapy, the minority child in group therapy can choose when to interact. In individual therapy, the pressure of attention given exclusively to the child may be an inhibiting factor. In group settings, the minority child may feel he is sometimes a helper, instead of always a receiver, as in individual therapy. Additionally, some of the socially oriented problems that minority children have, such as appropriate behavior in bicultural settings, self-image, or assertion problems, can be worked on and reality-tested in the group. Psychoeducational groups are especially appropriate for minority delinquent youth, school dropouts, and other behavioral problems that require a comprehensive treatment program that includes counseling, remedial education, and vocational training (Franklin, 1982). The traditional American Indian group therapeutic practices of "sweat lodge" and "talking circle" have also been found beneficial to youth who are in need of spiritual purification and affirmation of tribal identity (Manson, Walker, & Kirlaham, 1987).

Rationale and Criteria for Group Therapy

Group therapy as a treatment modality refers to an alliance of children or youth who are brought together to work on a common task, to use the group experience for support and mutual aid, for ethnic identity affirmation, for acculturation, for educational purposes, or to affect personality change. Hence, group therapeutic treatment involves different types of groups that have distinctive, though sometimes overlapping, goals. Goals range from those that are ethically and psychologically supportive to those that are educational and traditionally therapeutic.

When Group Therapy is Indicated or Contraindicated

The decision to recommend a minority child or youth for group therapy should be based upon a thorough individualized assessment. The following questions should be considered in selecting group therapy for a minority child or youth:

1. What is the nature of the minority child's problem?
2. What type of group therapy is indicated?
3. Should the approach be primary or auxiliary?
4. When in the treatment process should group therapy be introduced?
5. Can the youth benefit from an ethnically homogeneous or heterogeneous group?
6. Does the minority youth possess adequate motivation and English-language skills to interact in a group?

Group therapy can be an especially effective modality for minority youth experiencing problems with the following:

1. Acculturation process
2. Ethnic awareness and identity
3. Bicultural socialization skills
4. Feelings of isolation and loneliness
5. Poor ego functioning in key areas such as impulse control

Some minority youth will be fearful of exposure in groups where self-disclosure of intimate information related to self and family is required or encouraged. Some youth may lack the impulse control to tolerate the provocation and stirring up of intense feelings. The following criteria are suggested to help identify and exclude minority youth who may *not* benefit from group therapy (Yalom, 1985):

1. Lack of motivation
2. Inadequate English-language skills to participate in an ethnically heterogeneous group

3. Poor impulse control to a degree that violent behavior could occur in the group
4. An immature ego structure that restricts ability to hear other group members
5. Excessive demands for the therapist's total attention
6. Parental objections to group therapy (P. Lee, Juan, & Hom, 1984)

Goals of Group Therapy

Therapeutic goals of group therapy with minority youth include the following:

1. Educational focus that includes English conversational group (Tannenbaum, 1991)
2. Ethnic awareness and identity (Edwards & Edwards, 1984; P. Lee et al., 1984)
3. Bicultural social skill development (Bilides, 1991)
4. Activity and art therapy (Yamamoto & Yap, 1984)
5. Treatment of health and mental health problems (McKinley, 1991)

Practical Considerations for the Pregroup Phase

Despite a wealth of group-work literature attesting to the significance of race and ethnicity in the therapeutic encounter, most practitioners who begin group therapy with ethnic minority children are probably ill prepared to do so. There is perhaps no topic of discussion that takes place in a multiracial or multiethnic gathering of any sort that heightens anxiety levels more than a discussion of race and ethnicity itself; indeed, even when not introduced and highlighted, race and ethnicity is always an issue. It is a salient interpersonal factor having great significance for both group members and leaders. If race and ethnicity are not properly considered and integrated, even a well-conceptualized therapy group will not be able to actualize its goal and, in some cases, may produce unintentional damages to its group members. The following case study of a therapy group illustrates how a therapy group can affect minority group members.

✿ CASE STUDY
A Therapy Group

A therapy group consisted of one female and two male adolescent White students, two Blacks male students, two Hispanic female students, and one male Asian American student. The group discussed how to improve poor peer relationships. While different ethnic minority students were paired together according to racial lines, the White therapist found herself sitting next to the Asian student. As soon as the session started, the Black students and the Hispanic students were calling each other ethnic names and exchanging racial slurs. When these students ran out of words to insult each other, they turned to the Asian student, calling him the "Mommy's [therapist's] boy." While the group therapist was trying to control the unruly behaviors of the acting-out students, the Asian American student burst into tears and abruptly left the group. The same Asian student was reported absent from school for the next week. At the second week's group session, the therapist was given a notice by the school attendance officer informing her that the Asian American student had transferred to another school.

A multitude of problems negatively affected the minority children in this group. In addition to the group therapist's inability to provide proper structure and guidelines for the group, there are some critical issues related to race and ethnicity in the groups that the therapist failed to master. Such critical issues and their affects on the subsequent group process and group outcome will be detailed in the following discussions.

Selection of Candidates for Groups

Who should be included in group therapy depends on the stated purpose of the group. Include persons whose problem(s) will be aided by the group's purpose. If the focus of the group is on educational achievement or on therapeutic gains, group cohesiveness and intense interaction are desired. Membership selection does not need a stringent and restrictive criteria. Contrarily, if this is a therapeutic group for problem solving and personality change, group variables such as age, gender, ethnicity, acculturation level, motivation for participation in the group, ability for self-expression, and group size can be very significant factors. This will require careful planning and strategic preparation in the selection of group members. Similarly, if the purpose of the group is to enhance racial and ethnic awareness and identify, homogeneity should be a primary consideration for selecting group members.

The optimal size of the treatment group should be between six and eight members. This size is large enough to allow for interactions, but small enough to enable individual needs to be met. The children should be the same gender and about the same age, because latency-age children generally relate well to youngsters of their own gender. Adolescent groups can include both genders. However, because minority group children, especially Asian Americans, Hispanic Americans, and American Indians, normally are discouraged from discussing sexuality issues in public, their free participation in a gender-mixed group should not be expected, especially at the beginning stage of group therapy.

The "curative factors" (Yalom, 1985), effectiveness, and power of a group depend to a large degree on who participates. The "traditionalist" ethnic minority youth who has recently arrived in the United States may find group interaction intimidating, confusing and, therefore, nonproductive. American-born ethnic minority children are more likely to display acculturated behaviors reflecting their socialization in the United States and, therefore, may find group interaction more responsive to their needs. Although American-born minority youth may be prospective candidates for a group requiring more intensive interaction, the nonnative minority youth can take advantage of a concrete task group or an educational group focusing more on information giving and less on the open exchange of personal opinions and feelings (Tannenbaum, 1991).

Minority Children's Conceptions of Groups

Purpose usually denotes the specific reason(s) for which the group is formed and expresses the type of goals that the group will try to help its members meet. This group purpose or objective needs to be carefully phrased in a culturally correct manner. Traditional group therapy may imply individual failure or family dysfunctioning and can alienate prospective ethnic minority group members or cause them to terminate prematurely. Minority children and their families generally find it difficult to admit they have emotional or psychological difficulties, because such problems arouse considerable shame and a sense of having failed one's family. They will respond more favorably if they perceive the group's purpose as an obligatory means to meet their responsibilities, such as doing well academically in school or improving behavior at home. Their acceptance of such group purposes is consistent with their traditional cultural collectivism and their social explanation for disorienting events, such as immigration or loss of job or income (Green, 1982). This type of explanation allows the individual to see himself or herself as a victim of some unfortunate but uncontrollable events, a result of nonpersonal determinants.

Minority Children's Expected Behavior in a Group

A group therapist should be cognizant of how an ethnic minority child may interact in a group. For a group member to benefit from group therapy, he or she usually believes in the "therapeutic" process characterized by the child's acceptance of the problem and the need and motivation for change (Garvin, 1981). Individual group members also believe that long-range goal setting and the process of "working through" problems are essential to correct past defective experiences or maladaptive behavior. Verbal, intimate, emotional, self-disclosing, and behavioral feedback are seen as central to the change process (Yalom, 1985).

In contrast, ethnic minority children in group therapy may find it difficult to accept the fact that they have problems or they may feel they have not tried hard enough to overcome their problems. Language difficulty or nonstandard English usage and their native cultural upbringings, as well as just living day-to-day in a racist society, cause many ethnic minority children to refrain from directly confronting other group members. These children are frequently taught that it is rude to put people on the spot. Free participation and the exchange of opinions in a group may contradict the minority cultural values of humility and modesty. "Don't be a showoff or engage in any behavior that smacks of being a braggart" is a common minority admonition. It is directly responsible for ethnic minority children assuming silent member roles in a group.

The appropriate pacing of self-disclosure and the management of communication are a delicate process in working with ethnic minority children in a group. Personal disclosure of problems is antithetical to the cultural values of preserving face (Asian American) and dignity (Hispanic American) and keeping one's troubles contained within the family. In contrast to other ethnic minority groups, Black youth from urban areas may appear to be overly verbose in a group. Such behavior is often a compensation for their victimized powerless role in their environment (Gibbs, 1989).

In a racially heterogeneous group, ethnic minority children were noted for specific, racially related behavioral patterns (Bilides, 1991). Such groups become microcosms of struggles and prejudices generally played out in larger societal contexts. Different racial-group children will seat themselves according to race. A student's dropout rate is expected to be high if he or she happens to be the only representative of a particular racial group. Uniting against a therapist from a different racial group sometimes helps group members break antibicultural patterns.

Along with the color hierarchy, where light color is experienced as superior to dark color, different ethnic groups within each racial group also exhibit different behavioral characteristics. For example, foreign-born Blacks (Caribbean Islands and Africa) who have assimilation problems are seen by Black Americans (born in America) as uncouth, pushy, or simply weird. For Hispanic children, speaking Spanish is not just an expression of identity but is used in groups to form alliances with some members and to exclude others. Among other topics, class issues appear to be most difficult for racially mixed group members to discuss and to resolve.

Minority Children's Expectations of the Therapist in Group Therapy

For political and philosophical, as well as personal, reasons, minority children are known to resist nonminority therapists (Sattler, 1977). Much of this resistance is based upon their perception that the White therapist does not have sufficient knowledge about them as minorities. A minority therapist leading a racially heterogeneous group may be ascribed a lower social status not only by White children but also by the minority children (M. Davis et al., 1974). It is important that a therapist be aware of such initial barriers based on racial identity. The therapist may need to address such an issue with the group early on to establish ascribed credibility with the group. If credibility cannot be established, the group will likely terminate prematurely (S. Sue & Zane, 1987).

Ethnic minority children and youth who have had no previous experience with group therapy may not understand the role of a group therapist and may confuse the therapist with a physician. Such children will regard the group therapist as the knowledgeable expert who will guide them in the proper course of action. Hence, the group therapist is seen as an authority figure and is respected as such. The children expect that the authority figure will be more directive than passive (McKinley, 1991). Being directive does not mean that the therapist should tell the children how to live their lives. It does involve directing the process of the group session. When minority children are unfamiliar with group therapy and generally uncomfortable speaking in public, they may need an invitation to speak. The therapist needs to be directive at first to set the tone for the children in the group. The therapist can explain that changes in behavioral interaction are permitted and safe, and sometimes necessary, in order to solve problems. A therapist should not prejudge that because a child in a group is not talking that the child is not paying attention. A child may in fact be paying avid attention to the group, but may be censoring his or her own input. Watching for subtle changes in nonverbal communication is crucial to understanding the dynamics of the group.

A group therapist needs to convene an air of confidence. When asked, the therapist should not hesitate to disclose personal educational background and work experience. This is particularly true if the group therapist is a young female who conducts groups with Asian American or Hispanic American children. The traditional hierarchical structure of these two groups favor aged or experienced males. Minority children need to be assured that their therapist is more powerful than their illness or problems and will "cure" them with competence and know-how.

Some minority children, due to curiosity, and friendliness common in collectivist cultures, may ask the therapist many personal questions about family background, marital status, number of children, and so on. The therapist will need to feel comfortable about answering personal questions in order to gain the children's trust and to establish rapport. Once trust and rapport with the therapist is established, some children may form a dependency on the therapist. It would be a mistake to assume that such overtures or apparent dependency patterns necessarily indicate transference and that such behavior should be discouraged or avoided. Given the interpersonal complexity of ethnic minority cultures, forming relationships that mirror those found in family groups or in friendship networks may be helpful to the children as a means of guiding the interpersonal process with the therapist (Tannenbaum, 1991).

Reciprocity and obligation are strongly emphasized in ethnic minority cultures. Some minority children may consider keeping appointments or following directives as doing something for the therapist in return for the therapist's concern. The therapist should neither condemn nor confront such behavior but capitalize on it to help the children resolve their problems.

Ethnic minorities handle sexuality generally with modesty and closeness. Physical contact is not taken as casually as it is in mainstream American society, especially heterosexual contact. Among different minority groups, with the possible exception of the Hispanic American group, lines of distinction are drawn between private and public shows of physical affection. The group therapist must be conscious of when and with whom to have such contact, especially in regard to group members of the opposite sex.

Homogeneous Versus
Heterogeneous Group Composition

For group therapy with ethnic minority children, the issue of group composition is very important. Race and ethnicity always play important roles in the group process and in the attainment of group goals. Unfortunately, literature in this area is lacking. The question "should the group be racially and ethnically homogeneous or racially and ethnically heterogeneous?" can best be answered by the stated purpose or goal of the group. If the goal of the group is to enhance ethnic identity of the group members, the group should be homogeneous in membership. Such groups are composed under the assumption that racially similar children will be more attracted to each other and more likely to engage in greater in-depth disclosures about themselves. Contrarily, if the goal of the group is to reduce racial prejudice, group members' racial and ethnic backgrounds should be different. The underlying assumption of such a heterogeneous group composition is that intergroup strife is best reduced by experiencing or engaging in positive interracial contact.

Most group therapists probably lead groups that have neither ethnic identity enhancement nor the reduction of racial tensions as their primary purpose. The question confronting the group therapist becomes what group composition is optimal when race, per se, is unrelated to the group's purpose. L. Davis' (1980) study indicates that Blacks prefer a racially mixed group in which they are approximately half of the population. In contrast, Whites, under similar conditions, appear to prefer group compositions in which Blacks are approximately 20% or less of total group membership. Such clear differences in racial preference for group composition have the potential to lead to group-member dissatisfaction, discomfort, and conflict.

In addition to color differences and potential power conflicts, verbal communication styles of ethnic minority children should be considered when assessing group composition. Asian, American Indian, and Hispanic American children are taught not to interrupt and not to push to make their point. Some minority children may take longer to answer a question. In a group of very verbose, articulate, and aggressive White youth, the minority youth may be hesitant to speak up. Confrontation inevitably occurs at some point in a problem-solving group. Minority youth are unaccustomed to such interaction and may not know what to say.

In view of minority children's cultural characteristics that discourage admission of failure and personal problems, free expression and confrontation, heterogeneous grouping involving various subgroupings should be avoided (Ho, 1984). Having to communicate in English adds an additional stress. Whenever possible minorities of a particular nationality and geographical location should be grouped together. Chinese students from Hong Kong should be grouped separately from Chinese from Taiwan or American-born Chinese. The same applies to Hispanic children from Mexico, Cuba, Puerto Rico, and other Latin American groups; foreign Blacks from native Blacks; and American Indian children from different tribes. The clear need for such categorical groupings is commonality in subculture and language efficiency essential for the group progress and the achievement of group goals. If all members of the group fluently speak the same dialect or the English language, a heterogeneous grouping with various subgroups from the same country or nationality is acceptable.

Most group therapists who work with minority children may not have sufficient numbers of children or youth from one homogenous setting. The multiethnic and multicultural diversity of contemporary America suggests that group therapy is more likely to be multiethnic than single-ethnic based. It is imperative that therapists be aware that haphazard heterogeneous groupings can produce disastrous results, hurting instead of helping the minority children.

If a heterogenous composition appears to be most feasible and practical in group therapy with minority youth, the therapist needs to attempt to avoid large racial or ethnic imbalances. Being "one of a kind" in a group is a difficult position to occupy, as it has the tendency to put too much pressure on the "different" member to represent and defend a given group (L. Davis, 1980).

Lastly, a therapist, when evaluating group composition for therapy with minority youth, should consider gender and age issues because these can enhance or retard the group process. Because some ethnic cultures discourage open discussion of sexuality, ethnic minority children may feel uncomfortable being confronted by group members of the opposite sex. This is particularly true when the children are at the latency age. As they become adolescents, their interest in the opposite sex may entice them to attend and help sustain their interest in group therapy (McKinley, 1991).

Culturally Relevant Group Structure

The vertical and hierarchical role structure that forms an ethnic minority child's early relationship patterns with others also influences how he or she will interact in group therapy. The group's basic structure should clearly define the therapist in a leadership role. If a group therapist fails to assume a leadership role, especially at the beginning stage of therapy, a high dropout rate among group members is to be expected. Cultural traits such as discipline, deference, and loyalty toward an authority figure (therapist) generally have a positive effect on ethnic minority children, especially Asian Americans, American Indians, and Hispanic Americans, and enhance their ability to function as strong group members. Similarly, these three minority group cultures highly value restraint in expressing strong feelings or overt behaviors that may have sexual overtones. A group therapy structure that places great value on group catharsis, ventilation, and overt expressions of sexuality may contradict the values of these ethnic groups and cause premature termination of group participation. Contrarily, urban Blacks, who pride themselves on their ability to engage in heated boisterous confrontations, may be very vocal in group therapy (Franklin, 1982; Ridley, 1984). Additionally, the Black youth's self-flattering remarks should be taken lightly and viewed as jestful behavior. A Black youth's confrontative style sometimes can be interpreted as reflective feelings of powerlessness and resistance to authority, which the group therapist represents. At other times, the Black youth's confrontations can be used to test the validity of their point of view. The different communicative styles of various ethnic minorities presents an added challenge to a group therapist whose task is to select interventive strategies that are culturally relevant and responsive. When the group therapy is comprised of several ethnicities, the group therapist must provide a structure that allows the verbally active groups (e.g., Whites and Blacks) to express themselves, but at the same time moves the group to more structured tasks congruent with other minority children's expectations (e.g., Asians and Indians).

Ethnic minority children's expectations of a vertical group structure in which the therapist assumes a leadership role should not be misconstrued as their unresponsiveness to the mutual aid system concept. The key issue is how, on the part of the therapist, to facilitate the members in helping one another to achieve their individual and collective goals. The group therapist needs to assume a more direct and active role, especially at the beginning phase of treatment. As the group progresses, members feel more secure and comfortable with each other, realizing each has strengths to aid others in solving problems, rather than each depending solely on the group therapist. Only then can a more egalitarian interactive relationship be facilitated to maximize fully the usefulness of the group as a problem-solving modality.

Preparing Minority Children for the Group

The idea that members who are prepared for the group experience are more likely to benefit from it is receiving increased support (McKinley, 1991; Yalom, 1985). Preparation is particularly essential for ethnic minority children who have had no prior experience in a problem-solving group. To prepare an ethnic minority child for the group, the therapist needs to perform the following functions:

1. Describe to the child in concrete terms how a group can be used for support, ethnic identity affirmation, learning social skills, behavioral change, and problem solving. If it is feasible, the therapist can play a portion of a video tape highlighting the value and application of the group process.
2. Explain to the child that the group worker's role is different from that of a physician and describe some of the specific activities the therapist will perform in the group.
3. Point out to the child the importance of honest interpersonal exploration, including open expression and disclosure of inner feelings for developmental growth and for problem solving. It is vital that the group therapist solicit feedback from the child at this time and explain carefully to the child that discomfort and uneasy feelings are experienced by all members, especially at the first few sessions.
4. Share with the child that fear and discouragement are common feelings experienced by group members, and that problem solving is a gradual process that takes time and endurance.
5. Share with the child that the therapist is mindful of the anxiety and discomfort the child may experience and that the child can always choose not to be an active participant, such as being on the "hot seat" or the focal point of group discussion. Further, the child can always count on the therapist's support during moments of uncertainty and stress.
6. Assure the child that everything that transpires in the group will be confidential.

Because successful engagement of the child into the group and the successful utilization of the group process for personal change ultimately is dependent upon the development of a trusting relationship between the child, the child's family, and the group therapist, it is important that at this time the group therapist also engage the child's significant others. They too may have no previous knowledge of what group therapy is about. Should the child's participation in group therapy not be endorsed by the family, it is doubtful how much help the child can derive from the group. Considering the importance of the family in most ethnic minority cultures, it is imperative that the family support the group therapy effort. Otherwise, a minority child will not disclose intimate personal or family secrets that may alienate him or her from the family. Further, the level of help the child can expect from group therapy is related to how much the child continues to internalize his or her role within the family structure as a significant part of the child's identity. The group therapist needs to be accepted by the child's parents as a "member" of the extended family. Otherwise, the benefit derived from pregroup orientation may be useless or short-lived at best.

Considering how unfamiliar ethnic minority children and their families are with group therapy, properly preparing them prior to their participating in a group is an essential step and one a group therapist should pay particular attention to. Careful and strategic preparation will help the therapist establish credibility with minority children, and it will also help to reduce the dropout rate. At the same time it can facilitate and maximize future group processes. When all the pregroup tasks have been completed, the therapist can proceed to the group-interaction phase.

Practical Considerations for the Group-Interaction Phase

Leadership Style and Role of the Therapist

There is now sufficient evidence to suggest that certain therapist interactive styles may be more relevant to work with ethnic minority children in group therapy. Minority children's preferred interactive styles differ from those of middle-class Whites. These differences in leadership style are classified into four behavioral areas: respect, formality, concreteness, and activity.

Respect. Minority children growing up in their native culture and "internal environment" feel proud of their culture. They feel disrespect when they interact with the mainstream society, which often informs them that their native culture is "strange," "weird," and "inferior." Minority children's sensitivity to respect is especially keen when they are a member of the heterogeneous racial group and the group therapist is a member of the dominant society.

To convey respect, a group therapist needs to pay attention to interpersonal grace with warm expressions of acceptance, both verbally and nonverbally. The therapist can do this, for instance, by offering something to drink, suggesting the child remove his/her coat for comfort, or indicating a more comfortable chair. Such expressions serve to convey genuine concern and can add greatly to beginning and maintaining a positive relationship (Green, 1982).

To convey respect to minority children especially during the beginning phase of the group, the therapist should avoid constant direct eye contact with them. Because all minority children place a high value on what others think of them, the therapist should make a special effort to help the children avoid disgracing themselves in front of the group. For instance, prior to asking a child in front of the group if he or she has successfully completed a contracted task or home assignment, the therapist needs to be sure that a negative answer will not make the child feel disgraced. In addition, whatever the therapist can do to enhance the child's acceptance by the group will be reciprocated by the minority child who views externally derived evaluations as a part of one's system of self (Chestang, 1984; D. Johnson & Walker, 1987; Norbeck & De Vos, 1972).

Formality. To be formal and conventional is another leadership style that a group therapist needs to pay close attention to when working with minority children and their families. The group therapist should address the children's parents by their last name. If the minority client explicitly asks to be called by his or her first name, this request should be granted. Formality, although in some ways similar to respect, is subtly different. Although mainstream society may value informality over formality as a form of acceptable interaction, many minority cultures place great importance on formal interaction, especially when the minority person is unsure whether the therapist is to be trusted. To be formal in initial interactions with the minority children in a group, the therapist needs to establish a relationship with the group members in a manner that clearly places him or her in a leadership role. The leader that fails to establish a clear "leadership role" can expect a high dropout rate from the group members (S. Sue & Zane, 1987).

Concreteness. Minority children's need for concreteness may result partly from their stressful environment, which at times deprives them of such basic needs as shelter and food. Their young developmental age and struggle to master bilingualism cause many minority children to relate poorly to philosophical discussions and therapeutic strategies that are abstract and unclear. Minority children's responsiveness to concreteness does not mean that they are unresponsive or cannot be benefited by insight-oriented therapy. It simply means that a therapist's interactive style and strategies need to be specific, direct, and congruent with the minority child's ethnic reality and cognitive and language development (Tylim, 1982).

> ✿ CASE STUDY
> A Puerto Rican Student
>
> In a heterogeneous racial adolescent group, a Puerto Rican
> student philosophically and metaphorically said that she wished
> she could be a bird. Realizing this particular student's personal
> struggles with her family, pregnancy, and school and the overall
> overwhelming concern of the group, who could relate to this
> student's concern, the therapist "concretized" by asking the stu-
> dent to elaborate on her wish. The student replied that if she
> were a bird, she would fly away. The therapist further concret-
> ized by asking what sort of worries she would wish to leave be-
> hind. The student replied, "Everything—school, parents, getting
> a job, boyfriend, and the baby."

Activity. The group therapist must also consider the minority
children's responsiveness to active-interactive styles, especially at
the beginning phase of group therapy. Laid-back, passive, nondirec-
tive, and noninvolved therapeutic styles are incongruent with most
ethnic minority group styles and usually fail to accomplish "achieved
credibility" with the minority children. The extent to which a group
therapist needs to be active is mediated by such factors as the age of
group members, the nature of their problems, and the treatment
phase of the group.

Generally, at the beginning (testing) phase and the ending (termination) phase, a group therapist needs to be more active. At the beginning when members are testing out each other and the therapist
for trust and security, the therapist should take an active leadership
role to assist the group in achieving cohesiveness. At the termination
phase, a minority group member's deference to an authority figure
(therapist) may inhibit the open expression of cooperation, anxiety,
and other intimate feelings related to self and to other group members. The therapist needs to be active here to elicit such feelings and
expressions that are related to the reason they joined the group.

Hence, a therapist who is overly active can stifle group process,
but if he or she is not active enough, it can cause a high dropout rate
and a lack of group cohesiveness essential for problem solving and
personal change.

Structured Short-Term Concrete Goals

In work with ethnic minority children in groups, it has been found that they do not respond well to loosely targeted and abstract long-term goals, which they find incomprehensible, impractical, and unreachable. Instead, they prefer structured short-term goals with clear and concrete objectives (Edwards & Edwards, 1984; Inclan, 1985). A group therapist should not rule out the possibility, however, that some ethnic minority children, especially those who are born in this country or are highly acculturated, may respond well to highly personalized therapy focused on emotional areas. Recipients of the therapeutic work should be carefully selected, and it should not be attempted without a strong trusting relationship.

Due to the being-in-becoming cultural orientation of some ethnic minority children, especially American Indians and Hispanic Americans (Ho, 1987), a group therapist may find these clients reluctant in setting goals or in planning particular activities or interventions to achieve goals. Those children who come from traditional backgrounds or tribal groups have been taught that to plan for or count on something in the future may actually deter its occurrence (Edwards & Edwards, 1984). A group therapist should not interpret such reluctance as client resistance. Instead, attentive and respectful listening of the children's concerns about rigid goal setting and the group therapist's logical explanation for goal settings will go a long way to offsetting the minority children's cultural taboo for this task.

Culturally Relevant and Strength-Focused
Skills and Techniques in Problem Solving

In ethnic minority collectivist cultures, authority figures, such as parents and teachers, are honored and never openly challenged or criticized by children. Children are not allowed to show disrespect, disobey, raise their voices, or answer back. Accordingly, these ethnic minority children generally will expect the therapist, who is also an authority figure in a group, to be active and directive. Wishing to be respectful, the minority children in a group setting may adopt a passive dependent attitude, stay silent as much as possible, and avoid eye contact. A therapist needs to explain to the group that appropriate group interaction requires each to speak freely and openly. If the behavior of the group remains silent, the therapist may look down at the floor or away from the member, thus forcing the group members to look for the gaze and response of others in the group. The idea is to encourage the members to talk directly and openly to one another. Ho (1976b) describes an interaction in which the many silences of an Asian American group were broken when one group member ventured forth to talk about how much silence bothered him. The interaction was an important turning point for the group.

The ethnic minority children's strong sense of obligation can also be capitalized on in group therapy. The therapist's warm acceptance of the children can make them feel they should be mutually accepting of the therapist. The therapist can use the children's feelings of obligation to return favors or to challenge them to follow instructions or directives and to help with the group. The therapist can ask the children to assist other members who need help. Such concrete services can include making physical arrangements for group meetings and preparing drinks for the group. By providing the group therapist and the group such concrete services, the children's altruistic needs are met.

Ethnic minority children also value loyalties, including the loyalty that develops among group members and the therapist. This loyalty can be capitalized on to encourage regular group attendance and foster group cohesiveness.

In view of minority youth's sensitivity toward others, confrontative techniques, generally recognized as essential tools for unmasking psychological defense and resistance, should be used with caution. Minority youth highly value what others think of them and usually take confrontation and criticism as a personal attack, an unacceptable insult, and an interpersonal rejection. If a minority youth needs to be confronted about their impasse or persistent resistance responsible for their dysfunctional behavior, the therapist should refrain from a direct confrontation with the youth. Moreover, the therapist should stop others in the group from directly attacking the youth. Instead, the therapist can use an "indirect" means to help clients encounter their problems.

For instance, if a youth continues in a work setting to defy his employer in a passive-aggressive manner, the therapist should help the youth recognize the difficulty by commenting, "I wonder what others [outside the group] will say about 'our' behavior if they learn what 'we' did." Without directly assigning the youth a specific directive for improving relationship with others, the therapist may endorse such behavior and get the group to endorse it also. For example, the therapist can remark, "I might politely let my employer know that somehow I see the same thing differently than he does." The youth usually is perceptive and will test new directives or behavior. By reporting the success of a new behavior to the group, the youth gets an opportunity to be reaffirmed by others in the group.

Like all adolescents, minority youth generally have difficulty in understanding the effects of their behavior on others. Moreover, some Hispanic and Black youth, especially in urban settings, have a history of conflict with authority figures. These youth may appear unusually resistant, sullen, or hostile in the early sessions, especially because most of them have been referred by schools or social agencies. To overcome this initial resistance and to establish a trusting relationship, the therapist needs to be active, outgoing, directive, and open, encouraging the youth to discuss their anger and ambivalent feelings about being referred for therapy, fears about being labeled "weird" or "crazy" by their peers, and their reluctance to reveal their true feelings and concerns to the group.

If the therapist is of a different race than the rest of the group members, the therapist should also encourage group members to express their feelings relative to racial differences. By showing sensitivity to these issues the therapist can convey to group members that he or she understands their ethnic and situational realities. Further, the group members may realize that the therapist is real, sincere, and receptive to the meaningful discussions that are of utmost concern to them.

During the beginning phase of group therapy, some minority youth, especially those from urban settings, may expend a great deal of energy in challenging the therapist's authority and ability to maintain control of the sessions. The principles of heterogeneous grouping and pregroup screening are very applicable here, ensuring that the group is not comprised of all acting-out antisocial adolescents who can easily become uncontrollable under the negative influence of peer group dynamics (Franklin, 1982). The therapist must avoid being drawn into a power struggle with the group and, at the same time, must establish structure and set limits for the sessions.

✿ CASE STUDY
A Mexican-American Youth

During the beginning phase of a racially heterogeneous group session, a Mexican American youth said to another member, "Shut up, you nigger liar." The therapist immediately intervened by reminding the group of the rules about respecting other members, no name calling ("capping"), no put downs, and so on. After the group members calmed down, the therapist took advantage of the opportunity to raise the cultural sensitivity of the group. The therapist asked the Mexican American male what other Black female group members had to do with the anger he had toward her. The group then discussed how and why people use racial and ethnic terms to insult others. The discussion generated commonalities, group cohesiveness, and mutual trust among group members.

Confronting minority youth in the group, a therapist also needs to understand the minority youth's interactive style, ages of the group members, and the nature of their presenting problems.

✿ CASE STUDY
Vin-Tran—A Vietnamese Boy

During an activity group therapy session, Vin-Tran, a 9-year-old Vietnamese boy, got so frustrated with his drawing that he tore up the paper and the crayons. The therapist gently offered him help, but Vin-Tran responded with a resounding "No!" The therapist backed off but continued to keep an eye on him in an inconspicuous manner. When Vin-Tran began to destroy another drawing, the therapist immediately but quietly stepped in and offered to keep the unfinished product. Vin-Tran did not object.

At the beginning of the next session, the therapist showed Vin-Tran that she had preserved and valued his unfinished project. This process continued for another session. At the beginning of the following session, Vin-Tran asked if the therapist had preserved the latest unfinished project. The therapist showed him the unfinished projects in a neatly covered box. Vin-Tran was delighted that the therapist took time off to arrange and preserve his unfinished projects. He asked the therapist if he could pick out one of his unfinished projects and finish it. The therapist nodded. After working for a short time on the unfinished project he had picked, Vin-Tran signalled nonverbally for the therapist to come over and then asked for her help in completing the project.

The therapist's intervention was guided by her sensitivity toward Vin-Tran's ethnic family background, his presenting problem, his age, and the stage of group therapy. Vin-Tran was referred for group therapy because of underachievement in school work, impulsivity, and destruction of property. Vin-Tran's parents were greatly disappointed by his behavior, especially at school. They compared him with his older brother who excelled in school. Vin-Tran had a very low self-concept, and he disliked whatever he made in activity group therapy. Whatever he disliked, he destroyed. He conveyed his anger not by words but by actions.

The therapist made a special attempt not to offer him help because that would reinforce his low self-worth and inadequacy. Because it was still the beginning trust-building phase of group therapy and because of Vin-Tran's unfamiliarity with talk therapy, the therapist refrained from engaging him verbally about his feelings of frustration and unworthiness. Instead, the therapist intervened through action, which was to quietly and faithfully save his unfinished product. The therapist's action also communicated to Vin-Tran that she cared about him and valued him. Through such action-oriented intervention, Vin-Tran began to feel warmth, acceptance, and trust toward the therapist. Once the rapport was established, the therapist would attempt to encourage Vin-Tran to verbalize his feelings and to overcome the barriers that caused his underachievement.

In working with ethnic minority children in group, the therapist is always confronted with helping group members resolve issues that are culture bound.

✿ CASE STUDY
Karen—A Choctaw American Indian Girl

In a heterogeneous racial group with older adolescents, the therapist noticed Karen, an American Indian of the Choctaw tribe, became depressed when the group discussed future plans after graduation from high school. Despite her ability to perform high quality academic work, Karen's recent academic performance had been erratic, and, in fact, that had prompted the teacher to refer her to the group. Encouraged by several group members' persistence in finding out what was underneath her usual silence, Karen finally broke into tears saying, "I get no support from my parents about going to college after high school graduation. I do not want you all to think that my parents do not love me. Actually, they love me too much, and they just do not want me to be away from home, to be 'educated' and lose my Indianness."

A White group member commented that she had a hard time understanding Karen's parents' point of view. Other White students responded, "They [Karen's parents] are weird." The therapist immediately intervened by encouraging the group to search for some explanations for Karen's parents' position. Another Puerto Rican female student responded by saying that her mother, who is a single parent, also did not wish for her to go off to college because she worked two jobs and expected the girl to help out with the house chores, including taking care of her two younger siblings. Another White student insisted that she just did not understand how going to college would cause Karen to lose her Indianness.

The topic of cultural conflict then became an issue of group discussion. The therapist engaged the group to refocus on Karen's dilemma. Group members began to choose sides—some decided that Karen should go on to college to better herself; others decided that Karen should obey her parents, with whom she feels most secure and loved. The therapist challenged the group to offer Karen the third option, allowing her to pursue a college education without alienating her family. The group first decided that there was no way that the third option would work, but later agreed that they would think about it at home and discuss the topic more at the next session.

Right after the next session started, Karen thanked the group for devoting so much time to her personal problem. She also volunteered that she might be able to resolve her dilemma by enrolling in a nearby college. In addition, she would regularly inform her parents of the new information and experience she received in college, as a means to protect her Indianness.

The therapist's sensitivity and respect for Karen's culture and value dilemma enabled Karen to express feelings that truly concerned her. By listening and incorporating the group's concerned discussions and invaluable inputs, Karen was able to free herself from viewing her and her parents' culture as a "terminal hypothesis," which suggests that a behavior is unchangeable. In this case, it meant choosing to be Indian over getting a (White) college education. Retaining one's ethnic identity (Indian) and obeying one's parents are Karen's cultural traits. Through group discussion and concern, Karen was helped to view such cultural traits as a resource (rather than an inflexible feature) that can be used or not, depending on the circumstances. The circumstances allowed Karen to creatively use her cultural resource to get an education without having to compromise her ethnic Indian identity.

In view of ethnic minority children's general unfamiliarity with group therapy, their high degree of tolerance, unwillingness to critique in deference to authority, and restrictive verbal participation in the group, periodic individual conferences should be scheduled regularly with each group member. The main purpose of the individual conference is to ascertain if the youth is benefiting from the group process. During the conference, which usually lasts between 10 and 15 minutes, the therapist can offer support and specific feedback or suggestions to the youth regarding expected behavior in future group sessions. It is important that the therapist refrain from exploring with the youth an issue or problem(s) that can best be dealt with in the group. The therapist's special attention and time spent with each youth in an individual conference will reduce the dropout rate and enrich youth interaction in the group, all helpful in producing the desired outcomes.

Evaluation and Termination

Ideally, termination should occur when a group member or a total group no longer needs therapy. In actual practice, a child may leave the group due to unexpected circumstances, including the relocation of the parents. A time-limited group may terminate when some group members' needs still are unmet. In instances where the therapist is leaving the group prematurely or unexpectedly, it is important that the therapist assumes the responsibility for this action and clarifies and works through the reasons. The children should never blame themselves for the sudden ending of the group.

As a process of group termination, the therapist needs to engage the group members to review their progress and what the group has meant to them. In instances where the youth need more therapy for continued growth and development, appropriate referrals should be made.

The process of termination can reactivate a child's feelings about previous endings and losses. Hence, the need for terminating the group should be discussed well in advance of the expected termination date in order to allow the children sufficient time to make it a positive experience and to reduce anxiety, withdrawal, and acting-out behavior among group members. As a means to help the minority children mourn the loss of the group, a therapist might plan for a special party to acknowledge the group's last session.

The collectivist culture from which the minority children come may cause them to experience "family" transference during group termination stage. There may be continued resistance to termination, and attempts to perpetuate the relationship between group members, as well as between group members and the therapist beyond the ending date of the group (Tannenbum, 1991).

Appendix:
Ethnic-Competence-Skill Model in Psychological Interventions with Minority Ethnic Children and Youth

Here are some statements made by therapists who work with minority children. How often do you feel this way when you work with minority children?

Circle one number for each statement. ANSWER EVERY QUESTION.

In work with minority children, I . . .	Always	Frequently	Occasionally	Seldom	Never
A. Realize the child's ethnic minority reality, including the effects of racism and poverty on the child.	5	4	3	2	1
B. Am able to understand and "tune in" to the child's cultural dispositions, behaviors, and family structure which may include close extended family ties.	5	4	3	2	1
C. Am able to utilize cultural mapping to ascertain the child's problem.	5	4	3	2	1
D. Clearly delineate agency functions and respectfully inform the child of my professional expectations of him/her.	5	4	3	2	1
E. Am able to reaffirm the child's life skills and coping strategies within a bicultural environment.	5	4	3	2	1
F. Am able to assess the accomplishment of therapeutic goals according to the child's collectivist culture.	5	4	3	2	1
G. Understand the child's ethnicity, race, language, social class and differences in minority status, such as refugees, immigrants, or native born.	5	4	3	2	1
H. Am able to discuss openly racial and ethnic differences and issues and respond to culturally based cues.	5	4	3	2	1
I. Am able to identify the eco-systemic sources (racism, poverty and prejudice) of a minority child's problems.	5	4	3	2	1

In work with minority children, I . . .	Always	Frequently	Occasionally	Seldom	Never
J. Am able to formulate goals consistent with the child's emphasis on collectivism and interdependence.	5	4	3	2	1
K. Am able to "frame" the change within the traditional, culturally acceptable language	5	4	3	2	1
L. Am able to reconnect and restore the child to his/her larger world or environment.	5	4	3	2	1
M. Am able to objectify and make use of my own culture/ethnicity and professional culture (psychiatry, social work, psychology, etc.), which may be different than the child's own culture and ethnicity.	5	4	3	2	1
N. Am able to adapt to the child's interactive style and language, conveying to the child that I understand, value, and validate his/her life strategies.	5	4	3	2	1
O. Can identify the links between eco-systemic problems, and individual concerns or problems.	5	4	3	2	1
P. Am able to differentiate and select from three categories of goals: situational stress (e.g. social isolation, poverty), cultural transition (e.g., conflictual family-school practice), and transcultural dysfunctional patterns (e.g., developmental impasses and repetitive interactional behaviors).	5	4	3	2	1

In work with minority children, I . . .	Always	Frequently	Occasionally	Seldom	Never
Q. Am able to suggest a change or new strategy as an expansion of the "old" cultural stress or problem-solving response.	5	4	3	2	1
R. Am able to assist the child to incorporate the new changes in the child's original life strategy independent of the therapist's interaction.	5	4	3	2	1
S. Am sensitive to the child's fear of racist or prejudiced orientations.	5	4	3	2	1
T. Am able to understand the child's help-seeking behavior, which includes the child's conceptualization of the problem and the manner by which the problem can be solved.	5	4	3	2	1
U. Consider the implications of what is being suggested in relation to each child's cultural reality (unique dispositions, life strategies, and experiences.)	5	4	3	2	1
V. Am able to engage the child to formulate a goal that is problem or growth focused, structured, realistic, concrete, practical, and readily achievable.	5	4	3	2	1
W. Am able to apply change strategies that are consistent with the child's need and problem, degree of acculturation, motivation for change, and comfort in responding to the therapist's directives.	5	4	3	2	1

	Always	Frequently	Occasionally	Seldom	Never

In work with minority children, I . . . .

X. Consider the ethnic minority child's concept of time and space in a relationship during termination and make sure the termination is natural and gradual.

	Always	Frequently	Occasionally	Seldom	Never
	5	4	3	2	1

HOW TO SCORE

1. Enter the number you have circled for each question in the space below, putting the number you have circled to Question A over line A, to Question B over line B, etc.

2. Add the 4 scores on each line to get your totals. For example, the sum of your scores over lines A, G, M, and S gives you your score on skills during Pre-Contact phase; line B, H, N, and T give the score on Problem Identification, etc.

A ___ + G ___ + M ___ + S ___ = ___ Pre Contact

B ___ + H ___ + N ___ + T ___ = ___ Problem Identification

C ___ + I ___ + O ___ + U ___ = ___ Problem Specification

D ___ + J ___ + P ___ + V ___ = ___ Mutual Goal-Formulation

E ___ + K ___ + Q ___ + W ___ = ___ Problem Solving

F ___ + L ___ + R ___ + X ___ = ___ Termination

207

References

Abad, V., Ramos, G., & Boyce, E. (1974). A model for delivery of mental health service to Spanish-speaking minorities. *American Journal of Orthopsychiatry, 44,* 585-595.

Abramson, P., & Imai-Marquez, J. (1982). The Japanese-American: A cross-cultural, cross-sectional study of sex guilt. *Journal of Research in Personality, 16,* 227-237.

Acosta, F., Yamamoto, J., & Evans, L. (1982). *Effective psychotherapy for low-income and minority patients.* New York: Plenum.

Acuna, T. (1981). Strategies for Hispanics. *International Journal of Family Therapy, 5,* 17-24.

Alegia, D., Rivera, T., & Marina, S. (1977). El Hospital Invisible. *Archives of General Psychiatry, 34,* 1354-1357.

Allen-Meares, R., Gibbs, S., & Arkoff, B. (1986). *Social work services in schools.* Englewood Cliffs, NJ: Prentice-Hall.

Angel, R., & Guarnaccia, P. (1989). Mind, body, and culture: Somatization among Hispanics. *Social Science and Medicine, 28,* 1229-1238.

Anti-Asian sentiment. (1986, November 6). *Wall Street Journal,* p. 13.

Aponte, H. (1979). Family therapy and the community. In M. Gibbs (Ed.), *Community psychology* (pp. 5-6). New York: Gardner Press.

Aponte, H. (1990). Ethnicity dynamics important in therapeutic relationship. *Family Therapy News, 21,* 3.

Arkoff, A., & Weaver, H. (1966). Body image and body dissatisfaction in Japanese Americans. *Journal of Social Psychology, 68,* 323-330.

Asian American Advisory Council. (1973). *Report to the Governor on discrimination against Asians.* Seattle: State of Washington.

Association on American Indian Affairs. (1976). *Indian child welfare statistical survey* (Report submitted to the American Indian Policy Review Commission, U.S. Congress). Washington, DC: Government Printing Office.

Attneave, C. (1982). American Indians and Alaska native families. In M. McGoldrick, J. Pearce, & J. Giordano (Eds.), *Ethnicity and family therapy* (pp. 55-83). New York: Guilford.

Attorney General's Youth Gang Task Force. (1988). *Report on youth gang violence in California* (Report No. 1620). Sacramento, CA: Author.

Badillo-Ghadli, S. (1977). Culture sensitivity and the Puerto Rican client. *Social Casework, 55,* 100-110.

Bandura, A. (1977). *Social learning theory.* Englewood Cliffs, NJ: Prentice-Hall.

Banks, J. (1984). Multiethnic education in the USA: Practices and promises. In T. Corner (Ed.), *Education in multicultural societies* (pp. 121-123). London: Croom Helm.

Barnes, G., & Welte, J. (1986). Alcohol consumption of Black youth. *Journal of Studies on Alcohol, 47,* 53-61.

Bean, F., et al. (1984). Generational differences in fertility among Mexican Americans. *Social Sciences Quarterly, 65,* 573-582.

Beauvais, et al. (1989). American Indian youth and drugs, 1976-87: A continuing problem. *American Journal of Public Health, 79,* 634-636.

Beiser, M., & Attneave, C. (1982). Mental disorders among Native American children: Rate and risk periods for entering treatment. *American Journal of Psychiatry, 139,* 193-198.

Bell, P., & Evans, T. (1981). *Professional education, counseling the Black client: Alcohol use and abuse in Black America.* Center City, MN: Hazeldon.

Bellah, R., et al. (1985). *Habits of the heart: Individualism and commitment in American life.* Berkeley: University of California Press.

Bennett, F., et al. (1980). Middle ear function in learning-disabled children. *Pediatrics, 66,* 253-260.

Bennett, L. (1982). *Confrontation: Black and White.* Baltimore, MD: Penguin.

Bentz, C. (1977). Cultural exclusion and character. *American Journal of Psychiatry, 122,* 852-858.

Berlin, I. (1986). Psychopathology and its antecedents among American Indian adolescents. *Advances in Clinical Psychology, 9,* 125-152.

Berry, J. (1980). Acculturation as varieties of acculturation. In A. Padilla (Ed.), *Acculturation, theory, models, and some new findings.* Boulder, CO: Westview Press.

Berry J., & Annis, R. (1974). Acculturative stress: The role of ecology, culture, and differentiation. *Journal of Cross-Cultural Psychology, 5,* 382-406.

Bilides, D. (1991). Race, color, ethnicity, and class: Issues of biculturalism in school-based adolescent counseling groups. *Social Work with Groups, 13,* 43-58.

Billingsley, A. (1968). *Black families in White America.* Englewood Cliffs, NJ: Prentice-Hall.

Billingsley, A. (1987). Black families in a changing society. In J. Dewart (Ed.), *The state of Black America.* New York: National Urban League.

Boulette, T. (1980). Priority issues for mental health promotion among low-income Chicanos. In R. Valle (Ed.), *Hispanic national support systems.* Sacramento: California Department of Mental Health.

Bowby, G. (1958). *Maternal care and mental health.* Geneva, Switzerland: World Health Organization.

Bowen, M. (1978). *Family therapy in clinical practice.* New York: Aronson.

Boyd-Franklin, N. (1989). *Black families in therapy.* New York: Guilford.

Brice, J. (1982). West Indian families. In M. McGoldrick, J. Pearce, & J. Giordano (Eds.), *Ethnicity and family therapy.* New York: Guilford.

Brislin, R., et al. (1973). *Cross-cultural research methods.* New York: John Wiley.

Bromerly, M. (1987). New beginnings for Cambodian refugees or further disruptions? *Social Work, 32,* 236-239.

Bronfenbrenner, U. (1979). *The ecology of human development: Experiments by nature and design.* Cambridge, MA: Harvard University Press.

Brown A., & Forde, D. (1967). *African systems of kinship and marriage.* New York: Oxford University Press.

Brown, E. (1973). A comparative study of Alaskan Native adolescent and young adult secondary school dropouts. In B. Oviatt (Ed.), *A perspective of the Alaskan native school dropout.* Salt Lake City: Social Service Resource Center of Utah.

Brown, E., & Shaughnessy, T. (1982). *Education for social work practice with American Indian families.* Washington, DC: U.S. Department of Health and Human Services.

Brunswick, A. (1979). Black youth and drug-use behavior. In G. Beschner (Ed.), *Youth and drug abuse: Problems, issues and treatment.* Lexington, MA: Lexington Books.

Bryde, G. (1971). *Modern Indian psychology.* Vermillion: University of South Dakota.

Bryde, J. (1967). *The Sioux Indian student: A study of scholastic failure and personality conflict.* Pine Ridge, SD: ERIC Document Reproduction Services.

Bureau of Indian Affairs. (1971). *Information office statistics.* Washington, DC: Author.

Bureau of Research and Training. (1979). *National Mental Health Needs Assessment of Indochinese Refugee Populations.* Philadelphia: Pennsylvania Department of Public Welfare, Office of Mental Health.

Buriel, R., et al. (1982). Relationship of traditional Mexican American culture to adjustment and delinquency among three generations of Mexican American male adolescents. *Hispanic Journal of Behavioral Sciences, 1,* 41-55.

Burns, C., & Kaufmen, F. (1972). *Kinetic family drawings.* New York: Brunner/Mazel.

Bustamante Santa Cruz, B. (1975). The Cuban family. *Human Organization, 38,* 140-148.

Canino, I., et al. (1986). A comparison of symptoms and diagnoses in Hispanic and Black children in an outpatient mental health clinic. *Journal of the American Academy of Child Psychiatry, 25,* 254-259.

Carter, J., & Haizlip, T. (1972). *The counseling relationship.* Chicago: Science Research Associates.

Casal, L., et al. (1979). The Cuban migration by the sixties in its historical context. In L Casal (Ed.), *Black Cubans in the United States.* Miami: Office of Latin America and the Caribbean.

Casas, S., & Keefe, S. (1978). *Family and mental health in the Mexican American community.* Los Angeles, CA: Spanish-Speaking Mental Health Research Center.

Cauce, A. (1986). Social network and social competence: Exploring the effects of early adolescent friendships. *American Journal of Community Psychology, 14,* 607-629.

Centers for Disease Control. (1987). *AIDS weekly surveillance report—United States.* Atlanta, GA: Author.

Centers for Disease Control. (1988). *High-risk racial and ethnic groups—Blacks and Hispanics, 1970 to 1983.* Atlanta, GA: Author.

Center for Health Education and Social Systems Studies. (1985). *Health status of minorities and low-income groups.* Washington, DC: Government Printing Office.

Chadwick, B., & Strauss, J. (1975). The assimilation of American Indians into urban society: The Seattle case. *Human Organization, 34,* 4.

Chestang, L. (1984). Racial and personal identity in the Black experience. In B. White (Ed.), *Color in a White Society.* Silver Springs, MD: National Association of Social Workers.

Children's Defense Fund. (1985). *Black and White children in America: Key facts.* Washington, DC: Author.

Children's Defense Fund. (1986). *Welfare and teen pregnancy: What do we know? What do we do?* Washington, DC: Author.

Children's Defense Fund. (1987). *A children's defense budget.* Washington, DC: Author.

Children's Defense Fund. (1988). *Teens and AIDS: opportunities for prevention.* Washington, DC: Author.

Clark, K. (1952). Racial identity and preference in young children. In E. Maccoby (Ed.), *Readings in social psychology.* New York: Holt, Rinehart & Winston.

Coelho, G., & Stein, J. (1980). Change, vulnerability, and coping: Stresses of uprooting and overcrowding. In G. Coelho (Ed.), *Uprooting and development.* New York: Plenum.

Cohen, J., & Pearl, A. (1964). *Mental health of the poor.* Glencoe, IL: Free Press.

Coleman, J., et al. (1972). The locus of control and academic performance among racial groups. In S. Gutterman (Ed.), *Black psyche.* Berkeley: Glendessary Press.

Comas-Diaz C., & Jacobsen, F. (1987). Ethnocultural identification. *Psychotherapy, 50,* 232-241.

Comberg, S. (1982). Building on the strength of minority groups. *Practice Digest, 5,* 6-7.

Combs, D. (1978). *Crossing culture in therapy.* Monterey, CA: Brooks/Cole.

Committee for Economic Development. (1987). *Children in need: Investment strategies for the educationally disadvantaged.* New York: Author.

Costo, R. (Ed.). (1970). *Textbooks and the American Indian.* American Indian Historical Society.

Costo, R., & Henry, J. (1977). *Indian treaties: Two centuries of dishonor.* San Francisco: Indian Heritage Press.

Cota-Robles de Suarez, C. (1973). Sexual stereotypes—Psychological and cultural survival. *Regeneracion, 2,* 17-21.

Cummins, T. (1981). Cultural differences in guidance clinic patients. *American Journal of Social Psychiatry, 21,* 182-189.

Danphinais, P., & Rowe, W. (1981). Effects of race and communication style. *Counselor Education and Supervision, 21,* 72-80.

Davis, C., Padilla, A., & Paz, T. (1983). *U.S. Hispanics: Changing the face of America.* Washington, DC: Population Reference Bureau.

Davis, L. (1980). When the majority is the psychological minority. *Group Psychotherapy Psychodrama and Sociometry, 33,* 179-184.

Davis, M., & Rogler, T. (1974). Separate and together: All Black therapist group in the White hospital. *American Journal of Orthopsychiatry, 44,* 19-25.

de Anda, D. (1984). Bicultural socialization: Factors affecting the minority experience. *Social Work, 29,* 101-107.

Delgado, G. (1978). *Steps to an ecology of mind.* New York: Ballantine.

Deloria, V., Jr. (1969). *Custer died for your sins.* New York: Avon.

Dembo, R. (1988). Delinquency among Black male youth. In J. Gibbs (Ed.), *Young, Black, and male in America: An endangered species* (pp. 174-189). Dover, MA: Auburn House.

Development Associates. (1983). *Final report: The evaluation of the impact of the Part A Entitlement Program funded under Title IV of the Indian Education Act*. Arlington, VA: Author.

De Vos, G., & Abbott, K. (1966). *The Chinese family in San Francisco*. Unpublished master's thesis, University of California, Berkeley.

Dillard, J. (1983). *Multicultural counseling: Toward ethnic and cultural relevance in human encounters*. Chicago: Nelson-Hall.

DiSarno, N., & Barringer, J. (1978). Otitis media and academic achievement in Eskimo high school students. *Folia Phoniatrics, 39,* 250-255.

Dubanoski, R., & Snyder, K. (1980). Patterns of child abuse and neglect in Japanese and Samoan-Americans. *Child Abuse and Neglect, 4,* 217-225.

Duberman, L. (1975). *The reconstituted family: A study of remarried couples and their children*. Chicago: Nelson Hall.

Edgerton, R., & Karno, M. (1971). Mexican-American bilingualism and the perception of mental illness. *Archives of General Psychiatry, 24,* 286-290.

Edwards, D., & Edwards, M. (1984). Minorities: American Indians. In A. Minahan (Ed.), *Encyclopedia of social work* (pp. 142-150). Silver Springs, MD: National Association of Social Workers.

Enright, I., & Jaeckle, B. (1963). *Ethnicity and mental health*. New York: Institute of Pluralism.

Erikson, E. (1959). Identity and the life cycle. *Psychological Issues, 1,* 1-10.

Escobar, J., & Karrer, T. (1986). Symptoms of schizophrenia in Hispanic and Anglo veterans. *Culture, Medicine and Psychiatry, 10,* 259-276.

Falicov, C. (1982). Mexican families. In M. McGoldrick, J. Pearce, & J. Giordano (Eds.), *Ethnicity and family therapy* (pp. 134-163). New York: Guilford.

Falicov, C., & Karrer, B. (1984). Therapeutic strategies for Mexican-American families. *International Journal of Family Therapy, 6,* 18-30.

Farris, C. (1973). A White House conference on the American Indian. *Social Work, 18,* 80-86.

Felner, R., & Franklin, T. (1985). Adaptation and vulnerability in high-risk adolescents. *American Journal of Community Psychology, 13,* 365-379.

Fenz, W., & Arkoff, A. (1962). Comparing the need patterns of five ancestry groups in Hawaii. *Journal of Social Psychology, 58,* 82.

Fitzpatrick, J. (1971). *Puerto Rican Americans: The meaning of migration to the mainland*. Englewood Cliffs, NJ: Prentice-Hall.

Fitzpatrick, J. (1981). The Puerto Rican family. In C. Mindel & R. Habenstein (Eds.), *Ethnic families in America* (pp. 271-286). New York: Elsenier.

Flanagan, T., & McGarrell, E. (1985). *Sourcebook of criminal justice statistics*. Washington, DC: Government Printing Office.

Fogleman, B. (1972). *Adoptive mechanisms of the North American Indian to an urban setting*. [Microfilm]. Ann Arbor, MI: University Microfilms.

Franklin, A. (1982). Therapeutic intervention with urban Black adolescents. In E. Jones (Ed.), *Minority mental health* (pp. 272-296). New York: Praeger.

Furstenberg, F., & Gellas, T. (1987). *Adolescent mothers in later life*. Cambridge, England: Cambridge University Press.

Garcia, B. (1973). Self-concepts of Hispanic children. *American Journal of Social Psychiatry, 14,* 120-128.

Garcia, M., & Marks, G. (1989). Depressive symptomatology among Mexican-American adults: An examination with the CE 5-D Scale. *Psychiatry Research, 27,* 137-148.

Garmezy, N., & Rutter, M. (Eds.). (1983). *Stress, coping and development in children.* New York: McGraw-Hill.

Garvin, C. (1981). *Contemporary group work.* Englewood Cliffs, NJ: Prentice-Hall.

Gary, L., & Glasglow, D. (1983). *Stable Black families.* Washington, DC: Howard University Press.

Germain, C. (1973). An ecological perspective in casework practice. *Social Casework, 54,* 323-330.

Ghali, B. (1977). *Ethnic America.* New York: Basic Books.

Gibbs, J. (1987). Identity and marginality: Issues in the treatment of biracial adolescents. *American Journal of Orthopsychiatry, 57,* 265-278.

Gibbs, J. (1988). Conceptual, methodological, and sociocultural issues in Black youth suicide: Implications for assessment and early intervention. *Suicide and Life-Threatening Behavior, 18,* 73-89.

Gibbs, J. (1989). Black American adolescents. In J. Gibbs, L. Huang, & Associates (Eds.), *Children of color: Psychological interventions with minority youth* (pp. 179-223). San Francisco: Jossey-Bass.

Gibbs, J., Huang, L., & Associates, (Eds.). (1989). *Children of color: Psychological interventions with minority youth.* San Francisco: Jossey-Bass.

Gibson, G., & Vasquez, E. (1982, March). *Racism and its impact on Hispanics: Cognitive and affective teaching and learning.* Paper presented at the annual program meeting of the Council on Social Work Education, New York.

Gibson, M. (1988). *Accommodation without assimilation: Sikh immigrants in an American high school.* Ithaca, NY: Cornell University Press.

Giordano, J. (1976). Ethnicity and community mental health. *Community Mental Health Review, 1,* 4-14.

Glasser, I. (1983). Guidelines for using an interpreter in social work. *Child Welfare, 62,* 468-470.

Gold, M. (1977). *In praise of diversity: A resource book for multicultural education.* Washington, DC: Association of Teacher Education.

Goldstein, E. (1984). *Ego psychology and social work practice.* New York: Free Press.

Gonzales-Wippler, M. (1975). *Santeria: African magic in Latin America.* New York: Anchor.

Goodman, M. (1952). *Race attitudes in young children.* Boston: Addison-Wesley.

Gould, M., & Canino, I. (1981). Estimating the prevalence of childhood psychopathology. *Journal of the American Academy of Child Psychiatry, 20,* 462-476.

Grant, W. (1975). Estimates of school dropouts. *American Education, 11,* 42.

Grebler, L., Moore, J., & Guzman, R. (1973). The family: Variations in time and place. In L. Duran & H. Bernard (Eds.), *Introduction to Chicano studies* (pp. 48-62). New York: Macmillan.

Green, J. (1982). *Cultural awareness in the human services.* Englewood Cliffs, NJ: Prentice-Hall.

Grier, W., & Cobbs, P. (1968). *Black rage.* New York: Basic Books.

Guinn, R. (1978). Alcohol use among Mexican-American youth. *Journal of School Health, 48,* 90-91.

Gustafson, R., & Owens, T. (1971, May). *Children's perceptions of themselves and their teachers' feelings toward them.* Paper presented at the 51st Annual Meeting of the Western Psychological Association, San Francisco, CA.

Haley, J. (1976). *Problem-solving therapy.* San Francisco: Jossey-Bass.

Han, Y. (1985). Discriminant analysis of self-disclosing behavior and locus of control among Korean American and Caucasian American adolescents. *Pacific/Asian American Mental Health Research Review, 4,* 20-22.

Hanks, G. (1973). Dependency among Alaska Native school dropouts. In B. Oviatt (Ed.), *A perspective of the Alaskan Native school dropout* (pp. 274-292). Salt Lake City, UT: Social Service Resource Center.

Hanson, W. (1980). The urban Indian woman and her family. *Social Casework, 61,* 476-484.

Hare, B. (1975). *Relationship of social background to the dimension of self-concept.* Unpublished doctoral dissertation, University of Chicago.

Haviland, M., Horswill, R., O'Connell, R., & Dynneson, V. (1983). Native American college students' preference for counselor. *Journal of Counseling Psychology, 30,* 267-270.

Hawkes, G., & Taylor, M. (1975). Power structure in Mexican and Mexican American farm labor families. *Journal of Marriage and the Family, 31,* 807-811.

Henkin, H. (1987). Youth suicide: A psychosocial perspective. *Suicide and Life Threatening Behavior, 17,* 151-165.

Hill, R. (1972). *The strength of Black families.* New York: Emerson-Hall.

Hippler, A. (1974). The North Alaska Eskimos: A culture and personality perspective. *American Ethnologist, 1,* 449-469.

Hisama, T. (1980). Minority group children and behavior disorders—The case of Asian American children. *Behavior Disorders, 5,* 186-196.

Ho, M. (1976a). Evaluation: A means of treatment. *Social Work, 21,* 24-27.

Ho, M. (1976b). Social work with Asian Americans. *Social Casework, 57,* 195-201.

Ho, M. (1984). *Building a successful intermarriage.* St. Meinrad, IN: Abbey Press.

Ho, M. (1987). *Family therapy with ethnic minorities.* Newbury Park, CA: Sage.

Ho, M. (1989). Applying family therapy theories to Asian/Pacific Americans. *Contemporary Family Therapy, 11,* 61-70.

Ho, M. (1990a). *Intermarried couples in therapy.* Springfield, IL: Charles C Thomas.

Ho, M. (1990b). To work successfully with ethnic minorities. *Family Therapy News, 21,* 5-10.

Ho, M., & McDowell, E. (1973). The Black worker-White client relationship. *Clinical Social Work Journal, 1,* 161-167.

Hodgkinson, H. (1990, May). *Non-White demographics.* A speech delivered at the Second Annual Conference on Racial and Ethnic Violence on Campus, Norman, Oklahoma.

Holmes, T., & Masuda, M. (1974). Life change and illness susceptibility. In B. Dohrenwend (Ed.), *Stressful life events: Their nature and effects* (pp. 117-123). New York: John Wiley.

Houston, S. (1971). *Black and White identity formation.* New York: John Wiley.

Hsu, F. (1971). *The challenge of the American Dream: The Chinese in the United States.* Belmont, CA: Wadsworth.

Hsu, F. (1972). *American museum science book.* Garden City, NY: Doubleday.

Huffaker, C. (1967). *Nobody loves a drunken Indian.* New York: David McKay.

Hunt, P. (1987). Black clients: Implications for supervision of trainees. *Psychotherapy, 24,* 114-119.

Inclan, J. (1985). Variations in value orientations in mental health work with Puerto Ricans. *Psychotherapy, 22,* 324-334.

Irvine, S., & Carroll, W. (1980). Testing and assessment across cultures: Issues in methodology and theory. In H. Triandis (Ed.), *Handbook of cross-cultural psychology* (pp. 301-318). Boston: Allyn & Bacon.

Iuniga, B. (1987). Prevalence of psychological stress among Mexican Americans. *Journal of Health and Social Behavior, 27,* 120-129.

Ivey, A., Ivey, M., & Simek-Downing, L. (1987). *Counseling and psychotherapy: Integrating skills, theory and practice.* Englewood Cliffs, NJ: Prentice-Hall.

Jackson, G., & Cosca, C. (1974). The inequality of educational opportunity in the southwest. *American Educational Research Journal, 11,* 219-229.

Jackson, J. (1973). Family organization and ideology. In D. Miller (Ed.), *Comparative studies of Blacks and Whites in the United States* (pp. 76-82). New York: Seminar Press.

Jensen, A. (1969). How much can we boost IQ and school achievement? *Harvard Educational Review, 39,* 11-23.

Johnson, C. (1941). *Growing up in the Black belt.* Washington, DC: American Council on Education.

Johnson, D., & Walker, T. (1987). The primary prevention of behavior problems in Mexican-American children. *American Journal of Community Psychology, 15,* 375-385.

Josephy, A. (1971). *The Indian heritage of North America.* New York: Alfred Knopf.

Jourard, S. (1971). *Self-disclosure: An experimental analysis of the transparent self.* New York: John Wiley.

Kaplan, H., & Bloom, T. (1988). Explaining adolescent drug use: An elaboration strategy for structural equation modeling. *Psychiatry, 51,* 142-163.

Kardiner, A., & Ovesey, L. (1951). *The mark of oppression.* Cleveland: World Publishing.

Katz, L. (1978). The effects of conductive hearing loss on auditory function. *Psychiatry Ethnic of North America, 5,* 321-332.

Kendale, F. (1983). *Diversity in the classroom: A multicultural approach to the education of young children.* New York: Teacher College, Columbia University.

Kim, B. (1977-1981). *Annual service reports of the Korean Mental Health Center, Baltimore, MD.* Montclair, NJ: Association of Korean Christian Scholars in North America.

Kim, B. (1978). *The Asian Americans: Changing patterns, changing needs.* Montclair, NJ: Association of Korean Christian Scholars in North America.

Kim, H. (1980). Korean. In S. Thermstrom, T. Nann, & B. Pothier (Eds.), *Harvard encyclopedia of American ethnic groups* (pp. 782-791). Cambridge, MA: Harvard University Press.

Kitano, H. (1976). *Japanese Americans: The evolution of subculture.* Englewood Cliffs, NJ: Prentice-Hall.

Kleinfeld, J., et al. (1977). Boarding schools: Effects on mental health of Eskimo adolescents. *American Journal of Psychiatry, 134,* 411-417.

Kleinman, A., & Lin, T. (Eds.). (1981). *Normal and deviant behavior in Chinese culture.* Hingham, MA: Reidel.

Kleinman, A., & Sung, L. (1979). Why do indigenous practitioners successfully heal? *Social Science and Medicine, 13B,* 7-26.

Kline, F., Austin, W., & Acosta, F. (1980). The misunderstood Spanish-speaking patient. *American Journal of Psychiatry, 137,* 1530-1533.

Knight, C., et al. (1978). Acculturation of second- and third-generation Mexican American children. *Journal of Cross-Cultural Psychology, 9,* 87-96.

Knox, D. (1985). Spirituality: A tool in the assessment and treatment of Black alcoholics and their families. *Alcoholism Treatment Quarterly, 2,* 31-44.

Kochman, T. (1972). *Rappin' and Stylin' Out.* Urbana: University of Illinois Press.

Koh, T., & Koh, S. (1982). A note on the psychological evaluation of Korean school children. *Pacific/Asian American Mental Health Research Review, 1*, 1-2.

Krause, N., & Carr, L. (1978). The effects of response bias in the survey assessment of the mental health of Puerto Rican migrants. *Social Psychiatry, 132*, 81-83.

Kreisman, B. (1975). *Help-seeking in the inner city.* New York: Fordham University, Hispanic Research Center.

Krisberg, B. (1986). *The incarceration of minority youth.* Minneapolis: University of Minnesota, Humphrey Institute of Public Affairs.

Krush, T., et al. (1966). Some thoughts on the formation of personality disorder: Study of an Indian boarding school. *American Journal of Psychiatry, 122*, 867-876.

Labov, W. (1972). *Language in the inner city: Studies in the Black English vernacular.* Philadelphia: University of Pennsylvania Press.

LaFramboise, T., & Plake, B. (1983). Toward meeting the educational research needs of American Indians. *Harvard Educational Review, 53*, 45-51.

LaFramboise, T., & Rowe, W. (1983). Skills training for bicultural competence: Rationale and application. *Journal of Counseling Psychology, 30*, 589-595.

Lai, H. (1980). Chinese. In S. Thermstrom (Ed.), *Harvard encyclopedia of American ethnic groups* (pp. 781-794). Cambridge, MA: Harvard University Press.

Lapuz, L. (1973). *A Study of psychopathology.* Quezon City: University of the Philippines Press.

Lawrence, G., & Lurie, J. (1972). Communication problems between rural Mexican-American patients and their physicians. *American Journal of Orthopsychiatry, 42*, 777-783.

Lebra, T. (1976). *Japanese patterns of behavior.* Honolulu: University Press of Hawaii.

Lee, D. (1975). *Acculturation of Korean residents in Georgia.* San Francisco: R and E Research Associates.

Lee, E. (1982). A social system approach to assessment and treatment for Chinese-American families. In M. McGoldrick, J. Pearce, & J. Giordano (Eds.), *Ethnicity and family therapy* (pp. 527-551). New York: Guilford.

Lee, P., Juan, G., & Hom, A. (1984). Group work practice with Asian clients: A sociocultural approach. *Social Work with Groups, 7*, 37-48.

Levande, D. (1976). Family theories as a necessary component of family therapy. *Social Casework, 57*, 271-295.

LeVine, E., & Padilla, A. (1980). *Crossing cultures in therapy: Pluralistic counseling for the Hispanic.* Monterey, CA: Wadsworth.

Levitan, S. (1988). *What's happening to the American family?* Baltimore: John Hopkins University Press.

Lewis, R. (1984). The strength of Indian families. In *Proceedings of the Indian Child Abuse Conference* (pp. 301-312). Tulsa: National Indian Child Abuse Center.

Lewis, R., & Ho, M. (1976). Social work with Native Americans. *Social Work, 20*, 379-382.

Looney, J., & Lewis, J. (1983). *The long struggle: Well-functioning working-class Black family.* New York: Brunner/Mazel.

Los Angeles County Department of Mental Health. (1986). *Client and service summary statistics for the period 07/01/85-06/03/86.* Los Angeles: Author.

Lyman, S. (1977). Chinese secret societies in the Occident: Notes and suggestions for research in the sociology of secrecy. In S. Lyman (Ed.), *The Asian in North America* (pp. 13-19). Santa Barbara, CA: ABC-Clio.

Ma, S., Ma, T., & Chen, T. (1988, April). *Assessing suicide risk among Chinese-American adolescents.* Paper presented at the annual meeting of the American Orthopsychiatric Association, San Francisco.

Madsen, W. (1964). *The Mexican-American of South Texas.* New York: Holt, Rinehart & Winston.

Mahler, M. (1972). On the first three phases of separation-individuation process. *International Journal of Psychoanalysis, 53,* 333-338.

Mancini, J. (1980). *Strategic styles: Coping in the inner city.* Hanover, NH: University Press of New England.

Manson, S., Walker, R., & Kirlaham, D. (1987). Psychiatric assessment and treatment of American Indians and Alaska Natives. *Hospital and Community Psychiatry, 38,* 165-173.

Marishima, J. (1978). The Asian American experience: 1850-1975. *Journal of Ethnic and Special Studies, 2,* 8-10.

Marsella, T., Moore, J., & Guzman, R. (1973). Culture and personality perspective. *American Ethnologist, 1,* 449-459.

Martin, J., & Martin, E. (1985). *The helping tradition in the Black family and community.* Silver Spring, MD: National Association of Social Workers.

Mass, A. (1978). Asian as individuals: The Japanese community. *Social Casework, 57,* 160-164.

May, G. (1976). Personality development and ethnic identity. In L. Chestang (Ed.), *The diverse society* (pp. 128-141). Silver Springs, MD: National Association of Social Workers.

May, P., & Hymbaugh, K. (1983). A pilot project on Fetal Alcohol Syndrome for American Indians. *Alcohol, Health, and Research World, 7,* 3-9.

McAdoo, H. (1977). Family therapy in the Black community. *Journal of the American Orthopsychiatric Association, 47,* 74-79.

McAdoo, H. (1978). The impact of upward mobility of kin-help pattern and the reciprocal obligations in Black families. *Journal of Marriage and the Family, 4,* 761-776.

McAdoo, H. (Ed.). (1981). *Black families.* Beverly Hills, CA: Sage.

McKinley, V. (1991). Group therapy as a treatment modality of special value for Hispanic patients. *Social Work with Groups, 13,* 255-266.

McRoy, R., & Zurcher, L. (1983). *Transracial and inracial adoptees: The adolescent years.* Springfield, IL: Charles C Thomas.

Megargee, E. (1972). *The California psychological inventory handbook.* San Francisco: Jossey-Bass.

Meichenbaum, D. (Ed.). (1977). *Cognitive behavior modification: An integrative approach.* New York: Plenum.

Melendy, H. (1980). Filipinos. In S. Thermstrom (Ed.), *Harvard encyclopedia of American ethnic groups* (pp. 872-897). Cambridge, MA: Harvard University Press.

Menon, R., Burrett, M., & Simpson, D. (1990). School, peer group, and inhalant use among Mexican-American adolescents. *Hispanic Journal of Behavioral Sciences, 12,* 408-421.

Merian, L. (1977). The effects of boarding schools on Indian family life: 1928. In L. Merian (Ed.), *The Destruction of American Indian families* (pp. 78-91). New York: Association on American Indian Affairs.

Meshane, D. (1982). Otitis media and American Indians: Prevalence, etiology, psychoeducational consequences. In S. Manson (Ed.), *New directions in prevention among American Indian communities* (pp. 321-336). Portland: Oregon Health Sciences, University Press.

Milazzo-Sayre, B. L., Olmeda, E., Benson, P., Rosenstein, M., & Manderscheid, R. (1986). *Use of impatient psychiatric services by children and youth under age 18, United States, 1980* (Mental Health Statistical Note No. 175). Washington, DC: U.S. Department of Health and Human Services.

Millard, M. (1987, November 6). Problems of Asian juvenile offenders brings outcry for better system in S.F. *East/West News*, pp. 1, 8-9.

Miller, M., & Schoenfield, T. (1975). *The Native Americans*. Austin: National Education Lab.

Mindel, C., Habenstein, R., & Wright, C. (Eds.). (1988). *Ethnic families in America: Patterns and variations*. New York: Elsevier.

Mintz, S. (1973). Puerto Rico: An essay in the definition of national culture. In F. Cordasco (Ed.), *The Puerto Rican experience: A sociological sourcebook* (pp. 26-90). Totowa, NJ: Littlefield.

Minuchin, S. (1974). *Families and family therapy*. Cambridge, MA: Harvard University Press.

Miranda, M., & Kitano, H. (1976). Barriers to mental health: A Japanese and Mexican dilemma. In N. Herandez (Ed.), *Chicanos: Social psychological perspectives* (pp. 212-328). St. Louis: C. V. Mosby.

Mitchell, H., & Lewter, N. (1986). *Social theology: The heart of American Black culture*. New York: Harper & Row.

Mizo, E., & Delaney, A. (Eds.). (1981). *Training for service delivery to minority clients*. New York: Family Service Association of America.

Mokuau, N. (1987). Social workers' perceptions of counseling effectiveness for Asian American clients. *Social Work, 32*, 331-335.

Montero, D., & Dieppa, J. (1982). Resettling Vietnamese refugees: The service agency's role. *Social Work, 27*, 74-82.

Montiel, F. (1983). Hispanic families. *Journal of Marriage and the Family, 31*, 620-628.

Moore, K. (1986). Facts on births to U.S. teens. In M. Merger (Ed.), *Facts at a glance* (pp. 64-69). Washington, DC: Child Trends.

Morawetz, A., & Walker, G. (1984). *Brief therapy with single-parent families*. New York: Bruner/Mazel.

Morey, S., & Gilliam, O. (Eds.). (1974). *Respect for life*. Garden City, NY: Waldorf Press.

Mostwin, D. (1976). Uprootment and anxiety. *International Journal of Mental Health, 8*, 124-131.

Moynihan, D. (1965). *The Negro family: The case for national action*. Washington, DC: U.S. Department of Labor.

Muller, D., & Leonetti, R. (1974). Self-concepts of primary level Chicano and Anglo students. *California Journal of Educational Research, 25*, 57-60.

Murase, K. (1980). State and local public policy issues in delivering mental health and related services to Asian and Pacific Americans. In *U.S. Commission on Civil Rights: Issues of Asian and Pacific Americans* (pp. 170-178). Washington, DC: Government Printing Office.

Murillo, N. (1971). The Mexican American family. In N. Wagner (Ed.), *Chicano: Social and psychological perspectives* (pp. 145-162). St. Louis: C. V. Mosby.

Multicultural Drug Abuse Prevention Center. (1976). *First National Asian American Conference on Drug Abuse Prevention*. Los Angeles: Multicultural Resource Center.

Myers, B. (1976). Assessment of Black children. *Journal of the American Academy of Child Psychiatry, 23*, 156-162.

Naditch, M., & Morrissey, R. (1976). Role stress, personality, and psychopathology in a group of immigrant adolescents. *Journal of Abnormal Psychology, 85,* 113-116.

Nann, B. (1982). Settlement programs for immigrant women and families. In R. Nann (Ed.), *Uprooting and surviving* (pp. 221-226). Dordrecht, Holland: Reidel.

National Center for Health Statistics. (1986). *Health—United States, 1986.* Washington, DC: U.S. Department of Health, Education, and Welfare.

National Coalition of Advocates for Students. (1985). *Barriers to excellence: Our children at risk.* Boston, MA: Author.

National Technical Information Service. (1986). *American Indian health.* Washington, DC: U.S. Department of Health, Education, and Welfare.

Native American Research Group. (1979). *American Indian socialization to urban life: Final Report* (N119H Grant No. MH22719). San Francisco: Scientific Analysis Corporation.

Neighbors, H., & Taylor, R. (1985). The use of social service agencies by Black Americans. *Social Service Review, 59,* 259-268.

Nichols, P., & Anderson, E. (1973). Intellectual performance, race, and socioeconomic status. *Social Biology, 20,* 367-374.

Nobles, W. (1980). African philosophy: Foundations for Black psychology. In R. Jones (Ed.), *Black psychology* (pp. 23-36). New York: Harper & Row.

Norbeck, E., & DeVos, G. (1972). Culture and personality: The Japanese. In F. Hsu (Ed.), *Psychological anthology in the behavioral science* (pp. 12-21). Cambridge, MA: Schenkman.

Norman, B. (1980). Strengthening the ego. *American Journal of Orthopsychiatry, 28,* 107-182.

Norton, D. (1978). Black family life patterns: The development of self and cognitive development of Black children. In G. Powell, J. Yamamoto, A. Romero, & A. Morales (Eds.), *The psychosocial development of minority group children* (pp. 181-193). New York: Brunner/Mazel.

O'Connell, J. (1987). *A study of the special problems and needs of American Indian children.* Washington, DC: U.S. Department of Education.

Ogbu, J. (1985). A cultural ecology of competence among inner city Blacks. In M. Spencer & B. Gold (Eds.), *Beginnings: The social and affective development of Black children* (pp. 410-432). Hillsdale, NJ: Lawrence Erlbaum.

Okano, Y. (1977). *Japanese Americans and mental health.* Los Angeles: Coalition for Mental Health.

Okie, S. (1988, October 31). Children reach for new heights in study of growth hormones. *Washington Post,* pp. A1, A4.

Olden, C. (1953). On adult empathy with children. *The Psychoanalytic Study of the Child, 8,* 111-126.

Omi, A., & Winant, H. (1986). *Racial formation in the United States: From the 1960's to the 1980's.* Boston: Routledge & Kegan Paul.

Opler, M. (1967). Ethnic differences in behavior and psychopathology. *International Journal of Social Psychiatry, 1,* 11-17.

Ortiz, A. (1969). *Tewa world: Space, time, being, and becoming in a pueblo society.* Chicago: University of Chicago Press.

Ortiz, C. (1973). The Chicano family: A review of research. *Social Work, 18,* 22-23.

Osborne, W. (1971). Adjustment differences of selected foreign born pupils. *California Journal of Educational Research, 22,* 131-139.

Ozawa, M. (1986). Non-Whites and the demographic imperative in social welfare spending. *Social Work, 31,* 440-446.

Padilla, A., Carlos, M., & Keefe, S. (1979). Mental health service utilization by Mexican Americans. In M. Miranda (Ed.), *Psychotherapy with the Spanish-speaking: Issues in research and service delivery* (pp. 310-321). Los Angeles: University of California, Spanish-Speaking Mental Health Research Center.

Padilla, A., & Ruiz, R. (1973). *Latino mental health: A review of literature* (DHEW Publication No. HSM73-9143). Washington, DC: Government Printing Office.

Panitz, D., Scopetta, M., & Tillman, W. (1983). The role of machismo and the Hispanic family in the etiology and treatment of alcoholism in Hispanic American males. *American Journal of Family Therapy, 11*, 31-44.

Para, F. (1985). Social tolerance of the mentally ill in the Mexican-American community. *International Journal of Sociological Psychiatry, 31*, 37-45.

Passel, T., & Woodrow, B. (1984). *Hispanics: Social and psychological perspectives.* St. Louis: C. V. Mosby.

Penalosa, F. (1968). Mexican family roles. *Journal of Marriage and the Family, 30*, 680-689.

Pendagast, S., & Sherman, R. (1977). Diagrammatic assessment of family relationships. *Social Casework, 59*, 465-476.

Petersen, W. (1978). Chinese Americans and Japanese Americans. In T. Sowell (Ed.), *Essays and data on American ethnic groups* (pp. 154-162). Washington, DC: Urban Institute.

Pfister-Ammeude, M. (1973). Mental hygiene in refugee camps. In C. Zwingmann (Ed.), *Uprooting and after* (pp. 15-27). New York: Singer.

Phinney, J., & Rotherman, M. (1987). *Children's ethnic socialization: Pluralism and development.* Newbury Park, CA: Sage.

Pinderhughes, E. (1979). Afro-American and economic dependency. *Urban and Social Change Review, 12*, 24-27.

Pinderhughes, E. (1982). Afro-American families: The victim system. In M. McGoldrick, J. Pearce, & J. Giordano (Eds.), *Ethnicity and family therapy* (pp. 108-122). New York: Guilford.

Ploski, H., & Williams, J. (1983). *The Negro almanac: A reference work on the Afro-American.* New York: John Wiley.

Powell, G. (1985). Self-concepts among Afro-American students in racially isolated minority schools: Some regional differences. *Journal of the American Academy of Child Psychiatry, 24*, 142-149.

Powell, G., Yamamoto, J., Romero, A., & Morales, A. (Eds.). (1983). *The psychosocial development of minority group children.* New York: Brunner/Mazel.

Price, J. (1981). North American Indian families. In C. Mindel & R. Habenstein (Eds.), *Ethnic families in America* (pp. 314-338). New York: Elsevier.

Pryor Brown, L., & Peters, E. (1989). Stressful life events and psychiatric symptoms in Black adolescent females. *Journal of Adolescent Research, 4*, 140-151.

Rabkin, J., & Struening, E. (1976). *Ethnicity, social class and mental illness* (Working Paper Series No. 17). New York: Institute on Pluralism and Group Identity.

Rachal, J., Smith, M., & Taylor, L. (1980). *Adolescent drinking behavior* (Vol. 1). Research Triangle Park, NC: Research Triangle Institute.

Rahe, N., & Ja, E. (1978). Psychiatric consultation in a Vietnamese refugee camp. *American Journal of Psychiatry, 135*, 185-190.

Rainwater, L. (1966). The crucible of identity: The lower class Negro family. *Daedalus, 95*, 258-264.

Ramirez, M. (1969). Identification with Mexican American values and psychological adjustment in Mexican Adolescents. *International Journal of Social Psychiatry, 11*, 151-156.

Ramirez, M. (1983). *Psychology of the Americas: Mesitizo perspectives on personality and mental health.* New York: Academic Press.

Ramirez, M., & Castanada, A. (1974). Cultural democracy, bicognitive development, and education. New York: Academic Press.

Ramirez, M., & Price-Williams, B. (1974). Ethnic differences in delay of gratification. *Journal of Social Psychology, 93,* 23-30.

Red Horse, J. (1976). *Pre-parent testing: An analysis of early childhood development.* Unpublished manuscript, University of Minnesota, Minneapolis.

Red Horse, J. (1980). Family structure and value orientation in American Indians. *Social Casework, 61,* 462-467.

Red Horse, J. (1988). Cultural evolution of American Indian families. In C. Jacobs & D. Bowles (Eds.), *Ethnicity and race: Critical concept in social work* (pp. 186-199). Silver Spring, MD: National Association of Social Workers.

Reed, R. (1988). Education and achievement of young Black males. In J. Gibbs (Ed.), *Young, Black and male in America: An endangered species* (pp. 65-78). Dover, MA: Auburn House.

Rickel, A., & Allen, L. (1987). Preventing maladjustment from infancy through adolescence. In A. Kazdin (Ed.), *Developmental clinical psychology and psychiatry* (pp. 217-232). Newbury Park, CA: Sage.

Ridley, C. (1984). Clinical treatment of the nondisclosing Black client: A therapeutic paradox. *American Psychologist, 39,* 1234-1244.

Ritter, E., Smith, Y., & Chan, T. (1965). *Our Oriental Americans.* New York: McGraw-Hill.

Robinson, P., & Andersen, A. (1985). Anorexia nervosa in American Blacks. *Journal of Psychiatric Research, 19,* 183-188.

Rodriguez, F. (1983). *Education in a multicultural society.* Washington, DC: University Press.

Roscoe, B., & Peterson, K. (1982). Teacher and structural characteristics which enhance learning and development. *College Student Journal, 16,* 389-394.

Rosen, P., & Proctor, D. (1978). The study of the family. *Family Process, 4,* 1-20.

Rosenfeld, D., Chess, T., & Wilson, W. (1981). Classroom structure and prejudice in desegregated schools. *Journal of Educational Psychology, 73,* 17-26.

Rotherman, M., & Phinney, J. (Eds.). (1987). *Children's ethnic socialization: Pluralism and development.* Newbury Park, CA: Sage.

Rubin, R. (1974). Adult male absence and the self-attitudes of Black children. *Child Study Journal, 4,* 33-44.

Rueschenberg, E., & Buriel, R. (1989). Mexican American family functioning and acculturation: A family systems perspective. *Hispanic Journal of Behavioral Sciences, 11,* 232-244.

Ruiz, R. (1977). *The delivery of mental health. Report of the Task Panel on Special Population. Vol. IV.* Washington, DC: Government Printing Office.

Sabogal, F., Padilla, A., & Mizio, A. (1987). Hispanic familism and acculturation. *Hispanic Journal of Behavioral Sciences, 9,* 397-412.

Sata, L. (1983). Mental health issues of Japanese-American children. In G. Powell, J. Yamamoto, A. Romero, & A. Morales (Eds.), *The psychosocial development of minority group children* (pp. 112-123). New York: Brunner/Mazel.

Satir, V. (1972). *People making.* Palo Alto, CA: Science and Behavior Books.

Sattler, J. (1977). The effects of therapist-client racial similarity. In A. Gurman (Ed.), *Effective psychotherapy* (pp. 35-51). New York: Pergamon.

Sattler, J. (1988). *Assessment of children.* San Diego, CA: Jerome Sattler.

Scanzoni, J. (1971). *The Black family in modern society: Patterns of stability and security.* Chicago: University of Chicago Press.

Scanzoni, J. (1975). Sex roles, economic factors and marital solidarity. *Journal of Marriage and the Family, 37,* 130-144.

Schumm, W., Pearce, J., & Friedman, T. (1988). Differences between Anglo and Mexican American family members on satisfaction with family life. *Hispanic Journal of Behavioral Sciences, 10,* 39-54.

Schutz, W. (1958). *FIRO: A three-dimensional theory of interpersonal behavior.* New York: Holt, Rinehart & Winston.

Simmons, R. (1978). Blacks and high self-esteem. *Social Psychology, 41,* 54-57.

Skager, R. (1986). *A statewide survey of drug and alcohol use among students.* Sacramento, CA: Office of the Attorney General.

Sluzki, C. (1979). Migration and family conflict. *Family Process, 18,* 379-393.

Sollenberger, R. (1962). Chinese-American child-rearing practices and juvenile delinquency. *Journal of Social Psychology, 74,* 13-23.

Soloman, B. (1976). *Black empowerment.* New York: Columbia University Press.

Speck, R., & Attneave, C. (1974). *Family networks.* New York: Vintage.

Spencer, F., Keefe, S., & Carlos, M. (1981, May). *Cuban crisis. 1980: Mental health care issues.* Paper presented at the meeting of the Southeastern Psychological Association, Atlanta, Geogia.

Spergel, I. (1984). Violent gangs in Chicago: In search of social policy. *Social Service Review, 58,* 199-226.

Spiegel, J. (1971). Transactions inquiry: Description of systems. In J. Papajohn (Ed.), *Transactions: The interplay between individual, family and society* (pp. 23-41). New York: Science House.

Spielberger, C. (1975). The measurement of state and emotional anxiety. In L. Levi (Ed.), *Emotions—Their parameters and measurement* (pp. 178-192). New York: Raven Press.

Squires, S. (1987, April 20). Promising research on sickle-cell disease: Medical advances. *Washington Post,* p. 7.

Stack, C. (1974). *All our kin.* New York: Harper & Row.

Staples, R. (1978). *The Black family: Essays and studies* (Vol. 2). Belmont, CA: Wadsworth.

Stedman, J., & Adams, R. (1973). Teacher perception of behavioral adjustment as a function of linguistic ability in Mexican-American Head-Start children. *Psychology in the Schools, 10,* 221-225.

Stengel, R. (1985, January 23). Children having children. *Time,* pp. 78-90.

Steven, E. (1973). Marianismo. In A. Pescatello (Ed.), *Female and male in Latin America* (pp. 11-27). Pittsburg, PA: University of Pittsburg Press.

Stoker, D., & Meadow, A. (1974). Cultural differences in guidance clinic patients. *American Journal of Social Psychiatry, 20,* 186-202.

Stonequist, E. (1964). The marginal man: A study in personality and culture conflict. In E. Burgess & D. Bogue (Eds.), *Contribution to urban sociology* (pp. 362-379). Chicago: University of Chicago Press.

Stuart, P. (1977). United States Indian policy. *Social Service Review, 47,* 451-463.

Sturkie, K., & Flanzer, J. (1987). Depression and self-esteem in the families of maltreated adolescents. *Social Work, 32,* 491-496.

Sue, D. (1981). *Counseling the culturally different: Theory and practice.* New York: John Wiley.

Sue, S. (1977). Community mental health services to minority groups: Some optimism, some pessimism. *American Psychologist, 32,* 616-624.

Sue, S. (1985). Asian Americans and educational pursuits: Are the doors beginning to close? *Pacific/Asian American Mental Health Research Review, 4,* 25-26.

Sue, S. et al. (1976). Conceptions of mental illness among Asian- and Caucasian-American students. *Psychological Reports, 38,* 703-708.

Sue, S., & Morishima, J. (1982). *The mental health of Asian Americans.* San Francisco: Jossey-Bass.

Sue, S., Sue, D., & Sue, D. W. (1974). Delivery of community mental health services to Black and White clients. *Journal of Consulting and Clinical Psychology, 42,* 794-801.

Sue, S., & Zane, N. (1987). The role of culture and cultural techniques in psychotherapy: A critique and reformulation. *American Psychologist, 42,* 37-45.

Sung, B. (1971). *The story of Chinese in America.* New York: Collier.

Swinton, D. (1988). Economic status of Blacks. In J. Dewart (Ed.), *State of Black America, 1987* (pp. 98-121). New York: National Urban League.

Szapocznik, J., & Kurtines, W. (1980a). Acculturation, biculturalism, and adjustment among Cuban Americans. In A. Padilla (Ed.), *Acculturation: Theory, models, and some new findings* (pp. 27-42). Boulder, CO: Westview.

Szapocznik, J., & Kurtines, W. (1980b). Bicultural involvement and adjustment in Hispanic American youths. *International Journal of Intercultural Relations, 4,* 353-365.

Taborn, J. (1987). The Black adolescent mothers: Selected unique issues. In S. Battle (Ed.), *The Black adolescent parent* (pp. 172-191). New York: Haworth.

Tannenbaum, J. (1991). An English conversation group model of Vietnamese adolescent females. *Social Work with Groups, 13,* 41-55.

Taylor, R. (1976). Psychosocial development among Black children and youth: A reexamination. *American Journal of Orthopsychiatry, 46,* 4-19.

Thomas, M., & Hughes, M. (1986). The continuing significance of race: A study of race, class and quality of life in America, 1972-1985. *American Sociological Review, 51,* 830-841.

Thomas, P. (1967). *Down these mean streets.* New York: New American Library.

Thompson, M., et al. (1963). Twelve approaches to remedy the dropout problem. *Clearing House, 38,* 200-204.

Trankina, F. (1983). Clinical issues and techniques in working with Hispanic children. In G. Powell, J. Yamamoto, A. Romero, & A. Morales (Eds.), *The psychosocial development of minority group children.* New York: Brunner/Mazel.

Trimble, J. (1976). Value differences among American Indians: Concerns for the concerned counselor. *Journal of Counseling Across Culture.* Honolulu: University Press of Hawaii.

Tseung, W., & McDermott, J. (1975). Psychotherapy: Historical roots, universal elements and cultural variations. *American Journal of Psychiatry, 132,* 378-384.

Tsui, B., & Schutz, W. (1985). *Exploration in cross-cultural psychology.* San Francisco: Chandler & Sharp.

Tuddenham, R., Thomas, M., & Stuart, T. (1974). Mothers' reports of behavior on ten-year-olds. *Developmental Psychology, 10,* 459-495.

Tylim, I. (1982). Group psychotherapy with Hispanic patients: The psychodynamics of idealization. *International Journal of Group Psychotherapy, 32,* 339-350.

Ulibarri, H. (1970). Social and attitudinal characteristics of Spanish-speaking migrants and ex-migrant workers in the southwest. In J. Burma (Ed.), *Mexican-Americans in the United States* (pp. 471-486). Cambridge, MA: Schenkman.

U.S. Bureau of the Census. (1980a). *Subject report: American Indians.* Washington, DC: Government Printing Office.

U.S. Bureau of the Census. (1980b). *U.S. summary, characteristics of the population* (Vol. 1, pp. 9-20). Washington, DC: Government Printing Office.

U.S. Bureau of the Census. (1981). *General social and economic characteristics: U.S. summary* (P.C.80-1-C1). Washington, DC: Government Printing Office.

U.S. Bureau of the Census. (1982). *State and metropolitan area data book.* Washington, DC: Government Printing Office.

U.S. Bureau of the Census. (1983a). *General population characteristics, United States summary, 1980 census of population.* Washington, DC: U.S. Department of Commerce.

U.S. Bureau of the Census. (1983b). *Hispanic population* (Serial No. 98-10). Washington, DC: Government Printing Office.

U.S. Bureau of the Census. (1986). *We, the Black Americans.* Washington, DC: U.S. Department of Commerce.

U.S. Bureau of the Census. (1987a). *Statistical abstract of the United States.* Washington, DC: Government Printing Office.

U.S. Bureau of the Census. (1987). *Statistical abstracts of the United States: 1986: Table 1-32, No. 87.* Washington, DC: Government Printing Office.

U.S. Commission on Civil Rights. (1976). *Puerto Ricans in the continental United States: An uncertain future.* Washington, DC: Government Printing Office.

U.S. Commission on Civil Rights. (1978). *Social indicators of equality for minorities and women.* Washington, DC: Government Printing Office.

U.S. Congress, Office of Technology Assessment. (1986). *Indian health care* (OTA-H-290). Washington, DC: Government Printing Office.

U.S. Department of Commerce. (1984). *American Indian areas and Alaska native villages: 1980.* Washington, DC: Government Printing Office.

U.S. Department of Health, Education, and Welfare, Office of Special Concerns. (1974). *A study of selected socioeconomic characteristics of ethnic minorities based on the 1970 census: Vol. II. Asian Americans.* Washington, DC: Government Printing Office.

U.S. Department of Health and Human Services. (1981). *Fourth specific report to the U.S. Congress on alcohol and health.* Washington, DC: Government Printing Office.

U.S. Department of Health and Human Services. (1986). *Report of the Secretary's Task Force on Black and Minority Health.* Washington, DC: Government Printing Office.

U.S. Department of Health and Human Services. (1990). *Indian adolescent mental health.* Washington, DC: Government Printing Office.

U.S. Department of Justice, Bureau of Justice Statistics. (1987). *Bureau of Justice Statistics annual report.* Washington, DC: Author.

U.S. President's Commission on Mental Health. (1978). *Mental health in America: 1978* (Vol. 1). Washington, DC: Government Printing Office.

Varghese, B. (1983). Barriers to effective cross-cultural counseling. *Journal of Counseling Psychology, 24,* 420-429.

Vega, W., & Casas, S. (1986). Cohesion and adaptability in Mexican American and Anglo families. *Journal of Marriage and the Family, 48,* 857-867.

Vincenzi, H. (1987). Depression and reading ability in sixth grade children. *Journal of Social Psychology, 25,* 155-160.

Wa, D. (1980, September). *Emotion and mental health in traditional Chinese medicine.* Paper presented at Conference on Cultural Conception of Mental Health and Therapy, Honolulu.

Wahab, Z. (1973, March). *Barrio school.* Paper presented at the annual convention of the American Anthropological Association, New Orleans.

Wake, M. (1983). Acculturation and clinical issues affecting the mental health of Japanese Americans. *Pacific/Asian Mental Health Research Review, 2,* 5-6.

Walker, A. (1982). Embracing the dark and the light. *Essence, 128,* 67.

Wang, L., & Louie, W. (1979). *The Chinatown aftercare program: A report on a selected group of Chinese patients and their state hospital experience.* Unpublished manuscript.

Warner, W., Lawrence, D., & Devore, E. (1978). *Color and human nature.* Greenwood, MS: Negro University Press.

Washington, V. (1980). Teachers in integrated classrooms. *Elementary School Journal, 80,* 192-201.

Washington, V. (1982). Racial differences in teacher perceptions of first and fourth grade pupils on selected characteristics. *Journal of Negro Education, 51,* 60-72.

Weibel, O. (1984). Substance abuse among American Indian youth: A continuing crisis. *Journal of Drug Issues, 14,* 313-335.

Weiss, M. (1970). Selective acculturation and the dating process: The patterning of Chinese-Caucasian interracial dating. *Journal of Marriage and the Family, 32,* 273-278.

Welsh, P. (1988, May 1). The Black talent trap. *Washington Post,* p. C1.

Whitaker, C. (1989). [University of Minnesota Adolescent Health Program, Indian adolescent health survey]. Unpublished raw data.

Whitaker, C., & Keith, D. (1981). Symbolic experiential family therapy. In A. Gurman & D. Kniskern (Eds.), *Handbook of family therapy* (pp. 32-48). New York: Brunner/Mazel.

Wilson, W. (1987). *The truly disadvantaged.* Chicago: University of Chicago Press.

Wise, B. (1979). The health of American Indian children. *Health Service Report, 87,* 872-876.

Witkin, H., & Goodenough, D. (1981). *Cognitive styles: Essence and origins.* New York: International University Press.

Wong, W. (1989, June). Anti-Asian violence. *National Institute Against Prejudice and Violence,* p. 1-5.

Yalom, I. (1985). *The theory and practice of group psychotherapy.* New York: Basic Books.

Yamaguchi, T. (1986). Group psychotherapy in Japan today. *International Journal of Group Psychotherapy, 36,* 567-577.

Yamamoto, J., & Sasaki, Y. (1968). Cultural problems in psychiatric therapy. *Archives of General Psychiatry, 19,* 45-49.

Yamamoto, J., & Yap, J. (1984). Group therapy for Asian Americans and Pacific Islanders. *Pacific/Asian American Mental Health Research Review, 3,* 1-3.

Yee, A. (1973). Myopic perceptions and textbooks: Chinese-Americans' search for identity. *Journal of Social Issues, 29,* 99-113.

Young, D. (1969). The socialization of minority peoples. In D. Goslin (Ed.), *Handbook of socialization theory and research* (pp. 107-129). Chicago: Rand McNally.

Young, N. (1972). Independence training from a cross-cultural perspective. *American Anthropologist, 74,* 629-638.

Zimiles, H., et al. (1976). *Young Native Americans and their families: Educational needs assessment and recommendations.* New York: Bank Street College of Education.

Index